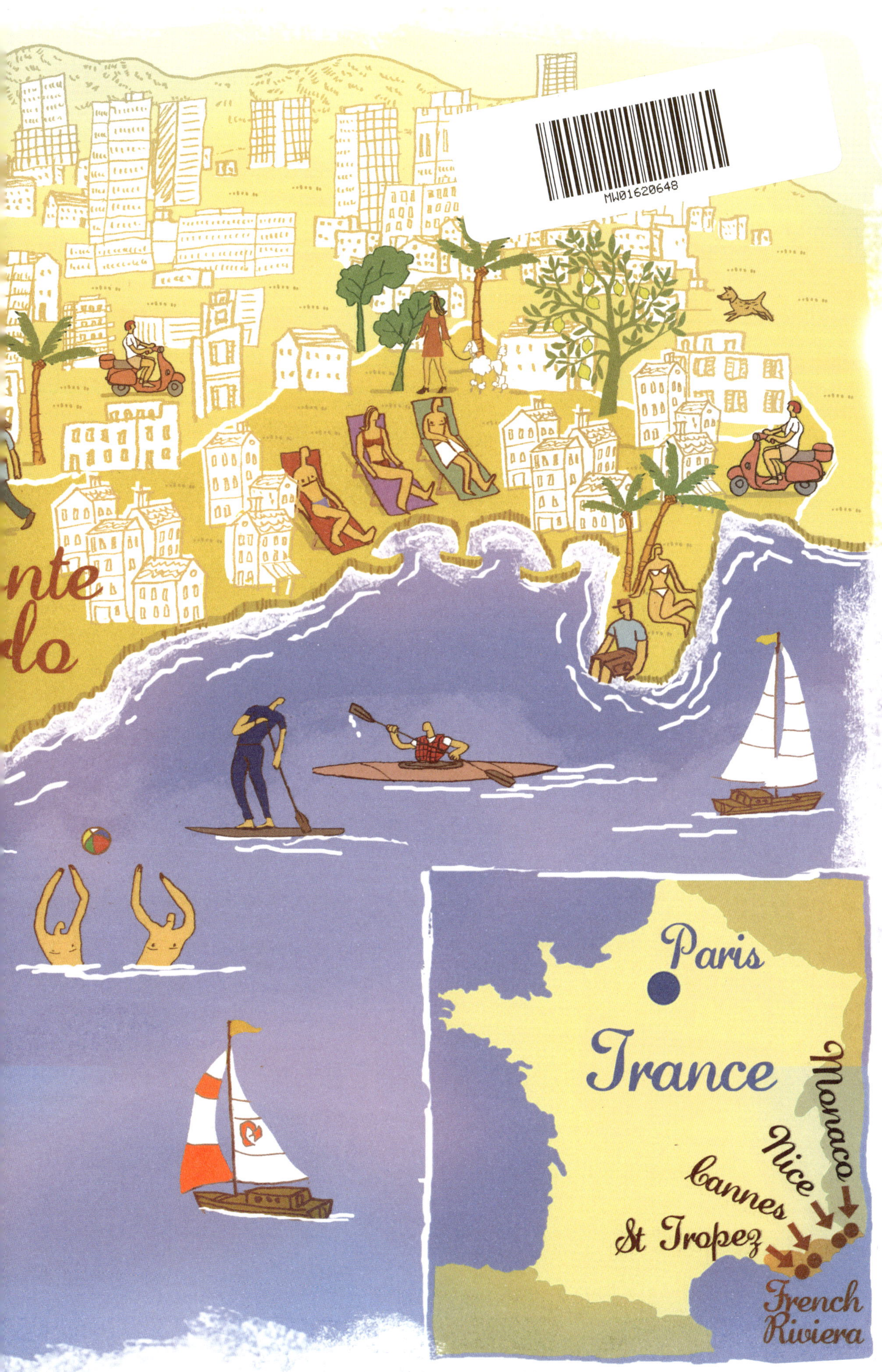
Paris
France
Monaco
Nice
Cannes
St Tropez
French Riviera

IN THE SPIRIT OF MONTE CARLO

For Her Excellency Maguy Maccario Doyle—
As a Monegasque, born and bred, her distinguished career has been devoted to the Principality of Monaco. She is one of its finest ambassadors—literally.

Endpapers: Map of Monte Carlo, © Robert Littleford.

601 West 26th Street, 18th Floor
New York, NY 10001, USA
Tel.: 212-989-6769 Fax: 212-647-0005
www.assouline.com
ISBN: 9781614282136
Printed in China.

PAMELA FIORI

IN THE SPIRIT OF MONTE CARLO

ASSOULINE

Contents

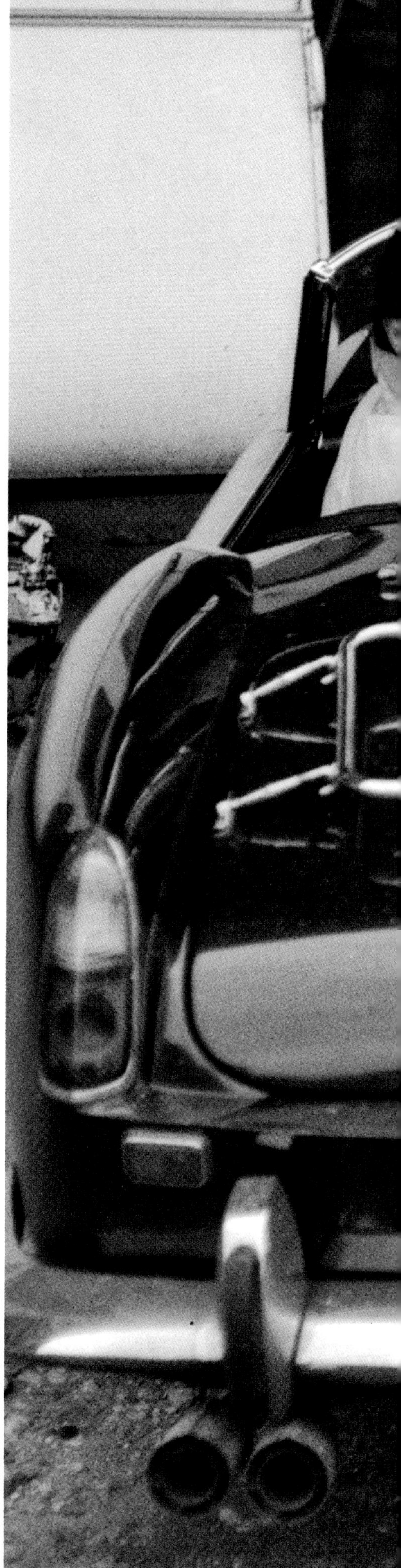

Alain Delon and Jane Fonda in 1964 during filming of *Joy House* (aka *Les Félins*).

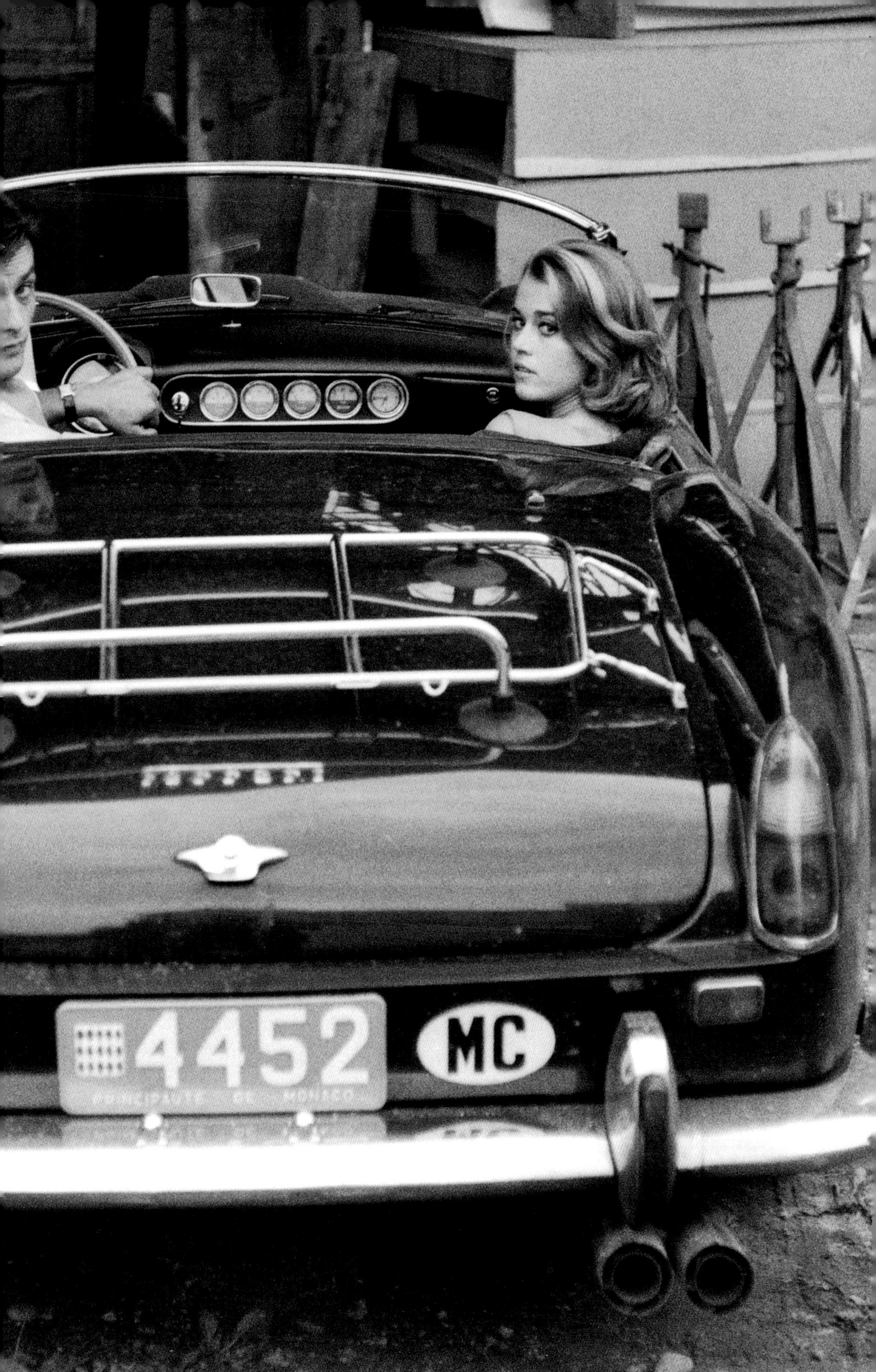
4452
MC

The Magic Kingdom

If I didn't know better, I'd swear that the palace of the Principality of Monaco was Cinderella's Castle in the Magic Kingdom at Disney World. However, unlike that fantasy playground, it was not born out of one man's fertile imagination, it's the real thing. What's more, an actual Prince and his Princess Bride live there, as has the Prince's family for more than 700 years.

Monaco occupies a tiny perch—smaller than New York City's Central Park—high above the French Riviera, between France and Italy. That it is the most expensive piece of real estate on the planet is all the more remarkable considering it was once poor, virtually uninhabitable, rather inaccessible, and facing a bleak future. The only sovereign state smaller than Monaco is the Vatican, which has its own incalculable wealth. (Whoever said that good things come in small packages was right on the mark when it comes to these two gems.)

The Principality's positive reversal of fortune can be directly traced back to the end of the nineteenth century, when a new community, Monte Carlo, was built within its borders. The story of this super-wealthy, sublimely luxurious resort town is the basis of this book, *In the Spirit of Monte Carlo*. As part of a series published by Assouline, it is the fourth book I have written about such world-class destinations. The other three—Capri, St. Barths, and Palm Beach—have several things in common but the most obvious is that they are all islands, completely surrounded by water, insular and perfectly content to be separated from the mainland.

Monaco is not an island (the Mediterranean laps only its southern side) but it might as well be. While reveling in its "apartness" and its exclusivity, it's far from homogeneous: Aside from the 6,000 natives known as Monegasques, it is home to more than a hundred nationalities, most of whom are millionaires and billionaires. If you want young and hip, head for St. Tropez. If you're looking for red-carpet glamour, better go to Cannes or to Cap d'Antibes, especially during the film festival. If you require all the conveniences of a big city, then nearby Nice is for you. However, you will also find traffic jams, crowds, crime, and all the temptations that flesh is heir to. Not that Monaco is scandal-free. In 1999 the multimillionaire banker Edmond Safra was found dead under mysterious circumstances: He was locked in the bathroom of his apartment in Monte Carlo when it caught fire (the murderer—his nurse—was captured, convicted, and imprisoned). When the daughters of Princess Grace and Prince Rainier were in their rebellious youth they raised a few eyebrows, as did as Prince Albert in his bachelor days. None of the above had the slightest effect on the population or on tourism.

To draw a comparison: St. Tropez is similar to Miami's South Beach, while Monaco is closer in spirit to Palm Beach, in that it is quiet and, while social, not wild and crazy. The paparazzi are not only unwelcome, they aren't allowed. An ample police force keeps the nation safe. (When was the last time you heard the expression "zero crime"?)

Monaco's pride and joy, Monte Carlo is a glorious Eden: perfectly manicured, architecturally grand, and floodlit at night to get the full effect of Casino Square, its magnificent centerpiece. Port Hercule houses the world's most imposing yachts. Chauffeur-driven Rolls-Royces and Bentleys, spanking-new Ferraris, Maseratis, and Aston Martins are common sights. On my last trip there, I noticed a white Rolls convertible, top down, drawing some attention in front of the Hôtel Hermitage where I was staying, but not nearly as much as it would have if parked in front of a deluxe hotel in Manhattan, Beverly Hills, London, or Paris.

The town has been the stuff of myths, movies, novels, and even a song, "The Man Who Broke the Bank at Monte Carlo." The French writer Colette discovered Audrey Hepburn on the steps of the Hôtel de Paris when Hepburn was making the movie *Monte Carlo Baby*. Colette supposedly exclaimed, "There's my Gigi," and cast her in that starring role in the Broadway play. Several

James Bond movies have used Monte Carlo as its location—Why not? It's a perfect stage set—and one of those Bonds, Sir Roger Moore, still lives there.

Yes, Monte Carlo reeks of luxury and old-fashioned glamour and, until recently, was regarded as the grande dame of the Côte d'Azur. But there are stirrings of change. Now a major banking and financial center, Monaco's main revenues no longer depend on casino gambling. An inundation of wealthy émigrés, many of them Russian, have taken up residence. Young, well-heeled couples can be seen walking with their children in strollers or prams. And those fancy cars and yachts may very well belong to billionaires in their thirties and forties.

The cavernous Buddha Bar is often packed, as it was the night I was there. Conspicuous was one empty table of ten that was soon filled when Prince Albert II arrived with his wife and their party. He gave a friendly nod to everyone in the room but otherwise was left to enjoy his meal with his companions.

I had three of the most exquisite meals in recent memory—at Alain Ducasse's Louis XV restaurant at the Hôtel de Paris, and at two of Joël Robuchon's places at the Hôtel Métropole. The lobby at the Métropole was aglow with a chic international crowd. More sedate but no less alluring was the lobby of the Hôtel Hermitage. The Hôtel de Paris was still attracting more stately guests, but that may change after its major face-lift, due to begin in the fall of 2014, is complete. No question about it, Monte Carlo is in alteration mode—and, predictably, it is not to everyone's liking.

My own first encounter with Monte Carlo was cinematic. The movie *The Red Shoes*, which came out in 1949, was being reshown at a theater in New Haven, Connecticut, in the early 1950s. My mother went there to visit her older brother and his family, and she took me and my sister with her (we lived in New Jersey). Anyone who has seen the film knows its tragic ending. Perhaps that was a bit too much drama for a kid of seven or eight, but I was entranced. *The Red Shoes* had everything an impressionable little girl could desire: a beautiful ballerina, a ballet based on a Hans Christian Andersen fairy tale, and a backdrop—the town of Monte Carlo—that was itself out of a fairy tale.

An actual visit in 1968 proved that Monte Carlo was every bit as beautiful as I had envisioned, and subsequent trips reinforced that early image. On one trip in the early 1970s, when I was a senior editor at *Travel + Leisure* magazine, my guide was a lovely young woman from the Monaco Tourist Office by the name of Maguy Maccario. We made an instant connection. When she was later transferred to New York and eventually became head of the office, our friendship continued and has to this day. Maguy Maccario Doyle is now, I'm happy to report, based in Washington, D.C., as Monaco's ambassador to United States. Her boss is Prince Albert II, who, like Maguy, grew up in Monaco.

When I was editor in chief of *Town & Country*, I realized that 2007 would be the twenty-fifth anniversary of the death of Princess Grace. I called Maguy to ask if the Principality might cooperate were *T&C* to publish a cover story—a retrospective, really—on Princess Grace's life dating back to her days as the Hollywood actress Grace Kelly. Not only was the answer yes, it led to a collection of attractions and events including an exhibition complete with vignettes at Sotheby's auction house in New York, which ran for eleven days and drew 20,000 people.

As the writer of the story, I traveled to Monaco with Maguy and with *T&C's* creative director, Mary Shanahan, to do the research. The most fascinating part was the day we visited a room in the royal palace where Princess Grace's personal belongings were stored in preparation for a major show in the Principality. There we witnessed racks of dresses, suits, and gowns, boxes of leather gloves and shoes, photos and letters—an intimate trove that to this day gives me goose bumps at the very thought.

I owe many things to Maguy Maccario Doyle, not the least of which is the inspiration for this book. She invited me to a screening of *Monte Carlo, naissance d'un mythe*, a documentary film about François and Marie Blanc, who were responsible for inventing Monte Carlo. I fancied myself something of a Monacophile, but this part of its history was altogether new to me. As I sat in the darkness in that small theater, the possibility of a book began to take shape. I guess you could say that my journey to Monte Carlo began and ended at the movies. How fitting.

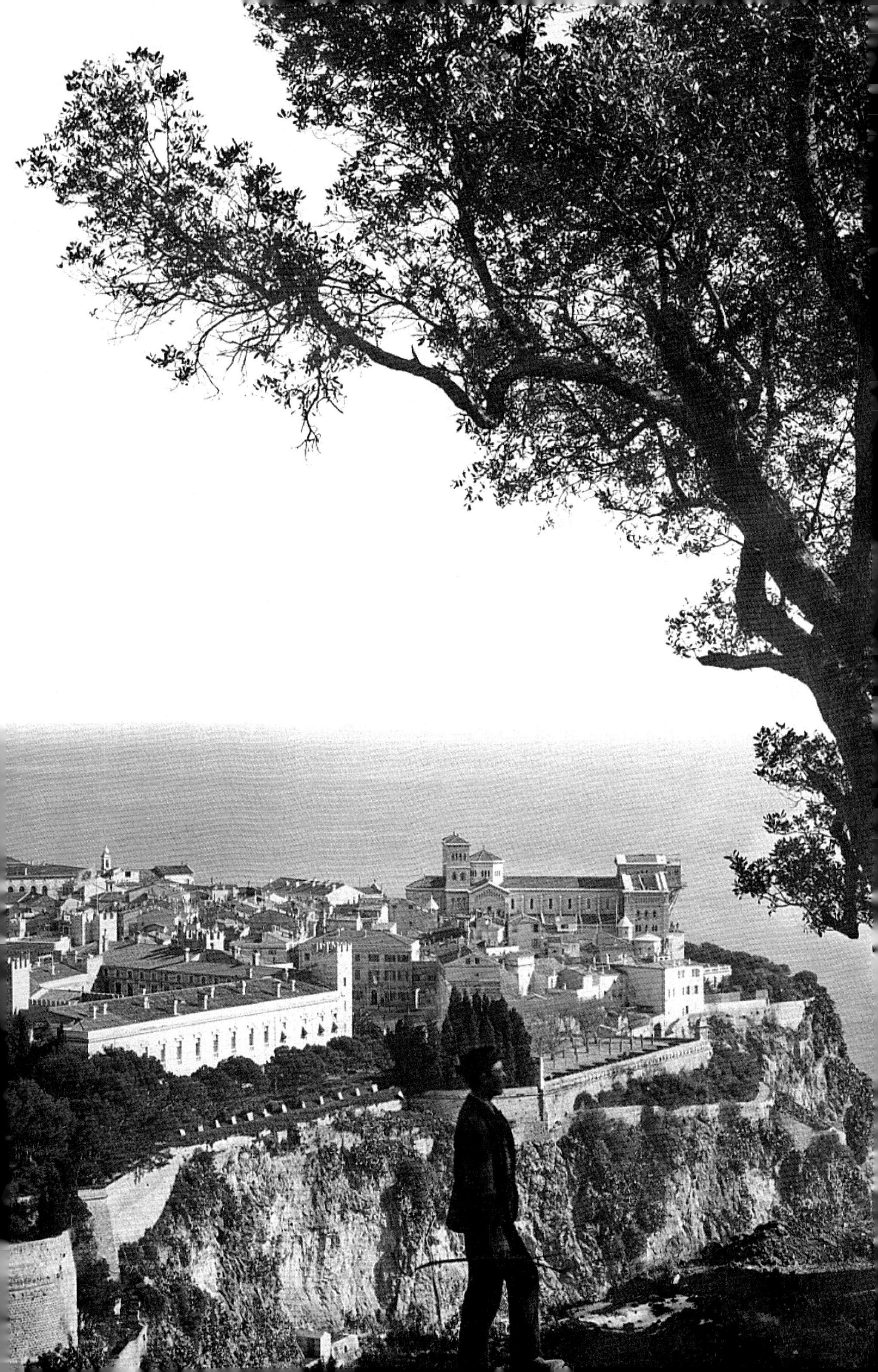

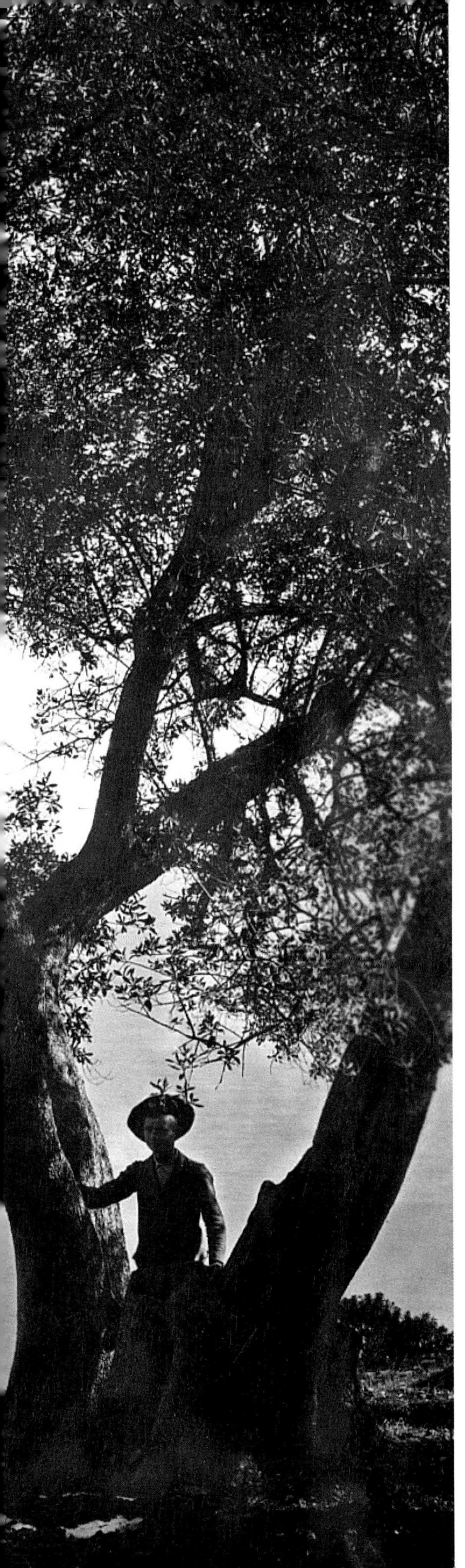

A Rocky Start

"There is nothing new about Monaco. The land is age-old, the sea that washes its shore is ancient. Even the Monegasques come from bloodlines lost in history. Humans have lived along this rocky Mediterranean coast ever since men and women learned to walk, make fire, and share crude tools."

—Martin Hintz,

Monaco: Enchantment of the World

What would become the impossibly glamorous and unfathomably rich Mediterranean principality of Monaco, with Monte Carlo as its shining star, was once both a rock and a hard place. Literally a rock—and actually called The Rock, or *Le Rocher* in French—it was seemingly impregnable and virtually inaccessible. And it was a hard place in that it was poor and inhabited by a primitive people, many of them seafarers and farmers, whose descendants are known as Monegasques. Aside from olive, lemon, and orange groves, the land was agriculturally barren.

View of the royal palace, situated atop *Le Rocher* ("The Rock"), 1880.

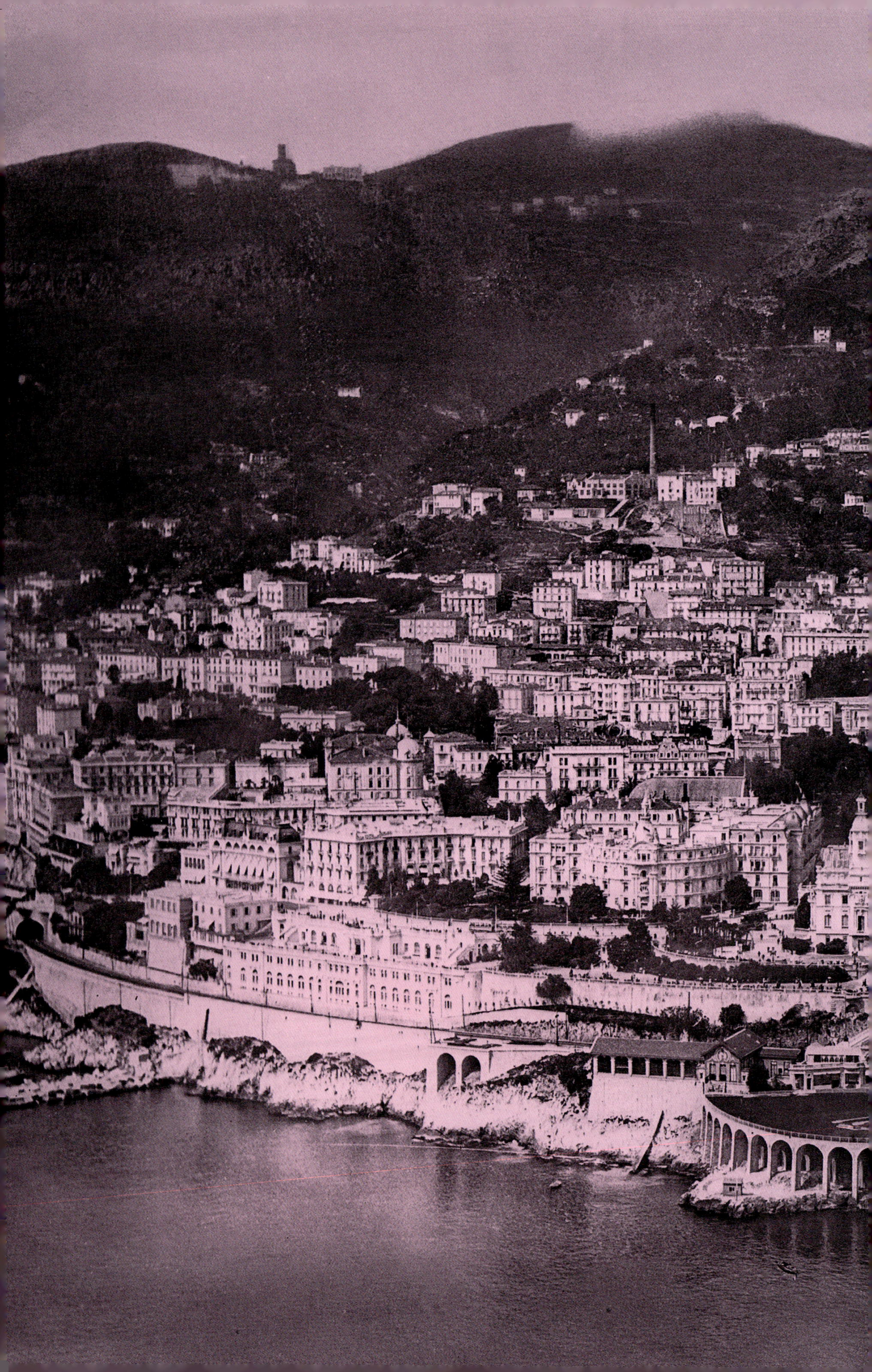

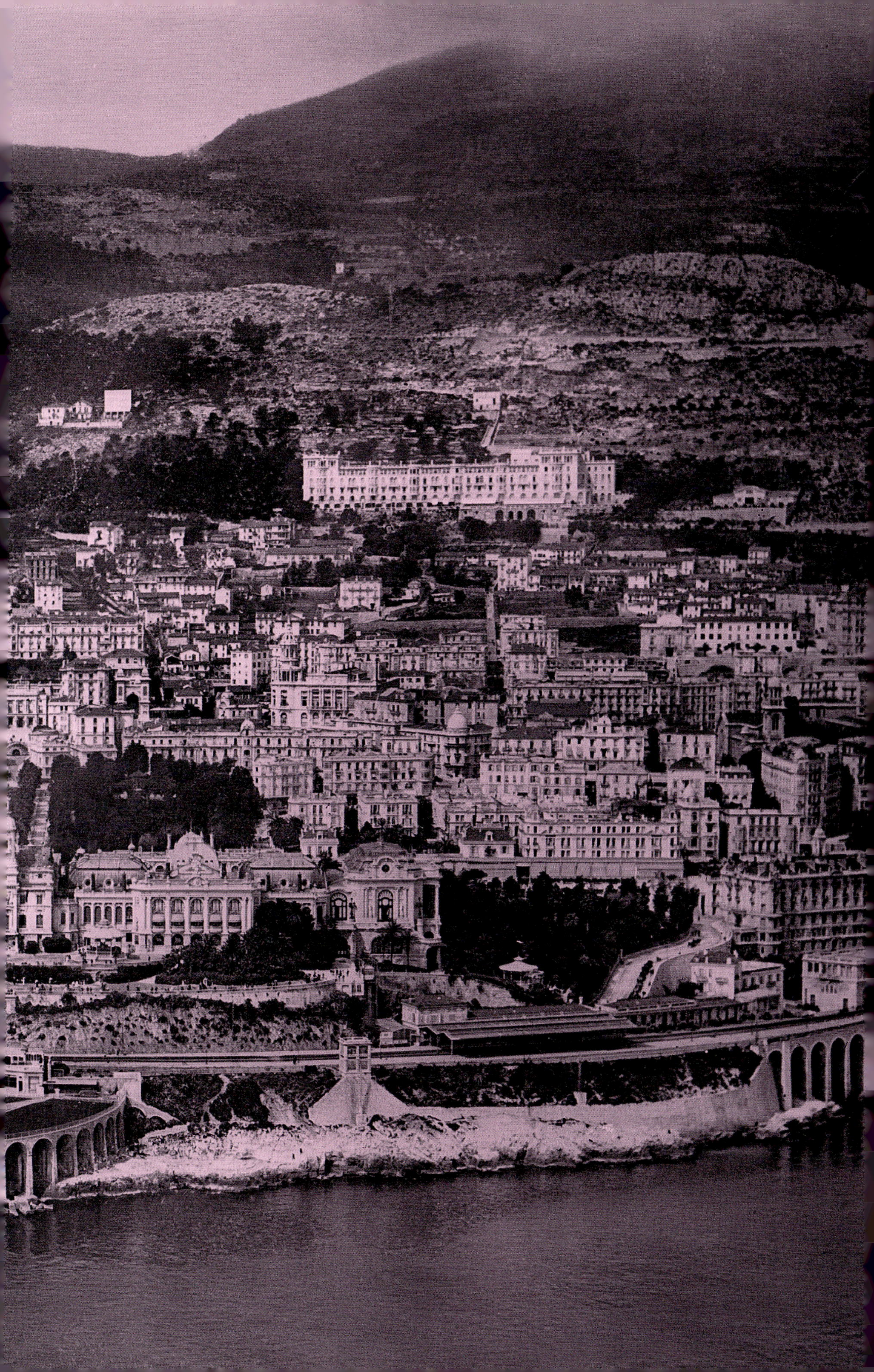

Monaco's history is as rocky as its landscape and harks back 300,000 years to the end of the Paleolithic era. The name comes from *Monoikos*, a colony founded by Phoenicians in the sixth century BC. An ancient myth claims Hercules passed through Monaco and turned away the gods who came before him. As a result, the main port of Monaco is occasionally referred to as the Port of Hercules.

Originally considered part of a region between Genoa and Provence, Monaco's original population from 1000 BC were called Ligurians (Genoa is the largest city in the Italian region of Liguria). It was invaded by Greeks and was briefly part of the Roman Empire. After the fall of Rome, Monaco was pillaged and plundered by the usual suspects: Vandals, Burgundians, Franks, Visigoths, and Ostrogoths. If all this weren't enough, the Saracens came a-sacking in the 800s AD.

Things somewhat settled down in the Middle Ages, when Germany (then Prussia), under King Henry VI, ceded Monaco to Genoa, which was then Monaco's largest neighbor. The Grimaldis, Monaco's ruling family off and on for 700-plus years and to this day, came from Genoese aristocracy. By aligning themselves with the Pope, they joined his other followers, who were called Guelphs. In opposition to the Guelphs were the Ghibellines, the faction that sided with the German Emperor Frederick Barbarossa. Monaco fell into Spanish hands for a period and for a long time was ruled by the French. Complicated? Inextricably. Turbulent? Indeed.

But as remote as Monaco was, The Rock was regarded as valuable and strategic, with a great deal of potential—if, that is, someone could figure out a way to penetrate and develop it. Surrounded on three sides by France and by the sea on the south, Monaco was beautiful but remote—its main advantage being a small and sheltered harbor.

Whoever would have dreamed that this minuscule and extremely wealthy haven would have ever been referred to as "poor Monaco," pitied by its neighbors. And yet it was. Other parts of the Côte d'Azur, such as Nice, Antibes, Cannes, and Beaulieu, were far easier to get to, thus attracting sun-seeking travelers from England, northern France, parts of Europe, even Russia, all trying to escape the harshness of winter. The richer these towns became, the poorer Monaco seemed by comparison—until, that is, the construction of Monte Carlo.

Promotional travel poster, 1900.
Previous pages: Monte Carlo and, in the distance, Beausoleil, 1914.

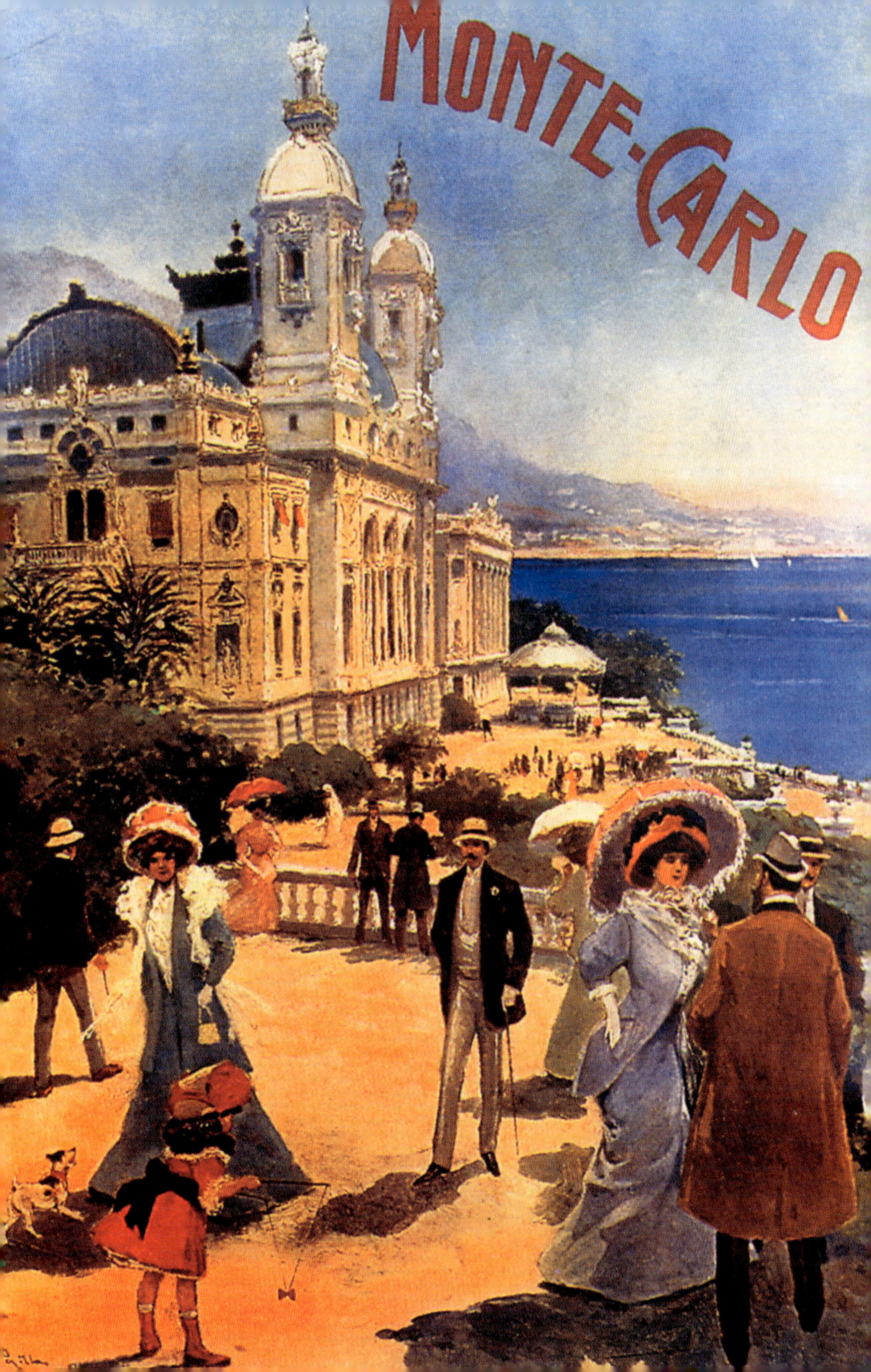
MONTE-CARLO

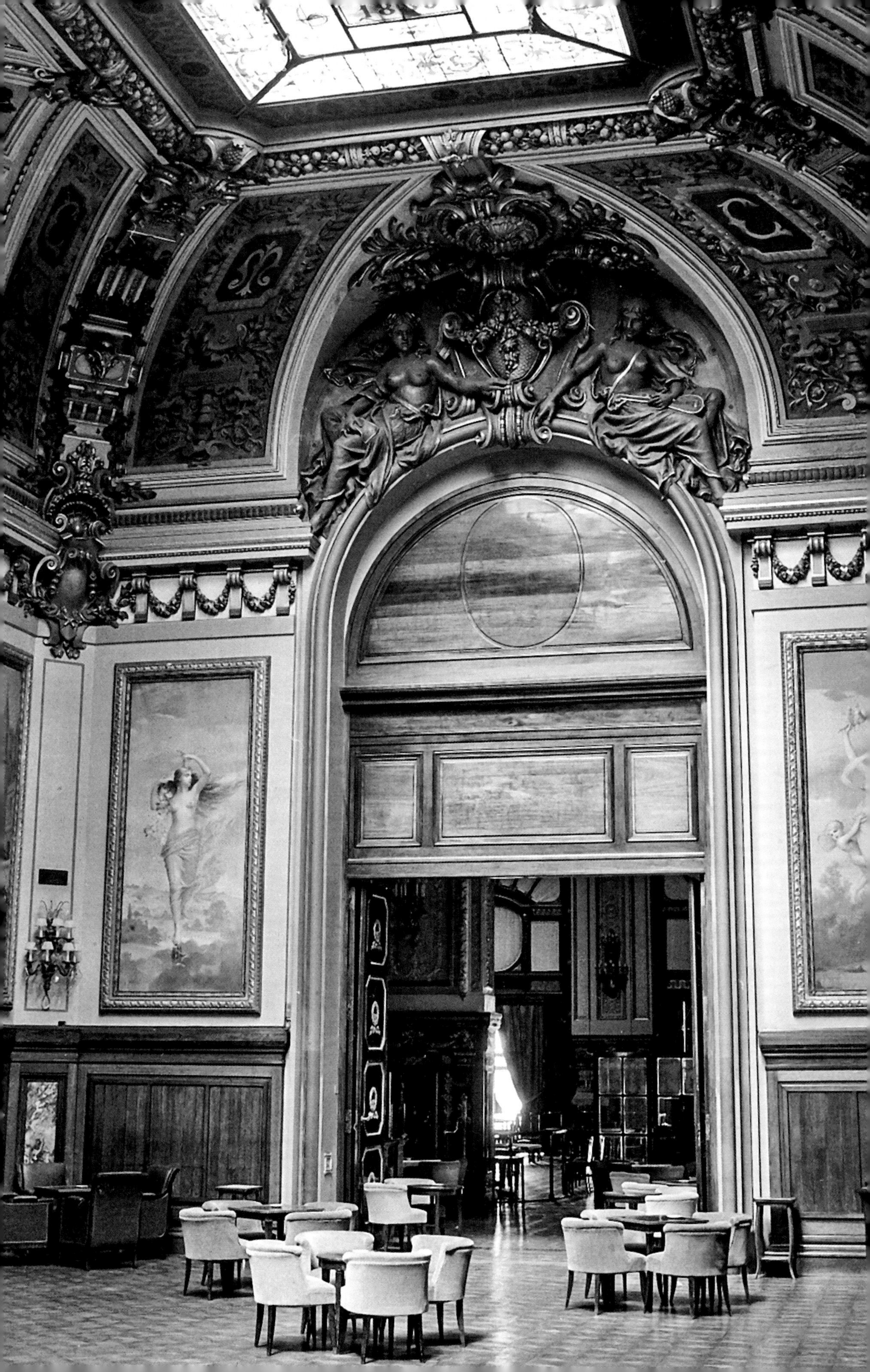

Monte Carlo Mirage

"If there is anything more delicious than the lovely terraces and villas of Monte Carlo, I do not wish to see them. There is nothing beyond the semi-tropical vegetation, the projecting promontories into the Mediterranean, the all-embracing sweep of the ocean... and the enchanting climate! One gets tired of the word beautiful."

—Mary Elizabeth Wilson Sherwood,

An Epistle to Posterity: Being Rambling Recollections of Many Years of My Life

The creation of Monte Carlo transformed everything for Monaco. The raw material—the gorgeous *mise en scène*—was there. Lacking was an infrastructure. Still, it was an opportunity at the ready. But more than a grand plan, the idea for Monte Carlo was a last-ditch effort on the part of the ruling Grimaldi family to save Monaco from bankruptcy. Once under Monaco's domain, the two neighboring villages of Menton and Roquebrune decided to claim their independence in 1848, a period of many revolutions in France. This was a huge and incalculable loss for Monaco, which depended on those towns for tax revenues. Prince Charles III was at his wit's end. At the urging of his lawyer and chief adviser, Monsieur A. Eynaud, and Princess Caroline, Charles's mother, the Prince decided to build a gambling casino and a sea-bathing facility. He needed and got permission from France, which at the time prohibited gambling (as did Italy). In 1848 he formed the Société Anonyme des Bains de Mer et du Cercle des Étrangers à Monaco, the forerunner of the powerful Société des Bains de Mer, or SBM, that still controls so much of Monte Carlo. The new quarter needed a name. One choice was Charleville, but it was already taken. The Prince finally settled on Monte Carlo—Italian for Mount Charles.

Casinos and spas as a dual attraction were becoming fashionable in Germany in the towns of Bad Homburg and Baden-Baden, so why not in Monaco? Easier said than done. A first attempt, in 1862, failed. After a few relocations—all of which flopped for one reason or another (lack of vision, lack of money, lack of commitment)—the perfect site was chosen: atop a plateau directly across from the palace, known as *Les Spelugues*, or The Caves.

Les Salons Privés, or private rooms, of the Casino, 1961.

Built to resemble an Italianate palazzo, the casino on the plateau was far from the success Prince Charles was hoping for. His first two concessionaires, both Frenchmen, abandoned the project after a dismal turnout (reports are that the casino had one visitor in its first year). A major reason was that the casino was so hard to reach, requiring at least four hours by horse and carriage from Nice and half that by sea, provided the waters were calm. The casino closed and remained empty until the arrival of an enterprising Frenchman named François Blanc, who, under Archduke Ferdinand, brought gambling to Germany. Aware of Blanc's achievements, Eynaud orchestrated a meeting at the palace with Blanc and his young German wife, Marie.

A brilliant and canny businessman, Blanc proposed a take-it-or-leave-it offer to reimagine the casino for 1.7 million gold francs, plus 50,000 francs a year and 10 percent of the profits. This also included being concessionaire to SBM for fifty years. The prince, recognizing an offer he could not refuse, accepted it on the spot. Thus began a fruitful relationship that was to alter and benefit Monaco in countless ways.

While Blanc thought big, his wife, Marie, twenty-seven years younger, possessed a natural flair for elegance and sophistication, even though she was the daughter of a Homburg cobbler. Together and over a period of twenty years they built what became the showplace of the French Riviera.

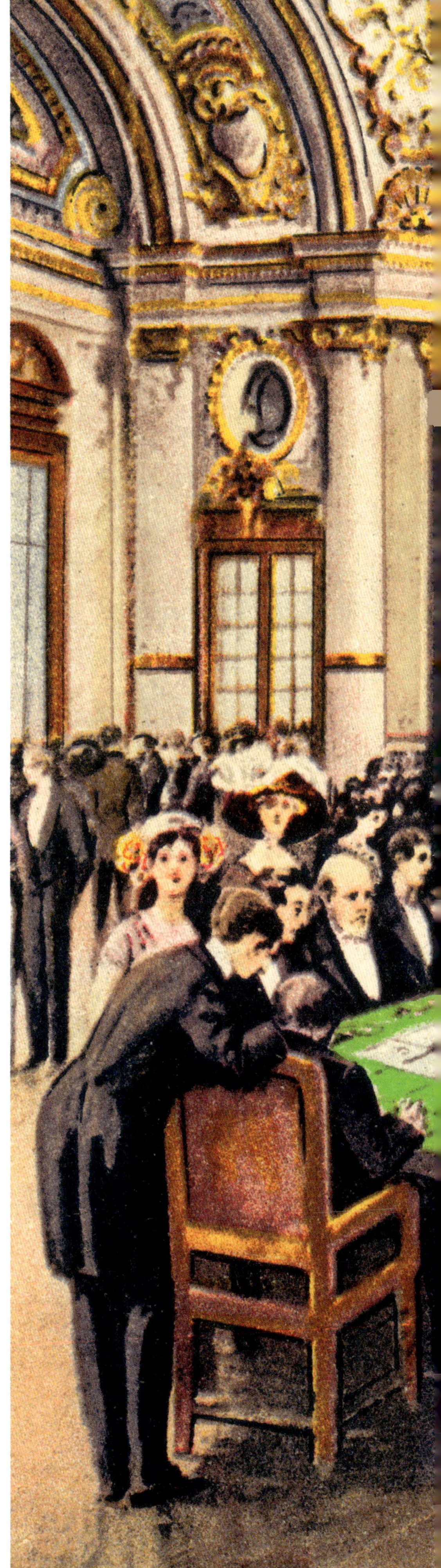

The roulette table in the Casino's Salles Schmitt.

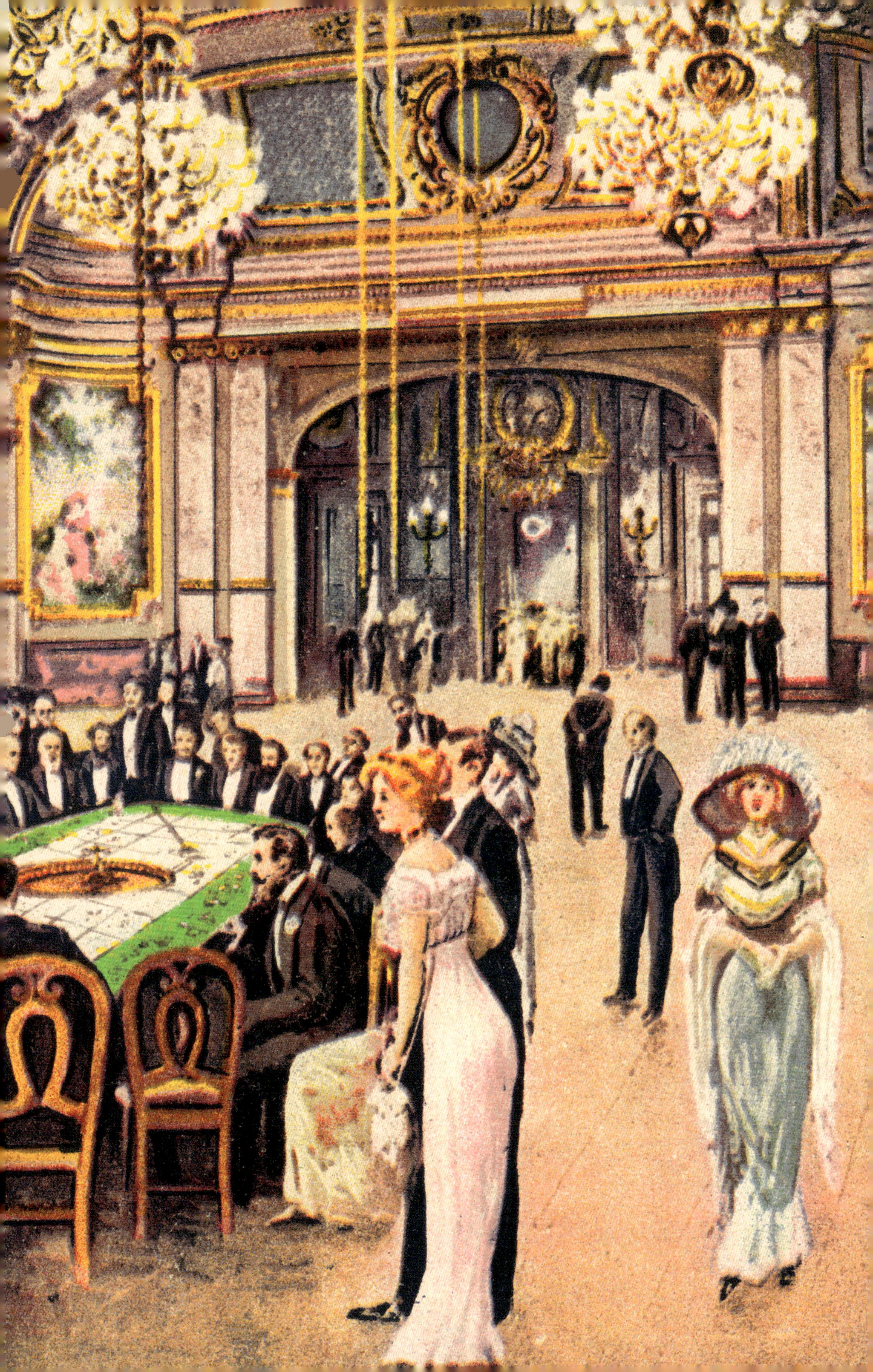

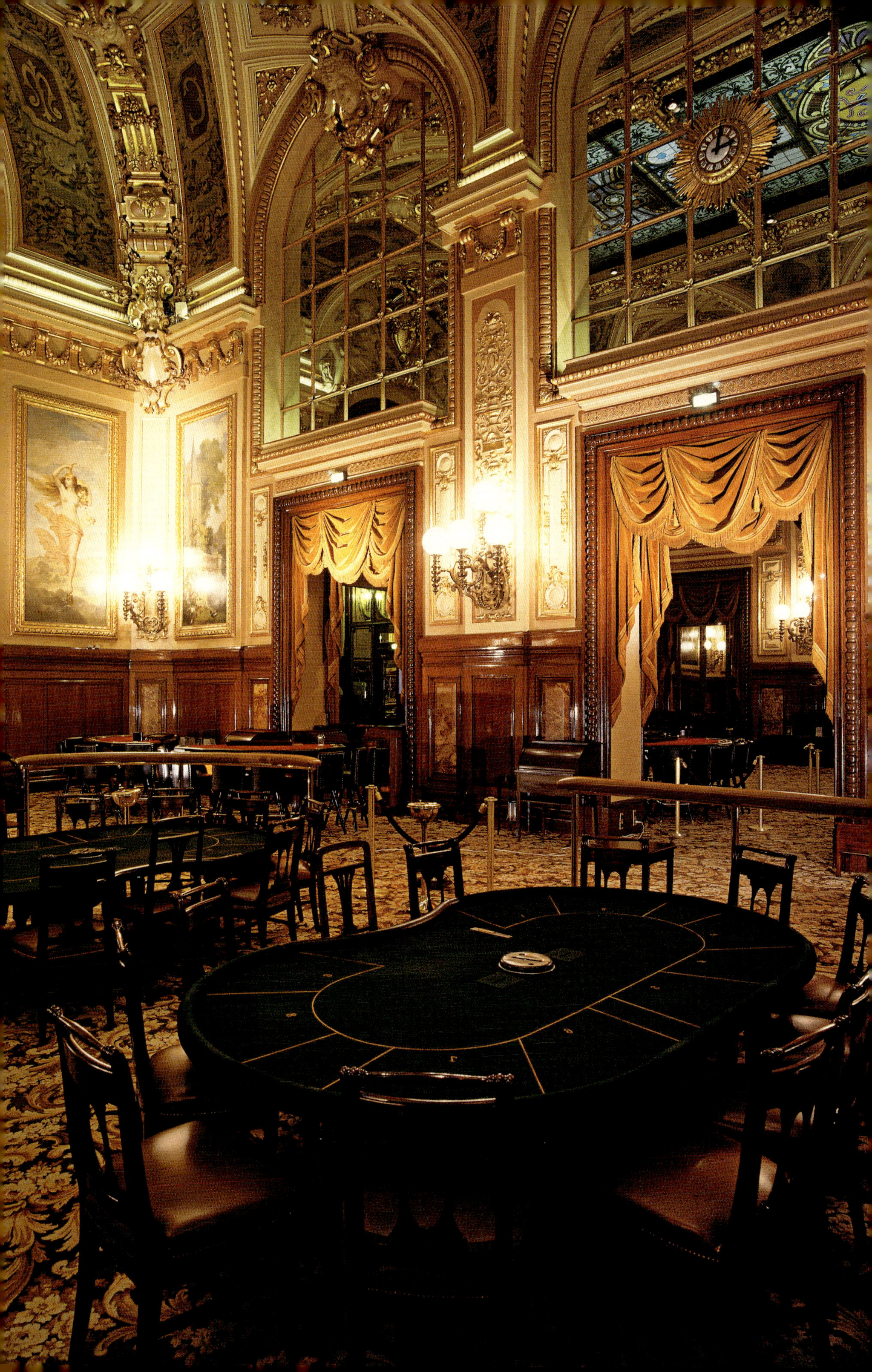

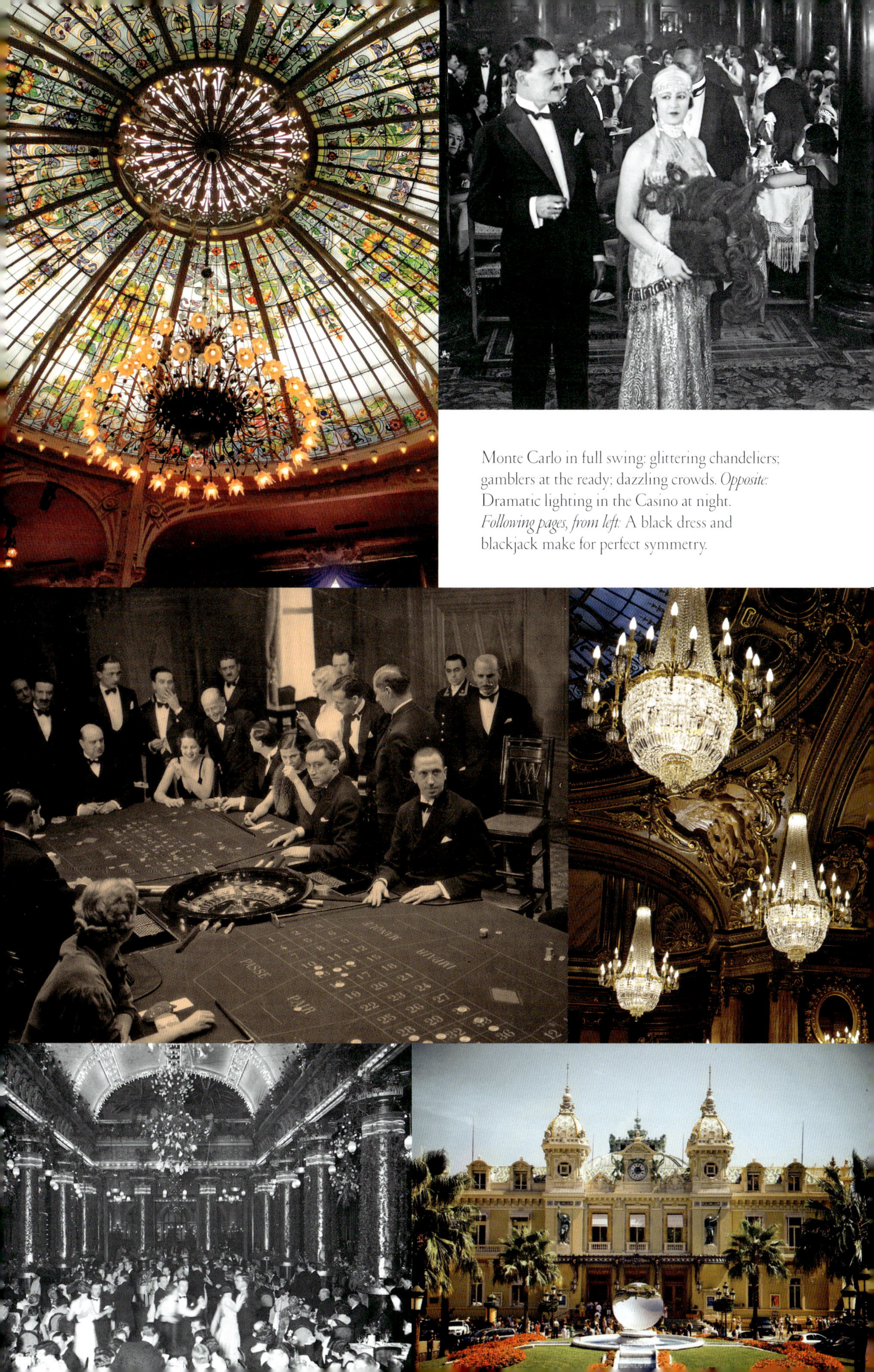

Monte Carlo in full swing: glittering chandeliers; gamblers at the ready; dazzling crowds. *Opposite:* Dramatic lighting in the Casino at night. *Following pages, from left:* A black dress and blackjack make for perfect symmetry.

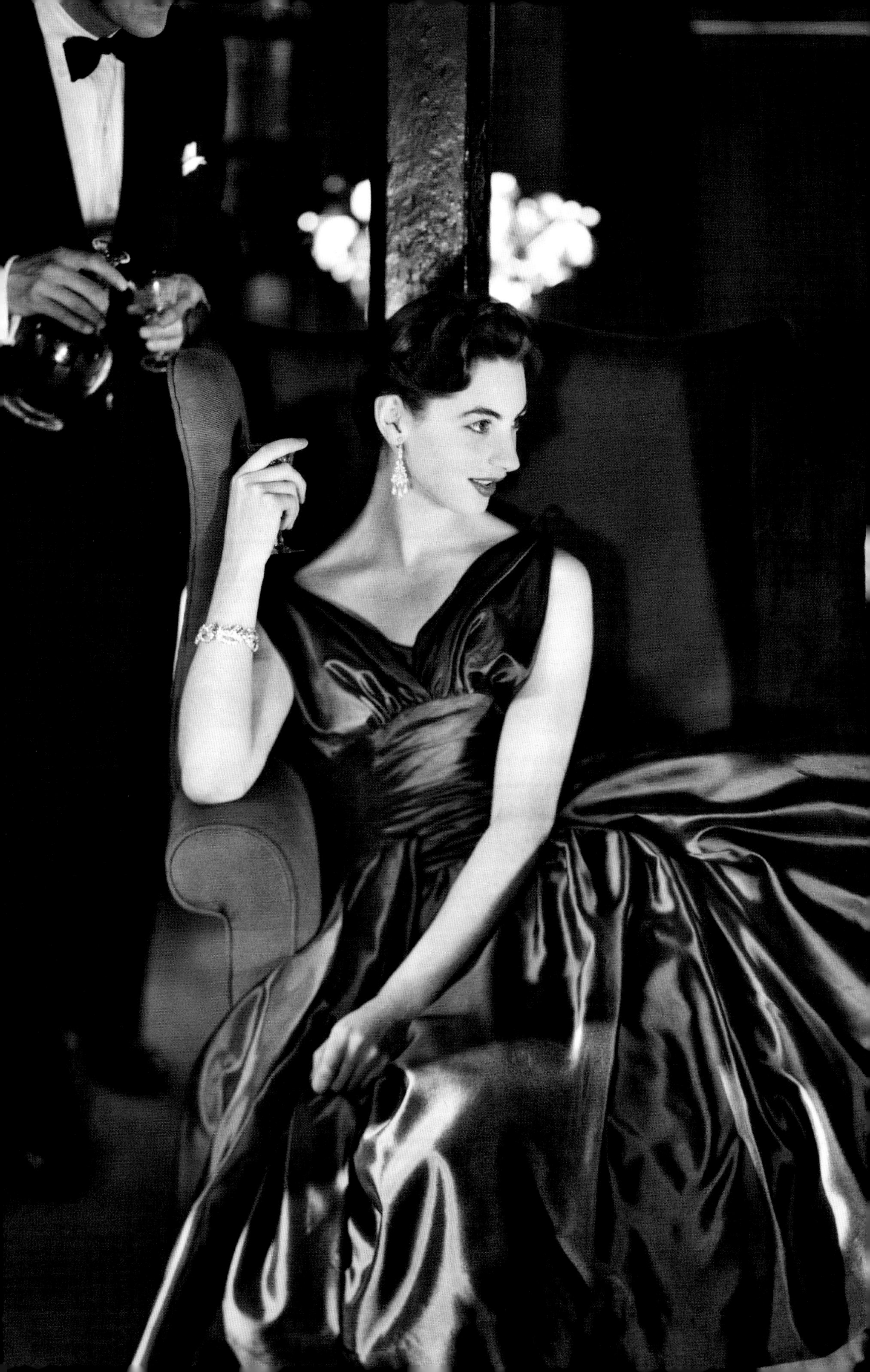

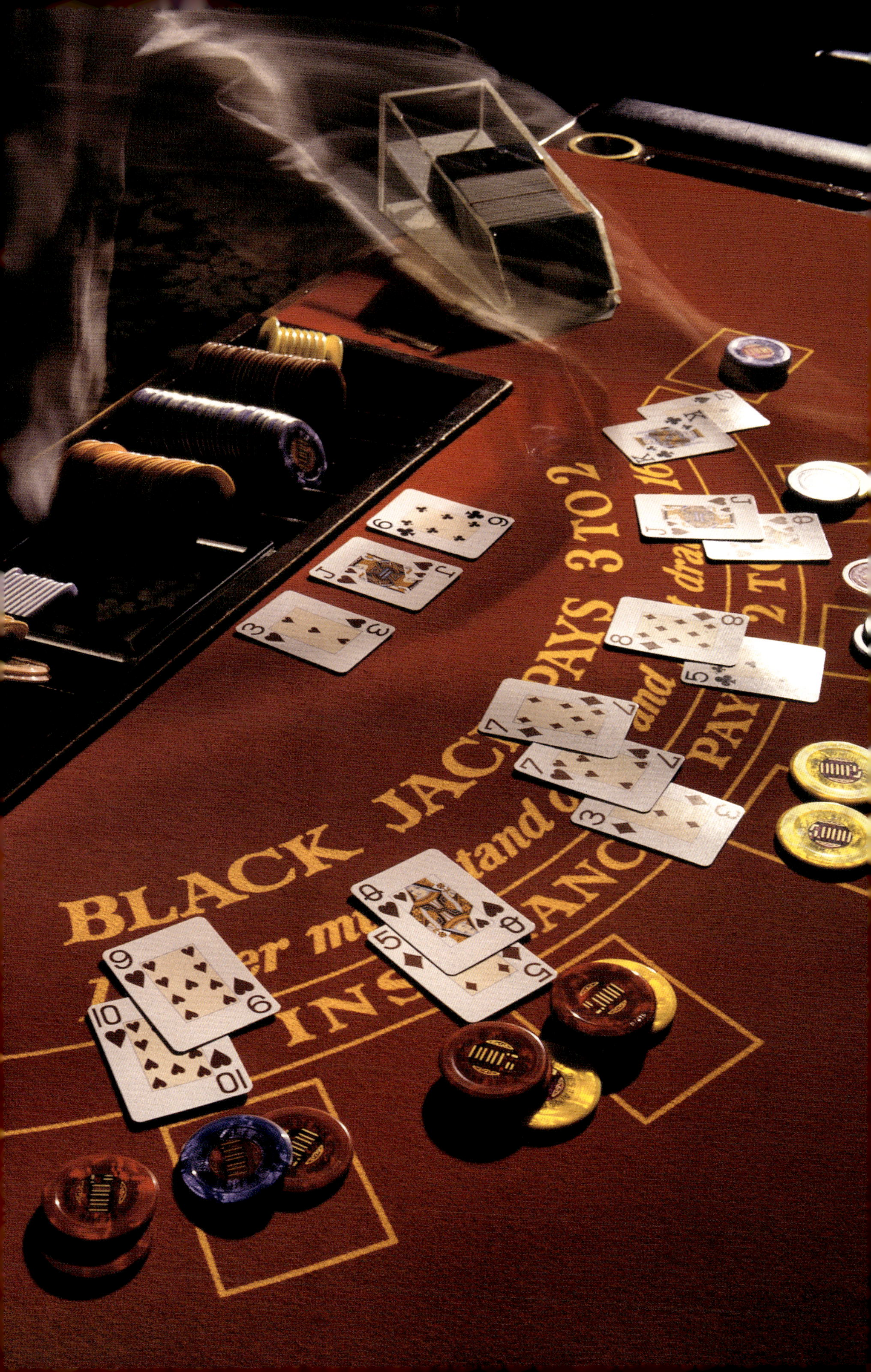
BLACK
PAYS 3 TO 2

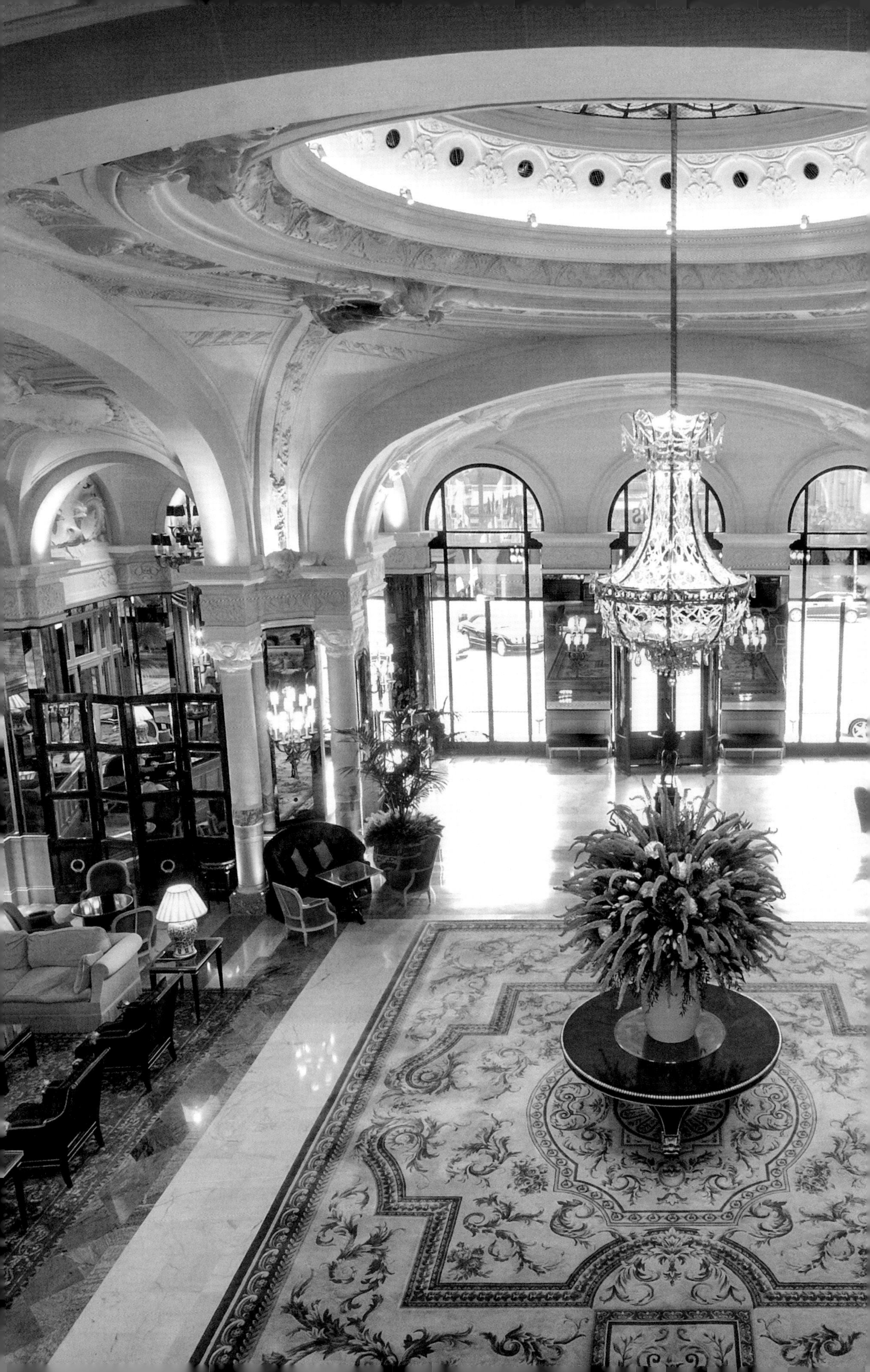

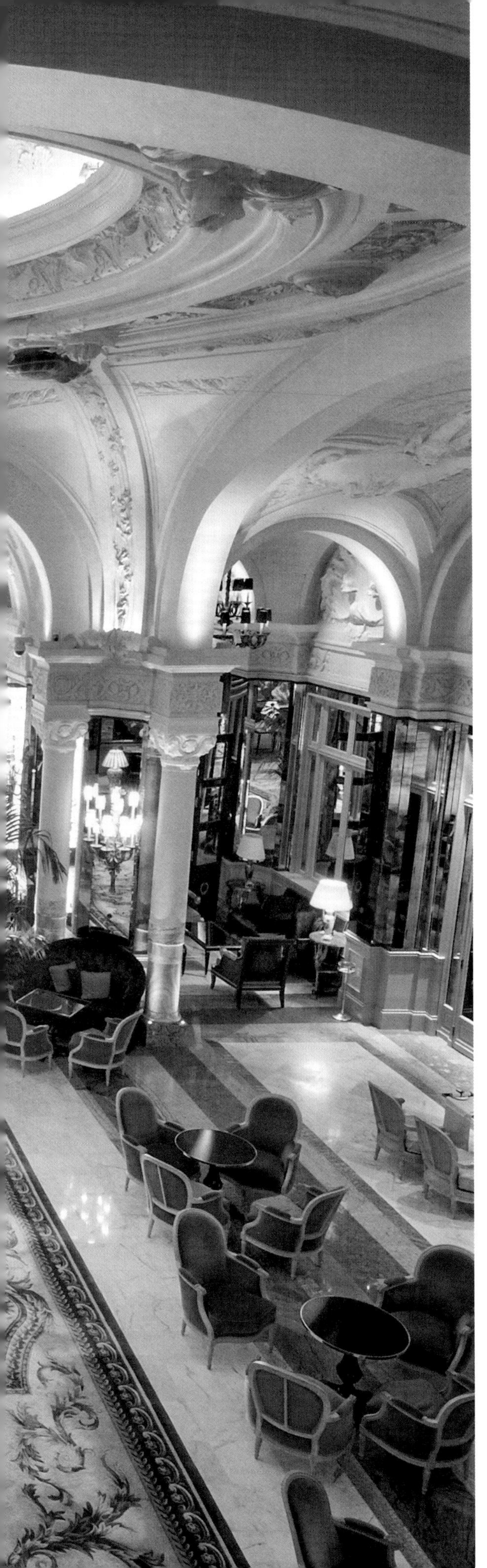

The casino was only part of Blanc's scheme, which also called for a luxury hotel, the legendary Hôtel de Paris; the construction of roads and tunnels; and the extension of the Paris-Lyon-Méditerranée railway, or PLM, to Monaco; and finally, an opera house. Employing 1,000 laborers and engineers, many of them Monegasques, Blanc's dream began to unfold. As it did, other developers, enterprises, and emigrés followed.

François Blanc was the Principality's visionary, or, put another way, he was to Monaco what Walt Disney was to America. His Mouse? A devilish contraption called the roulette wheel.

The supremely elegant lobby of the Hôtel de Paris.
Following pages: Flashy sports cars are a common sight in Casino Square.
Pages 28-29: The Café de Paris, in the foreground, today is dwarfed by high-rises.

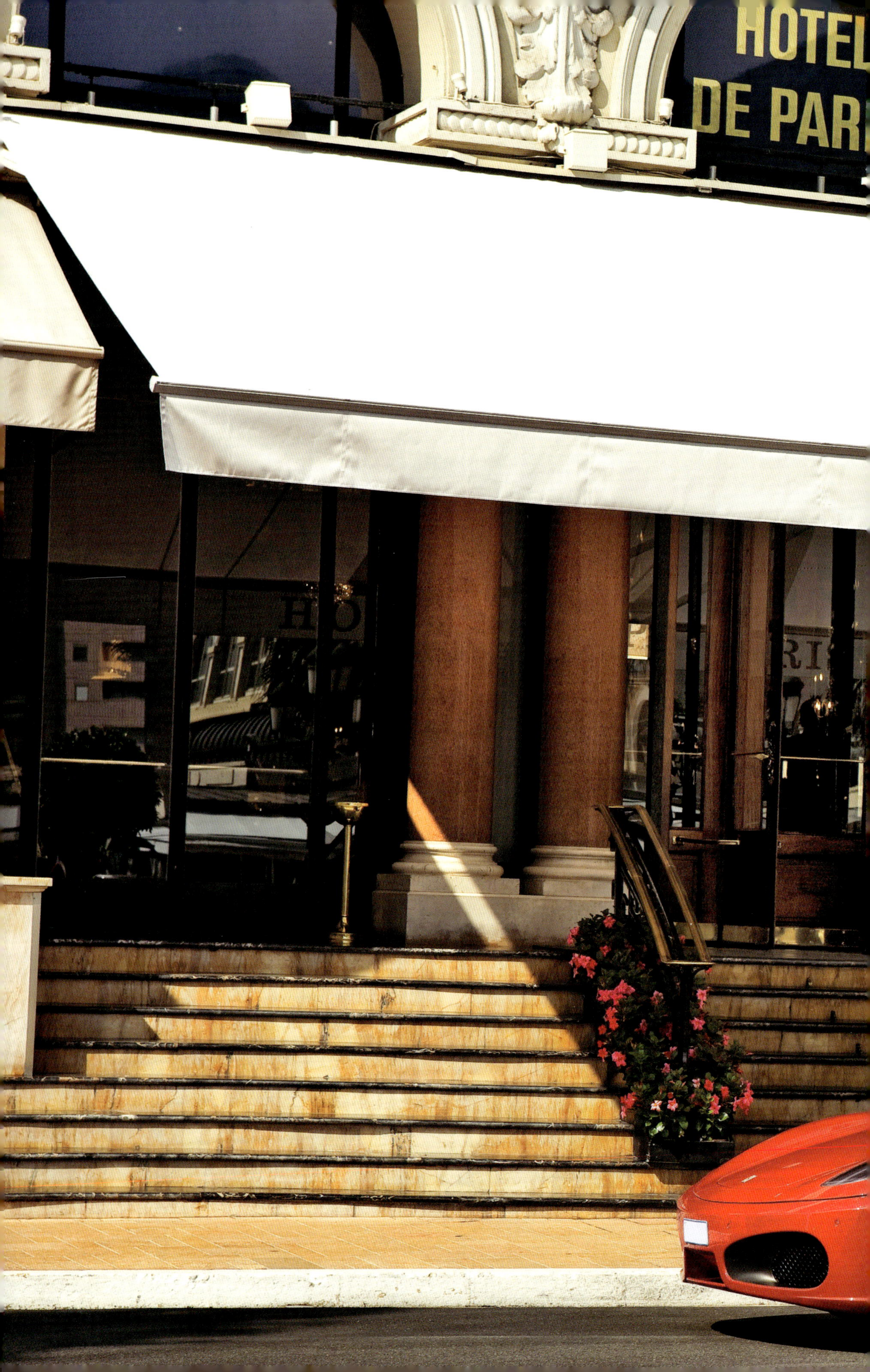
HOTEL
DE PAR

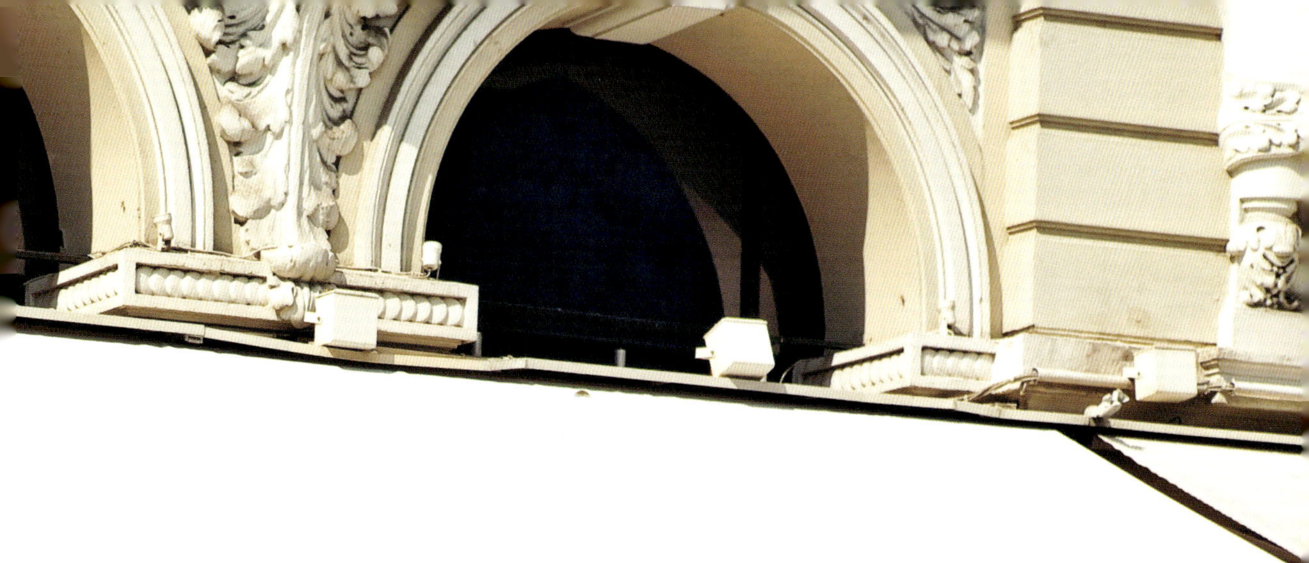
HOTEL DE PARIS

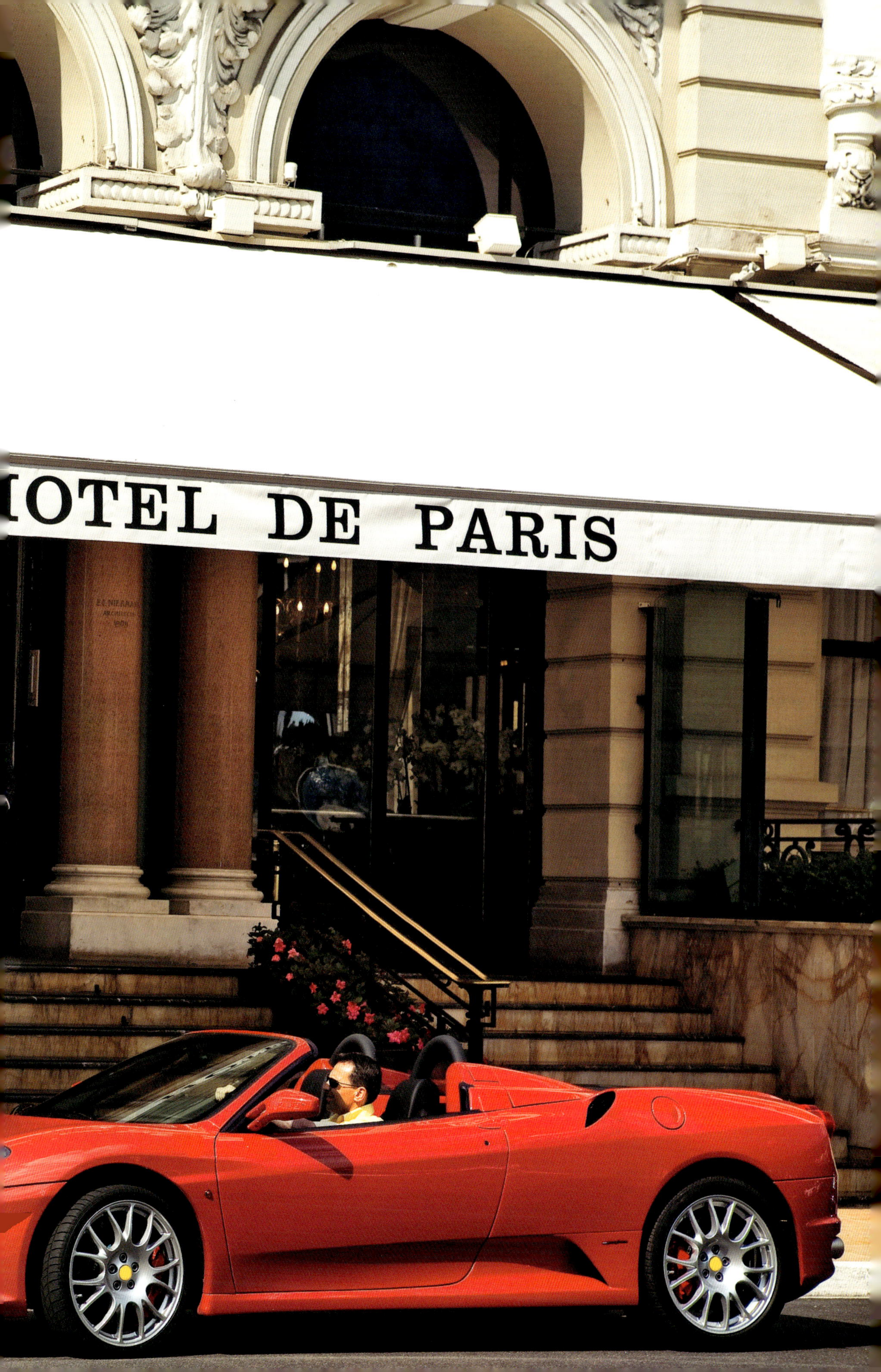

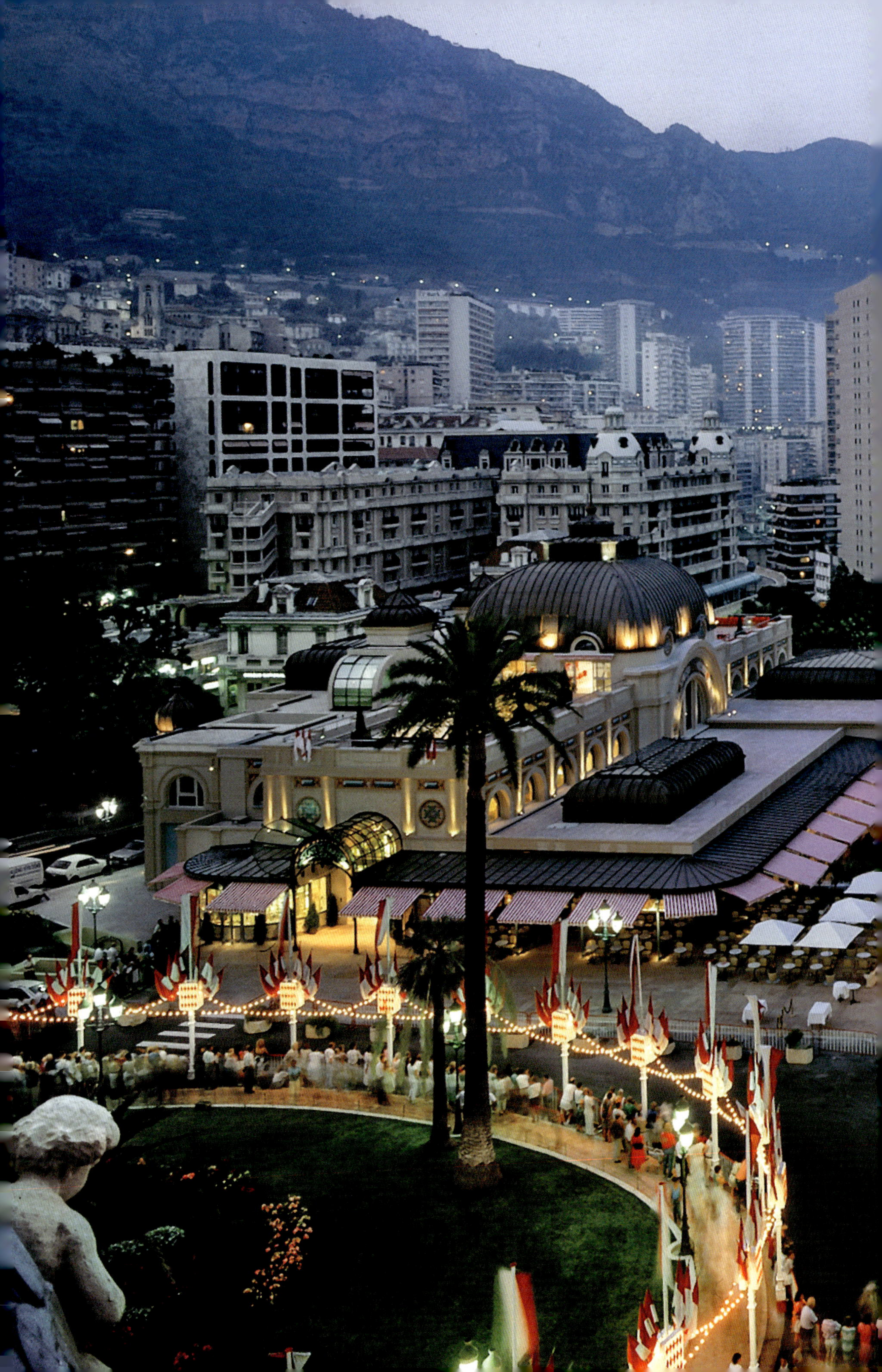

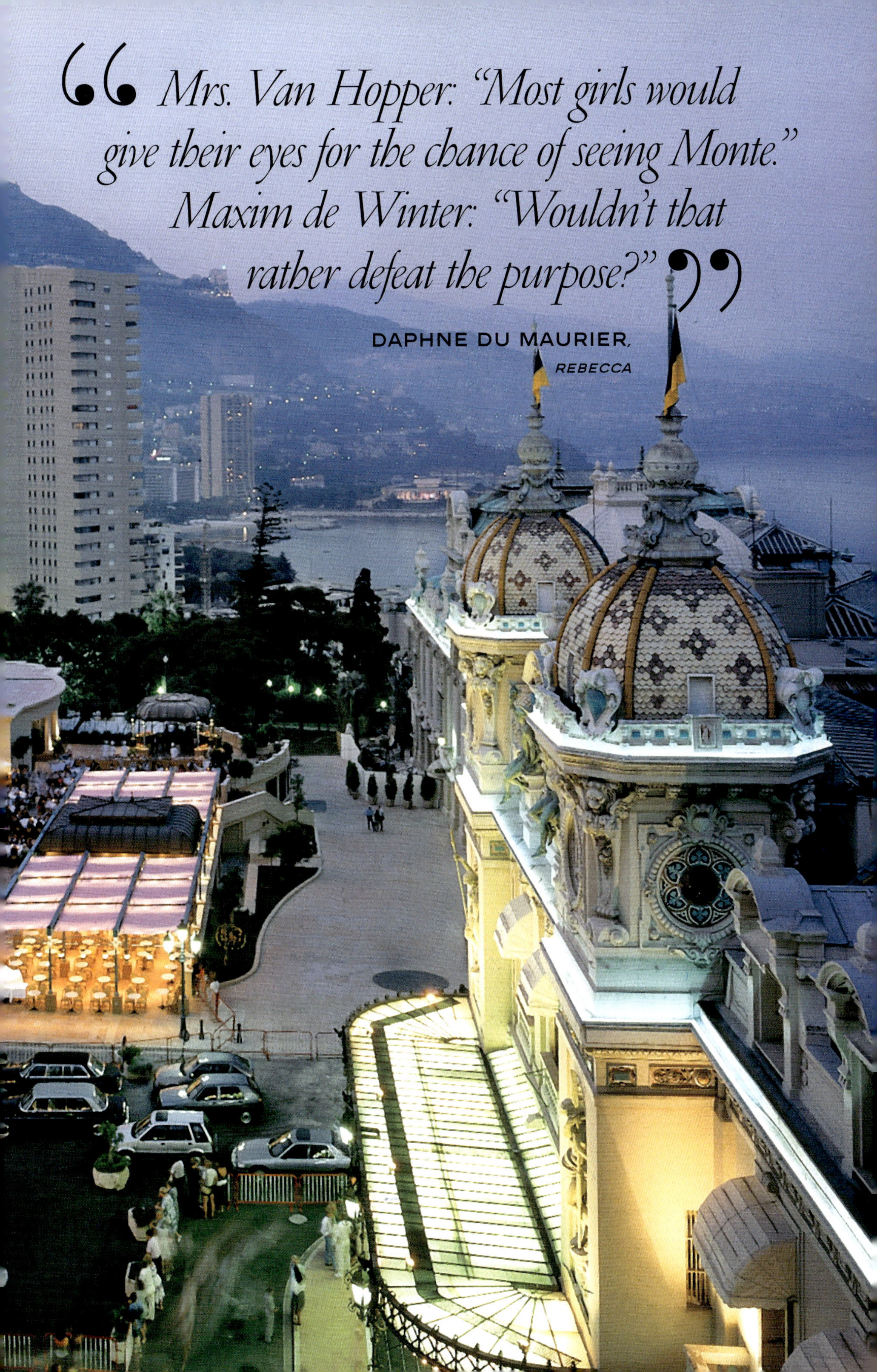

> “Mrs. Van Hopper: “Most girls would give their eyes for the chance of seeing Monte.”
> Maxim de Winter: “Wouldn't that rather defeat the purpose?””

DAPHNE DU MAURIER,
REBECCA

The Invincibles

"Each year, countless tourists from all over the world ask for an explanation of the Grimaldi motto, Deo Juvante*—"with God's help"—and are touched when they learn that it embodies seven centuries of cooperation between a dynasty and its people."*

—Alain Decaux, *Monaco and Its Princes*

No European family has ruled longer than the Grimaldis in the Principality of Monaco. Not the Tudors (128 years) or the Windsors (97 and still going strong) in Great Britain; nor the Hapsburgs (102 years) in Austro-Hungary. The Bourbons in France come closest (from 987 to 1792)—an impressive 705 years of domination. But the Grimaldis lead the noble pack at 717 years.

The Genoese clan dates back to the twelfth century and its founder, Otto Canella. Thirty-eight Grimaldis have followed in positions of power or privilege ever since, to the present monarch, fifty-six-year-old Prince Albert III. But it wasn't until the evening of January 8, 1297, that the Grimaldis held sway over Monaco in a conflict between the pro-German Guelphs, who manned the castle of Monaco, and the pro-Pope sect called the Ghibellines.

Dressed as a Franciscan monk—or so the story goes—a certain Francesco "Malizia" Grimaldi (Francesco the Malicious) ascended on foot to the castle on top of the famous rock. Begging shelter for the night, Malizia entered the fortress with his men and seized it from the Guelphs, returning Monaco to the Ghibellines. The Grimaldis have ruled Monaco—though not successively—from that fateful night.

Not every Grimaldi was a memorable or even honorable ruler, as is exactingly documented in the book *Monaco and Its Princes* by Alain Decaux (Perrin, 1997). There were three Honorés, two Louis, an Antoine, and a Florestan. In terms of their importance to Monte Carlo, however, the following princes made their indelible marks:

The official coat of arms of the Principality of Monaco.

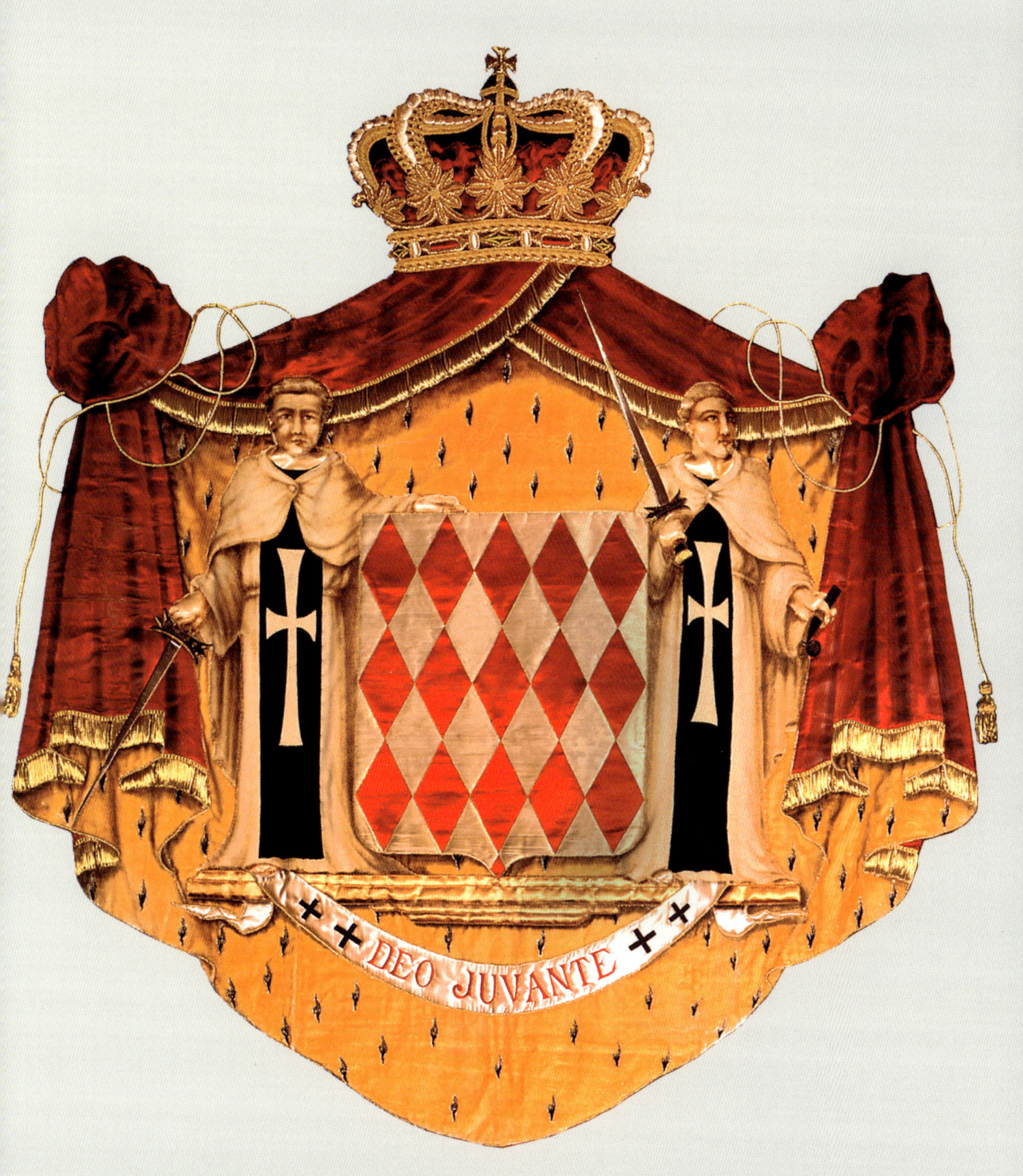
DEO JUVANTE

CHARLES III: On the strong advice of his mother, Princess Caroline, and his lawyer and chief consul, Monsieur A. Eynaud, Prince Charles hired the casino developer François Blanc to build the Monte Carlo of today, putting it on the map for all time. On April 2, 1863, Charles founded the Société des Bain de Mer (SBM) and permitted Blanc, who had built a gambling house in Bad Homburg, to conceive and run it.

Blanc was true to his word and created a town that rivaled all others on the French Riviera. Not even Nice, Cannes, or Antibes could compete with Monte Carlo's sumptuous setting. Moreover, it had casino gambling, where fortunes could be made and, far more often, lost.

In 1868, just five years later, the PLM (Paris-Lyon-Méditerranée) railway made its first stop in Monaco, thereupon opening Monte Carlo to rest of the world. That included not only European and Russian royalty and high-stakes gamblers but also prostitutes, get-rich-quick opportunists, and the hoi polloi. But, no question about it, Prince Charles III was Monaco's savior.

The casino raised so much money for the Principality in its first years that Charles made an extraordinary decision: In 1869 he exempted all Monegasques from paying land, property, or personal taxes. The drawback was that they were not permitted to gamble in the casino. Both of these declarations exist to this day.

PRINCE ALBERT I: The only child of Charles III, Albert must have had saltwater in his veins, or else he was simply a lonely boy looking to escape the solitude of confinement in a royal palace. He joined the Spanish army when he was merely seventeen, returning to Monaco in 1869 when Queen Isabella II of Spain was overthrown.

Albert's main occupation became oceanography, which led to serious scientific studies that took him far and wide, most importantly to the North Atlantic. His side interest in paleontology unearthed a collection of Cro-Magnon bones in caves located in nearby Ventimiglia, Italy. They are on display at the Musée d'Anthropologie Préhistorique in Monaco. But his crowning achievement was the founding of the Oceanographic Museum, situated on Monaco-Ville, within walking distance of the palace.

As sovereign, Albert also was responsible for Monaco's first constitution, executed in 1911, and signed a treaty establishing France as its protector.

Prince Charles III, the founder of Monte Carlo, painted by François Biard, 1869.
Following pages: The royal palace, the oldest edifice in Monaco. The structure we know today dates from the sixteenth century.

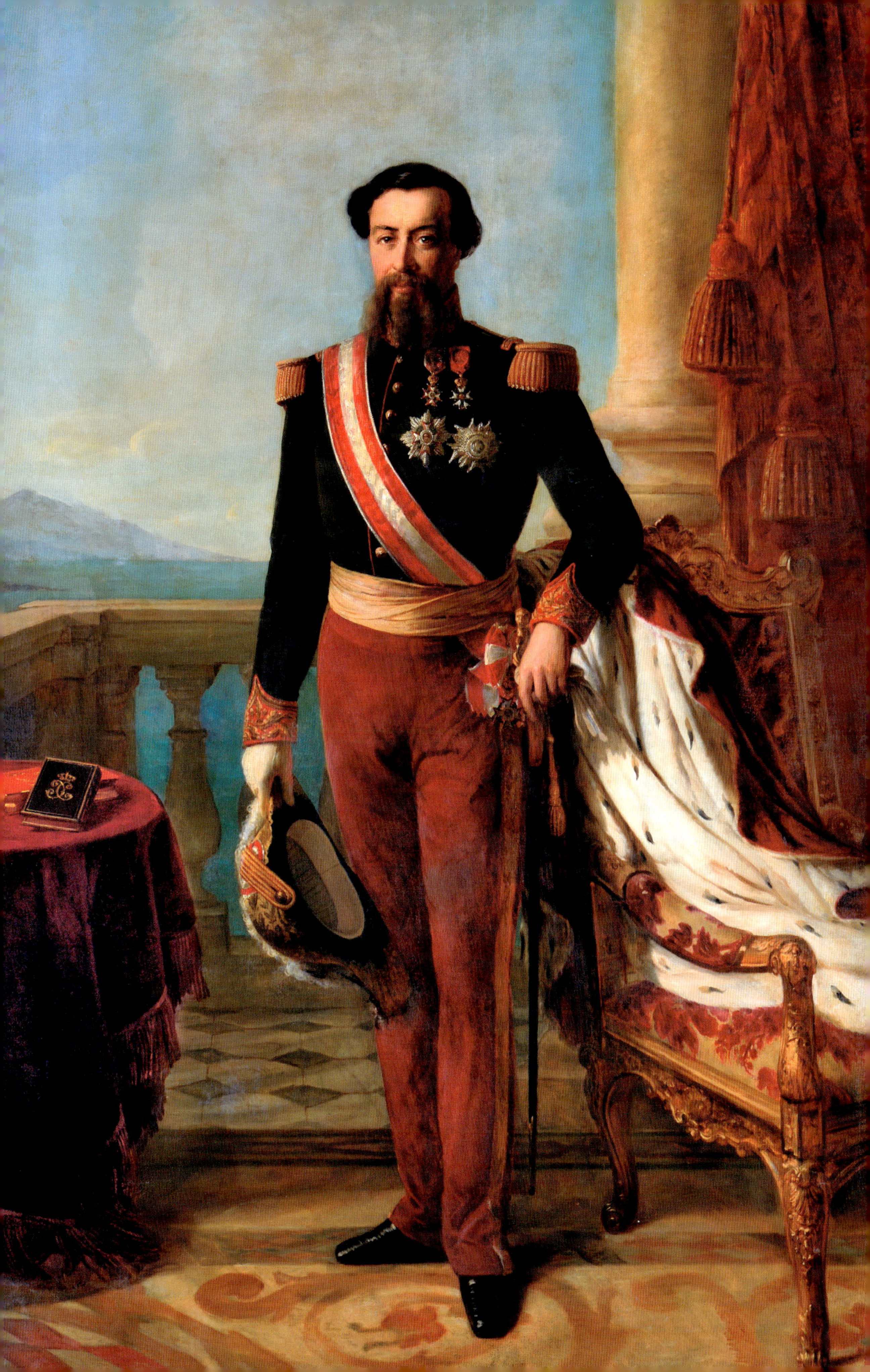

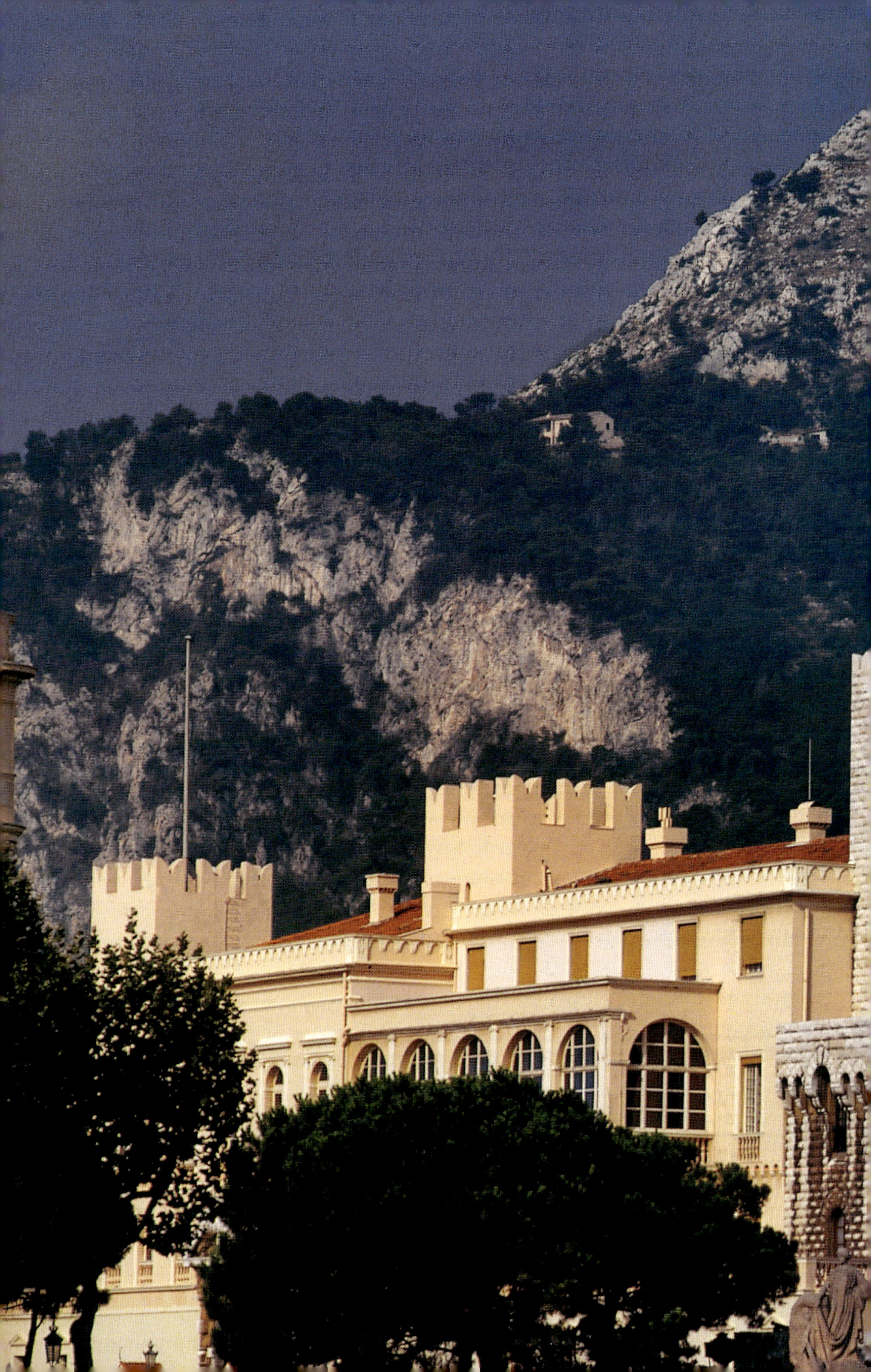

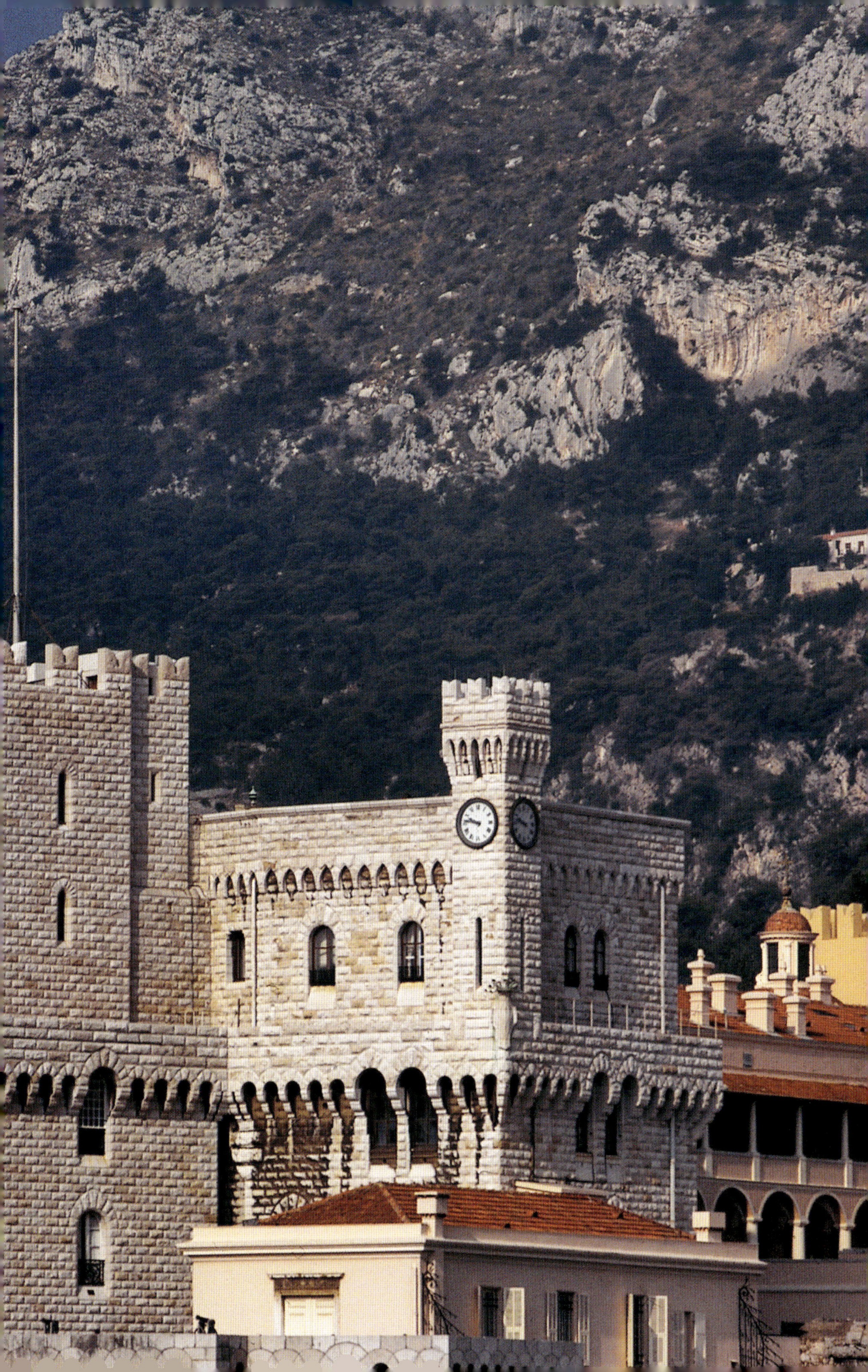

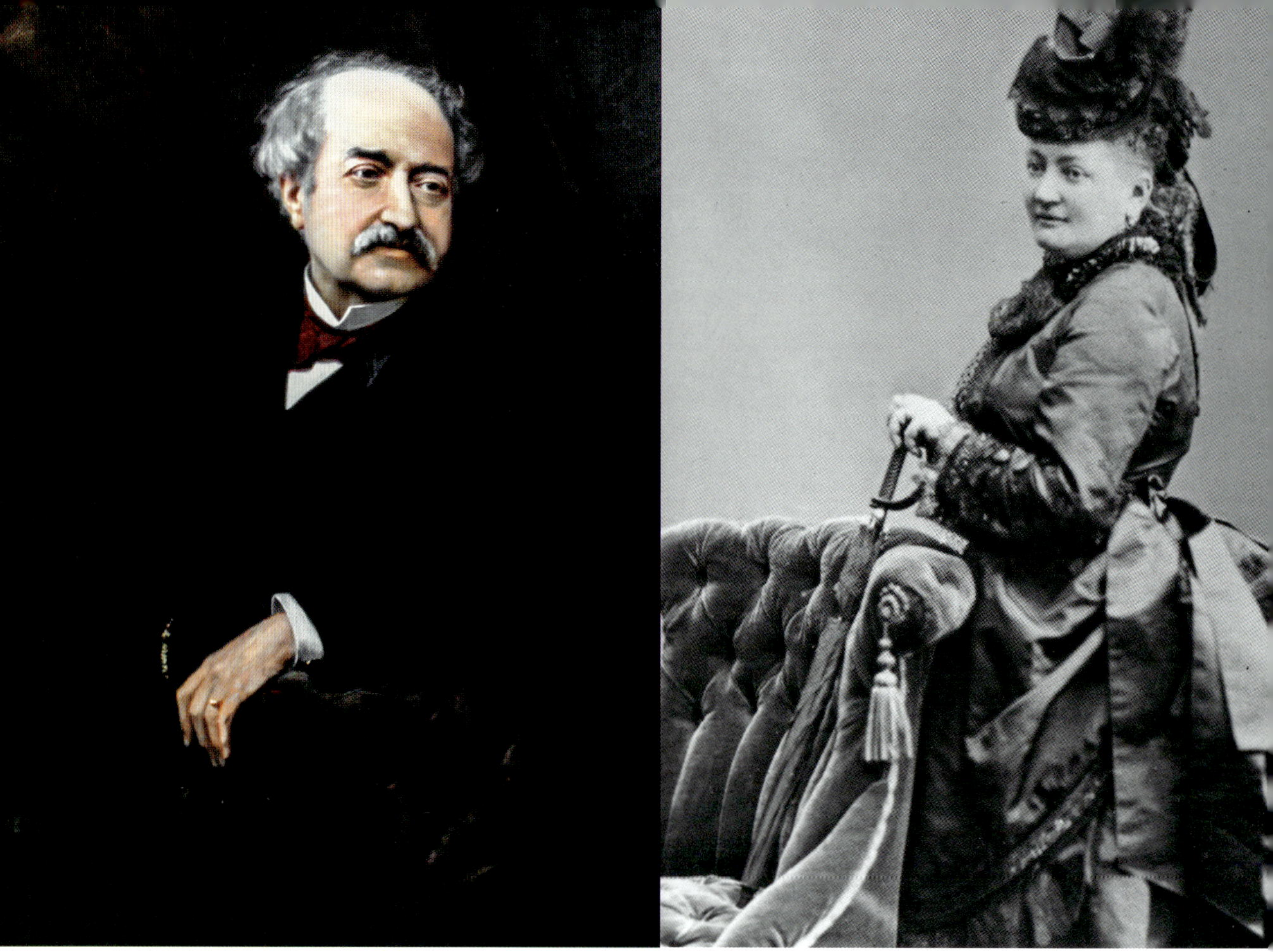

From left: Francois Blanc, Marie Blanc.

LOUIS II: Because he was raised in Baden-Baden, Germany, where his mother and her relatives lived, Prince Louis didn't meet his father, Prince Albert I, until he was ten years old. When he realized his father had no intention of giving him any role in Monaco, Louis attended a military academy, enlisted in the French cavalry, and served in Algeria. Finally, in 1910, Prince Albert beckoned his son to Monaco. When World War I began, Louis re-enlisted, went into battle, and was a decorated hero (among other honors, he received the Croix de Guerre). By the time he left the service, Louis was promoted from captain to major.

Louis succeeded Albert after Albert's death in 1922. Monaco's revenues from the casino had fallen in the postwar period, and gambling was now permitted in both France and Italy, giving Monte Carlo unforeseen competition. Louis's mission was to bring Monte Carlo back to its former glory. To accomplish this, he focused on sports, expanding Monaco's draw as a tourist mecca, by creating both the Monte Carlo rallye in 1911 and the Grand Prix of Monte Carlo in 1929. Eventually, high-end tourism returned. But then another jolt: World War II, which brought another somber period to Monaco, all of Europe and, eventually, to the United States and the Far East.

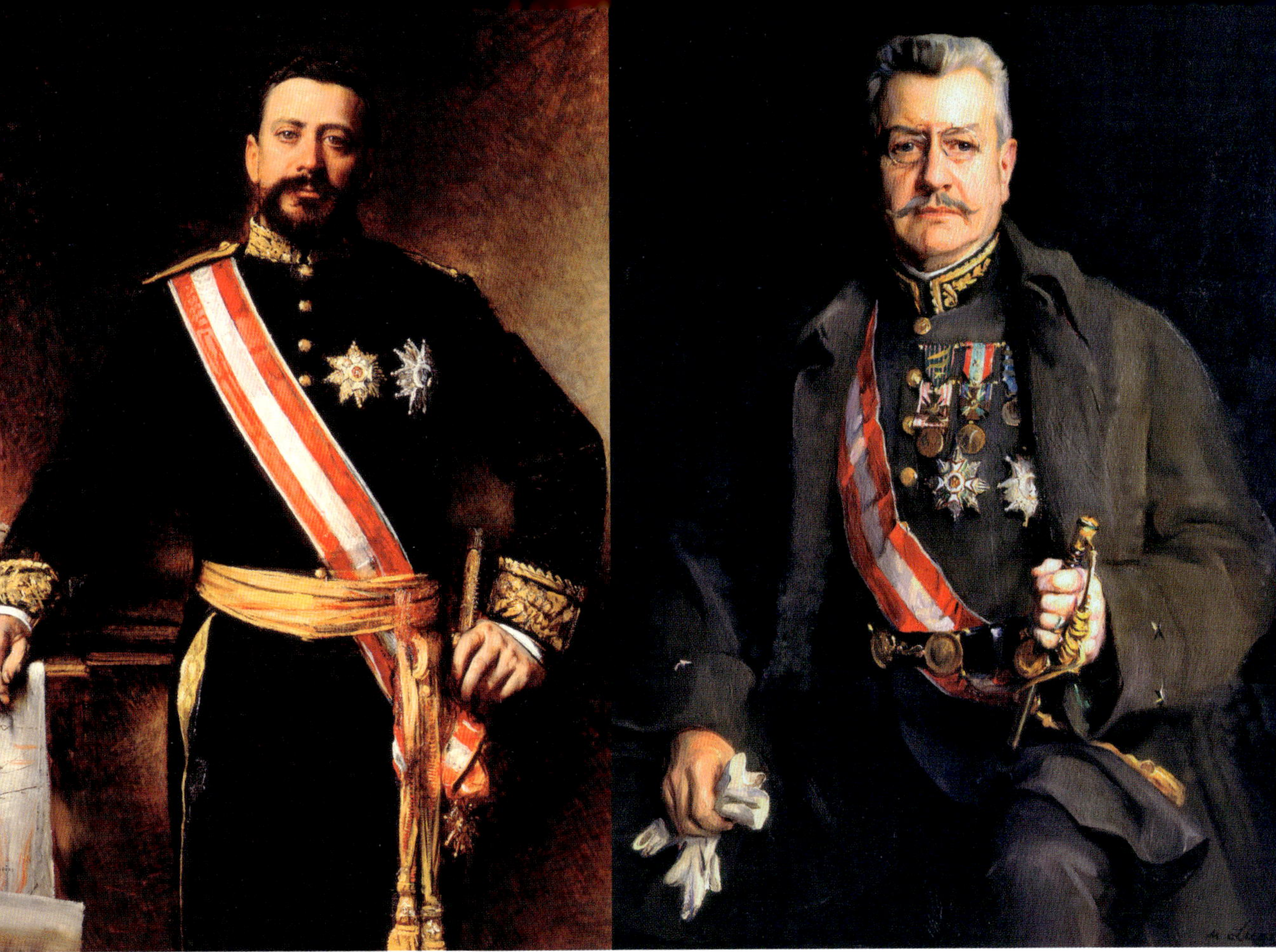

From left: Prince Albert I, Prince Louis II.

PRINCE RAINIER III: Son of Louis II, and the Principality's first truly modern leader, Rainier was also its most glamorous: polo player, race car driver, yachtsman, and man-about-Monaco. As the longest-reigning Grimaldi, he cleaned up the harbor, reclaimed land, developed real estate, encouraged bankers and stock brokers to open branches, and generally cared for the well-being of his people.

His most formidable rival was the Greek shipping tycoon Aristotle Onassis. Rich as Croesus, as the saying goes, Onassis was obsessed by Monte Carlo. He became a controlling shareholder in the SBM in the early 1950s and wanted to develop the town as a residence for the world's wealthiest people. Rainier, however, had something else in mind—a community where not only the superrich could thrive but one that also welcomed and provided for the middle class, particularly Monegasques. So vexed was Rainier by Onassis's growing influence on his domain that the prince complained that Monte Carlo might as well be called Monte Greco. By 1959 the relationship between the two men had eroded to the point where Rainier took charge by exercising his authority and creating 600,000 SBM shares that were non-transferable, making

"When I married Prince Rainier, I married the man and not what he represented or what he was. I fell in love with him without giving a thought to anything else."

PRINCESS GRACE OF MONACO

Portrait of Rainier III, Monaco's modern Prince Charming, 1950.

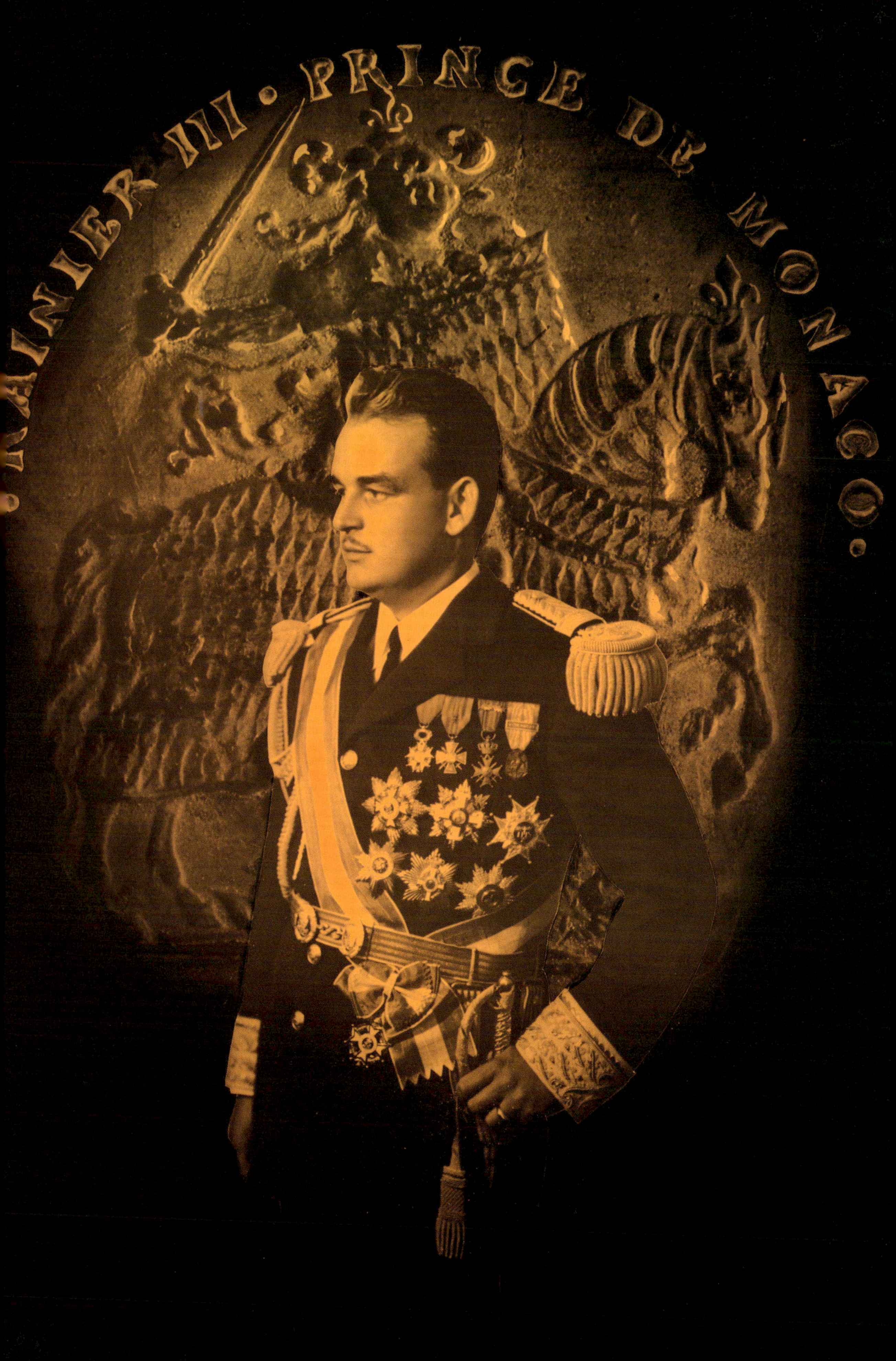
RAINIER III · PRINCE DE MONACO ·

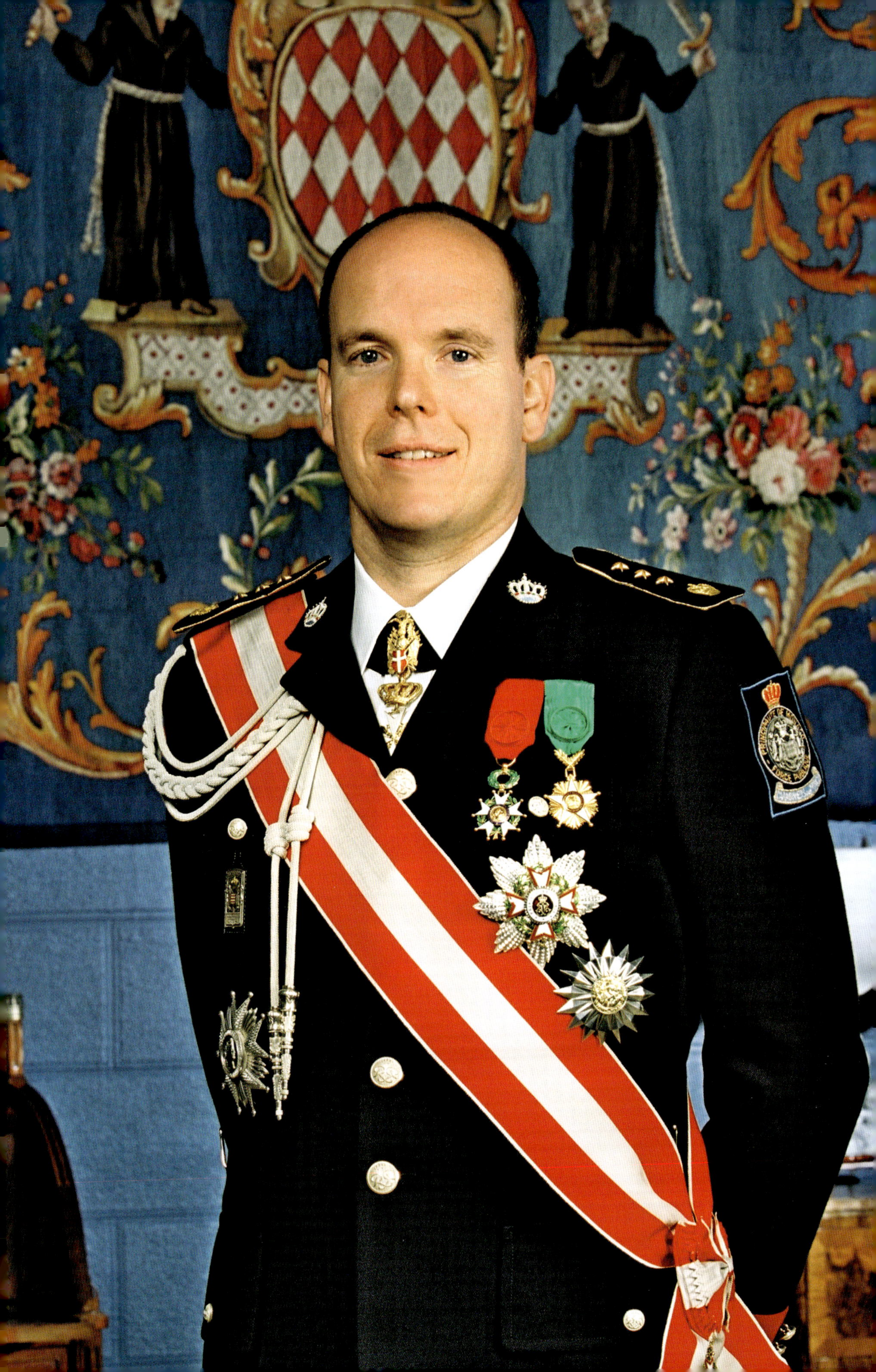

the Principality a majority shareholder once more. That clever move got rid of Rainier's nemesis once and for all.

Not everything in the 1950s was trying for Prince Rainier. A longtime and highly eligible bachelor, he sensed that the time had come for him to marry, raise a family, and plan for the future (i.e., provide an heir). While there were several possibilities among European royalty, Rainier stunned the world by choosing Hollywood actress Grace Kelly to be his bride. They wed on April 19, 1956, in what was then called "the wedding of the century." Part of the agreement was that Kelly would give up her dazzling career. She did so without hesitation, putting Hollywood behind her, and was henceforth known as Princess Grace of Monaco. America may have lost a rising star, but Monaco gained a ravishing princess who couldn't have arrived in Monaco at a more opportune time. She helped put Monte Carlo and Monaco back in the limelight by her beauty and regal presence.

Tragically, Princess Grace died after suffering injuries in an automobile crash in 1982. Although their marriage wasn't perfect, Rainier was grief-stricken. He carried on, but with great difficulty. Their three children—Caroline, Albert, and Stéphanie—took up the mantle that their mother had borne so elegantly. Rainier died in 2006 at age eighty-one. His son, the middle child and the Principality's rightful heir, assumed the title of His Sovereign Highness Crown Prince Albert. Enter a new era.

PRINCE ALBERT II: "The apple doesn't fall far from the tree," goes the adage. Like his father, Albert is an avid sportsman—a five-time Olympic bobsled team captain, a soccer player, and a sailor. And like his namesake, Albert I, he has a keen and abiding interest in oceanography, biodiversity, and the environment—not only in the Mediterranean basin but in barely habitable places such as the Arctic and the Antarctic, where his foundation conducts ongoing explorations and experiments.

Albert and Rainier have other things in common as well: Both had extended and robust bacherlorhoods, and both share a fascination with elegant, cool-looking blondes. In 2001 and at the ripe age of fifty-two, Albert married his longtime companion, Charlene Wittstock. A former Olympic swimmer from South Africa, Princess Charlene bears a striking resemblance to Albert's mother, Princess Grace. Only time will tell if she will elevate the Principality in the same way.

The same applies to Prince Albert. So far, he is making his mark both within and outside of Monaco, and is beloved by his people, who have nothing but the highest expectations for their Crown Prince.

Prince Albert II on Monaco's National Day, November 19, 2007.

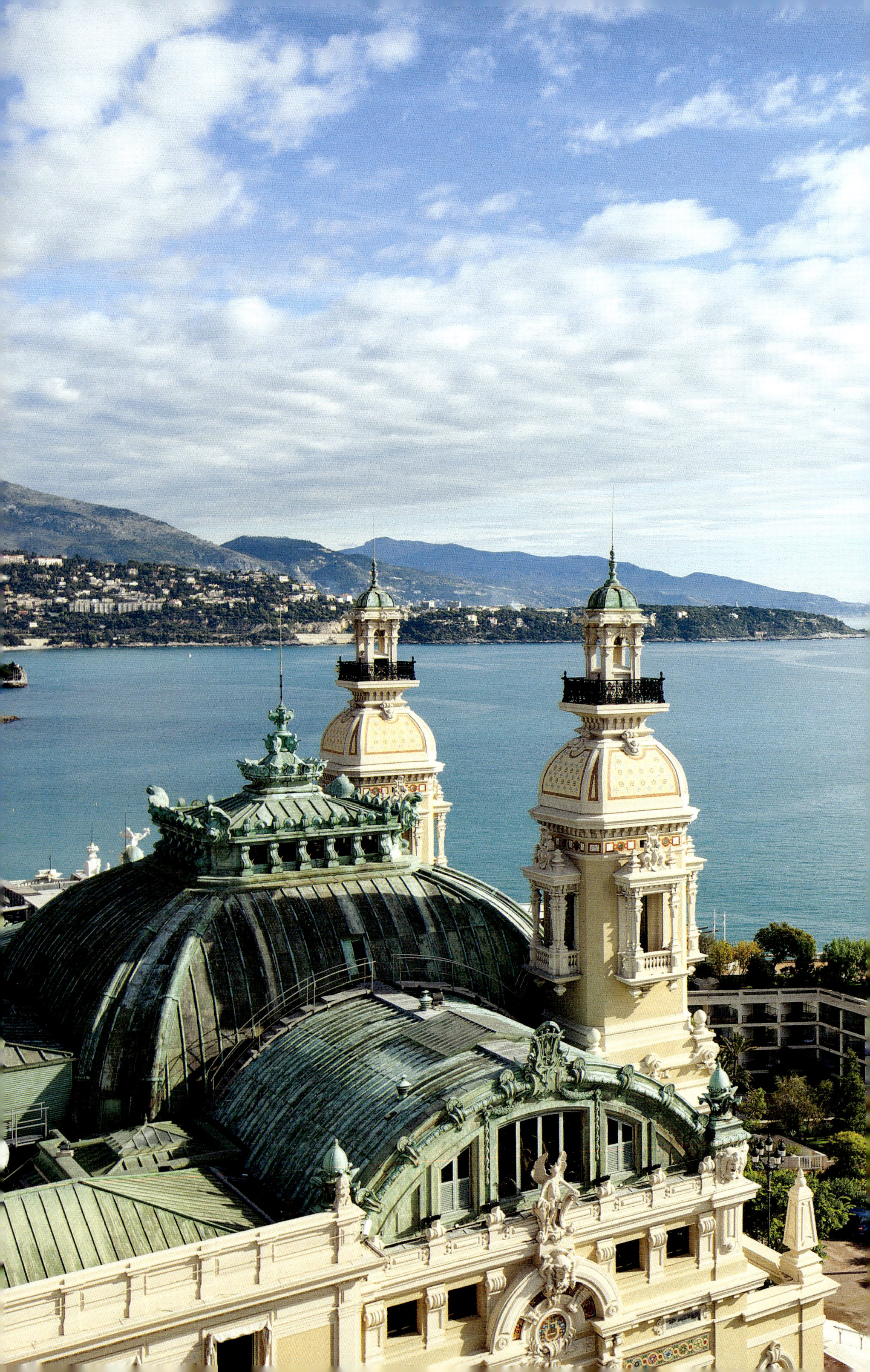

The Glittering Prize

"What happened in the next few years was little short of miraculous. An entire town sprang up on the plateau, with streets, tree-lined boulevards, plazas, a park, hotels, villas. A metropolis was born..."

—Alain Decaux, *Monaco and Its Princes*

All eyes were on Monte Carlo, the Côte d'Azur's shining star. Once the railway extension was in place, by 1870, along came the hungry crowds eager to place their bets and partake in the pleasures of a sparkling new destination.

Accompanied by their entourages, a roll call of royalty arrived in full regalia: Emperor Franz Joseph of Austria, Empress Eugénie, Tsar Nicholas of Russia, the king of Greece, King Leopold of Belgium, Napoléon III, and the British monarchs (including King Edward VII, who considered Monte Carlo a private playpen for his many assignations with high-priced courtesans like La Belle Otero). A former barren plateau was now a thriving oasis attracting the rich, famous,

View of the Mediterranean, with the Salle Garnier in the foreground.

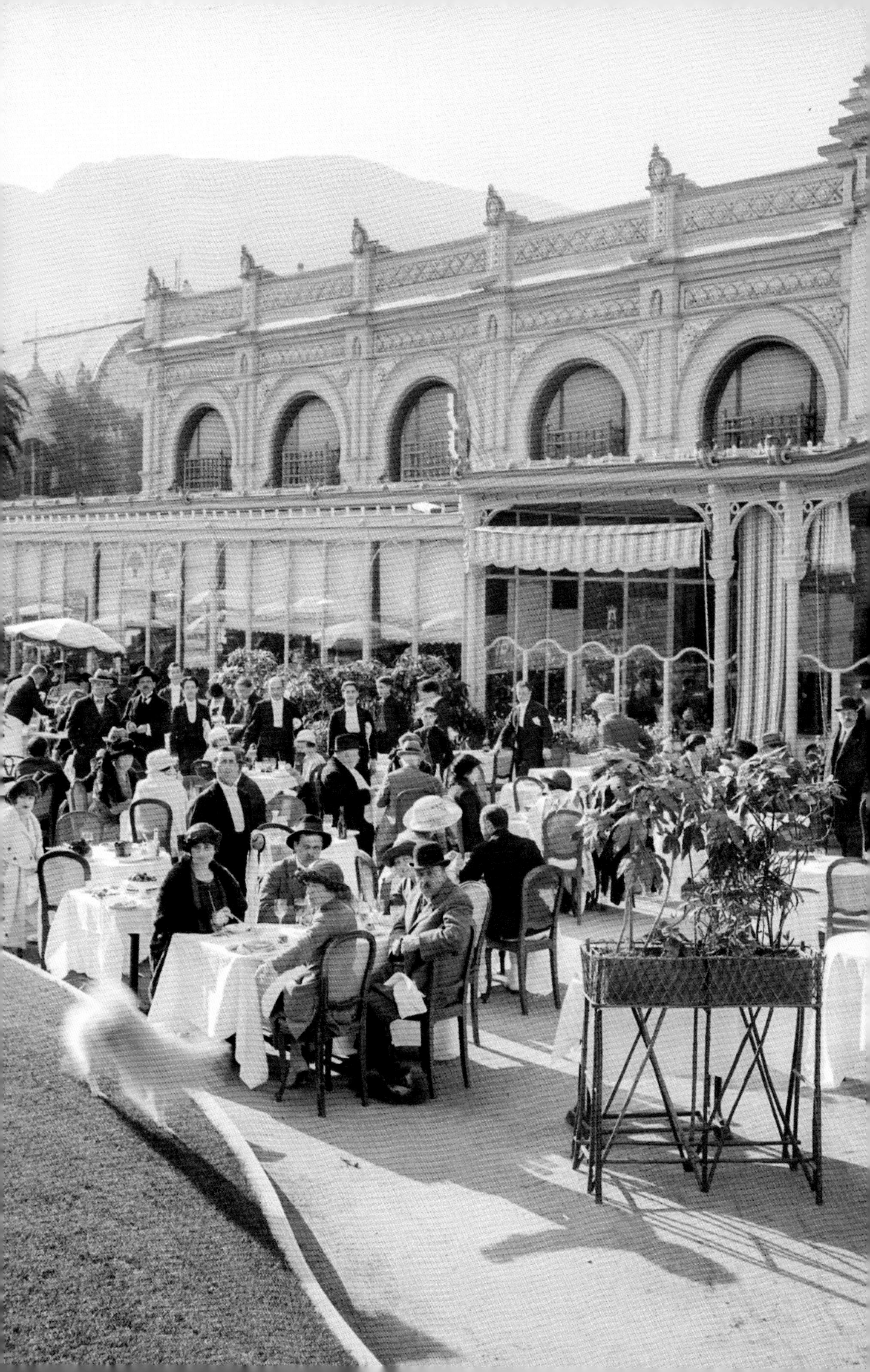

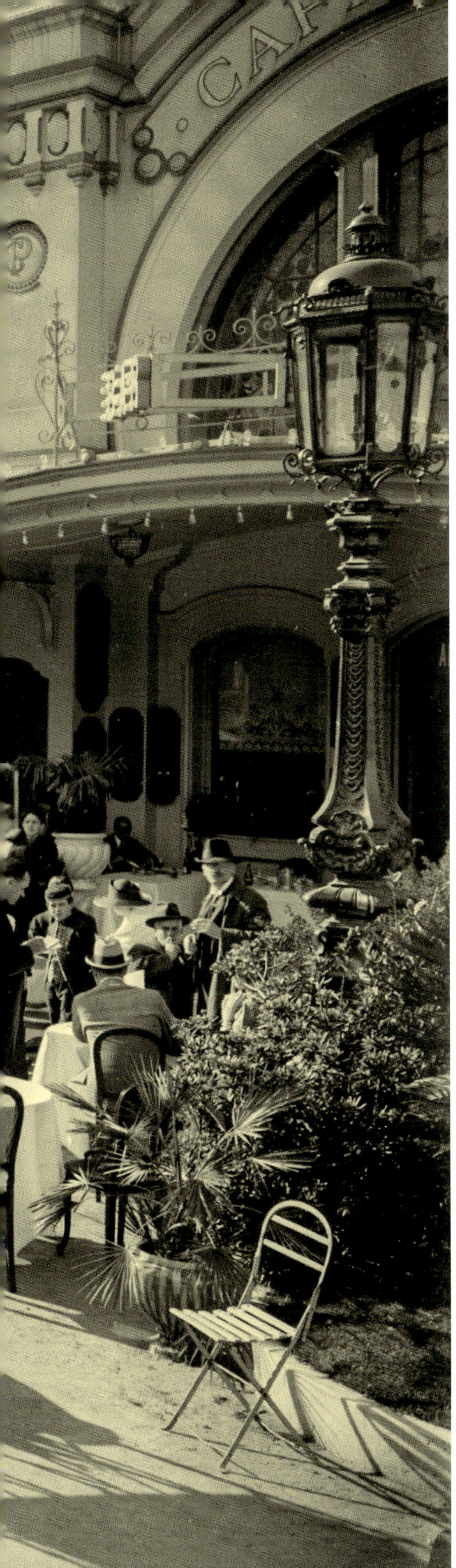

and infamous to its waters and to its gaming tables. Jules Verne, Alexandre Dumas, Hector Berlioz, the composer Massenet, Barons Haussmann and Rothschild, and others of the *beau monde* chose Monte Carlo, to the consternation of rival Riviera towns. Aside from the casino, people flocked to the Hôtel de Paris and the Café de Paris on either side of it. Charles Garnier, architect of the revered Paris Opéra, was summoned by Marie Blanc to build a smaller replica in a scant six months. Garnier, who had also had a hand in designing the casino, delivered—and, astonishingly, on time. Now Monte Carlo had the perfect trifecta: a splendid casino, a deluxe hotel, and a prominent cultural center for the arts. Is it any surprise Monte Carlo's ascension in the late nineteenth century corresponds with that of the Belle Époque in Europe and the Gilded Age in America?

In *The Poisoned Paradise*, a novel written in 1922, author Robert W. Service depicts Monte Carlo as "various kinds of a jewel. In the morning it glitters likes a diamond; in the afternoon it gleams like a great pearl of the Orient; in the evening it glows with the mellow lustre of a sapphire."

Not everyone, however, was impressed. Somerset Maugham dubbed Monte Carlo "a sunny place for shady people." The Dean of Canterbury charged that the town attracted "the scum of the world." There was further pushback from other Christian critics who

The terrace of the Café de Paris, 1921.

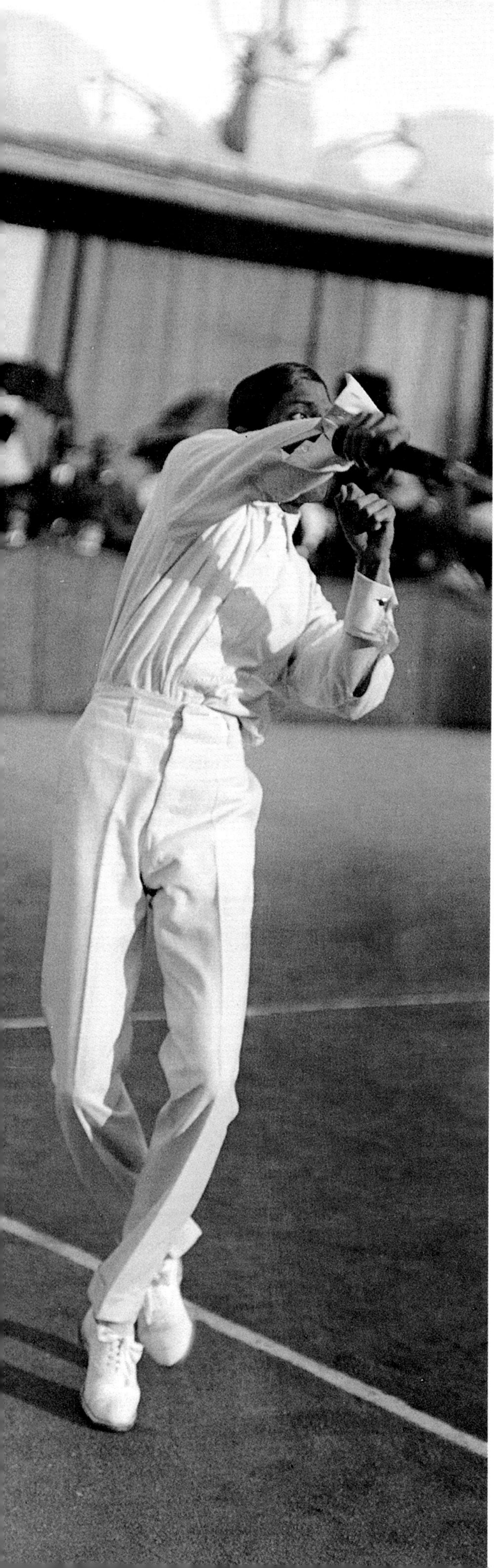

felt gambling represented evil and that Monte Carlo was no better than a mini Sodom and Gomorrah. In Jim Ring's 2004 history titled Riviera: *The Rise and Rise of the Côte d'Azur,* he quotes the Bishop of Gibraltar, who posed this question: "Is it right for Christian men and women ever to enter a place where they are sure to rub shoulders with the swindler, the harlot and the thief, whose chambers are built with the wages of iniquity, and whose riches are the price of blood?" The casino itself has been described variously as a "great lunatic asylum," "demoralizing," and "a centre of depravity."

Such verbal assaults didn't do much to discourage the throngs of revelers. Indeed, to "winter in Monte Carlo" was such a popular pastime that the expression almost became a cliché, akin to the present-day "summering in the Hamptons." More hotels sprang up, as well as posh villas and spas. Monaco's population doubled, and a building boom began.

Galas, balls, fancy social and sporting events, and fireworks were de rigueur. Men came with their wallets bulging; women were fairly dripping in emeralds, rubies, and diamonds and the latest Paris fashions. All were on parade day and night. No place on the planet was a more potent metaphor for glamour, luxury, and the high life than Monte Carlo—a tiny but richly packaged paradise.

The Maharaja of Indore, 1911, playing tennis at Condamine.

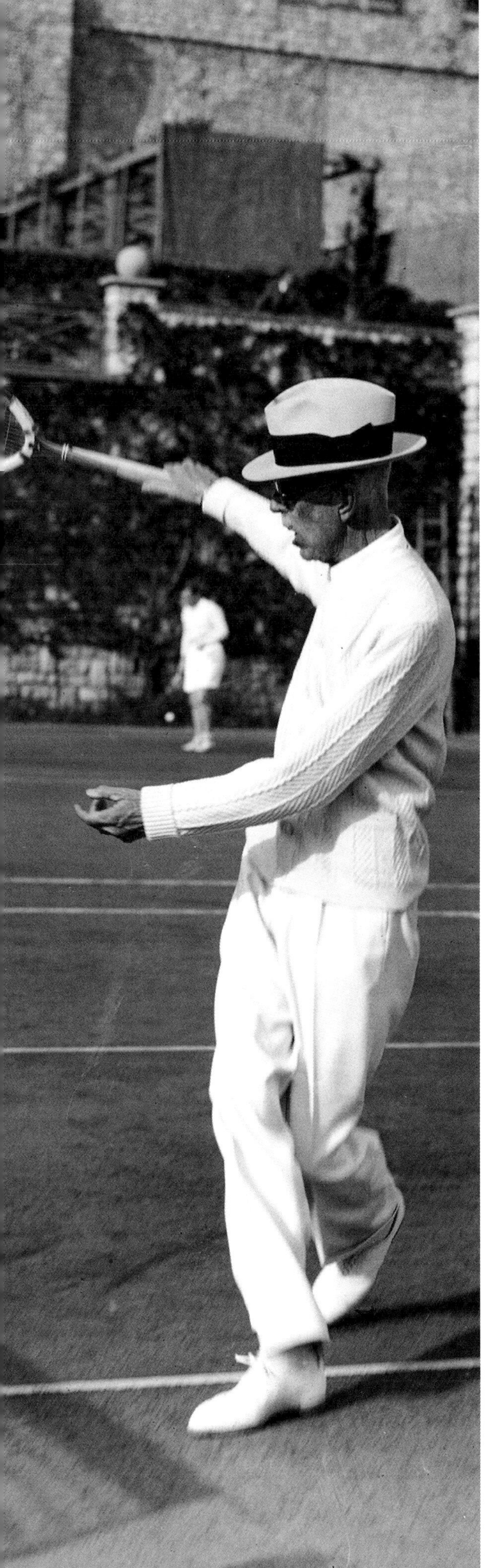

The package, as founded by Prince Charles III in 1863, was called the Société des Bains de Mer, or SBM, and is synonymous with Monte Carlo. The SBM doesn't control everything in the town, only the most precious jewels in its crown. Today, that adds up to five casinos, three performance venues, four hotels, four spas, four sports facilities, and twenty-nine restaurants and nightclubs. Not a bad collection after 126 years of operation, and definitely the major revenue source for the Principality and the House of Grimaldi. Without the SBM and Monte Carlo, Monaco wouldn't be nearly as wealthy.

What accelerated Monte Carlo's fortunes in the beginning was casino gambling—a tantalizing and expensive distraction. As anyone who understands this world knows all too well, "the house always wins." But that warning has never been a deterrent to those who can't resist the spin of a roulette wheel or a seat at the blackjack table. In the 1953 British movie *Affair in Monte Carlo*, starring Merle Oberon and Leo Genn, Genn takes the recently widowed Oberon to the casino and tries to explain such risk-taking: "No one who doesn't gamble can ever understand the attraction to the pursuit by someone who cannot resist the urge to place a bet, no matter how much of a long shot, no matter how far-fetched."

Gustave V, King of Sweden, at the Monte Carlo Sporting Club, 1938.

"Then one day as she was passing the window of a tourist agency she stopped to stare at a vivid poster depicting a sea of turquoise blue, a terraced town that seemed carved from ivory, a background of amethystine mountains, palms, pigeons, gorgeous flowers. Underneath was the name—Monte Carlo."

ROBERT W. SERVICE,
THE POISONED PARADISE **(1922)**

A travel poster announcing that "Chic People Winter in Monte Carlo," 1937.

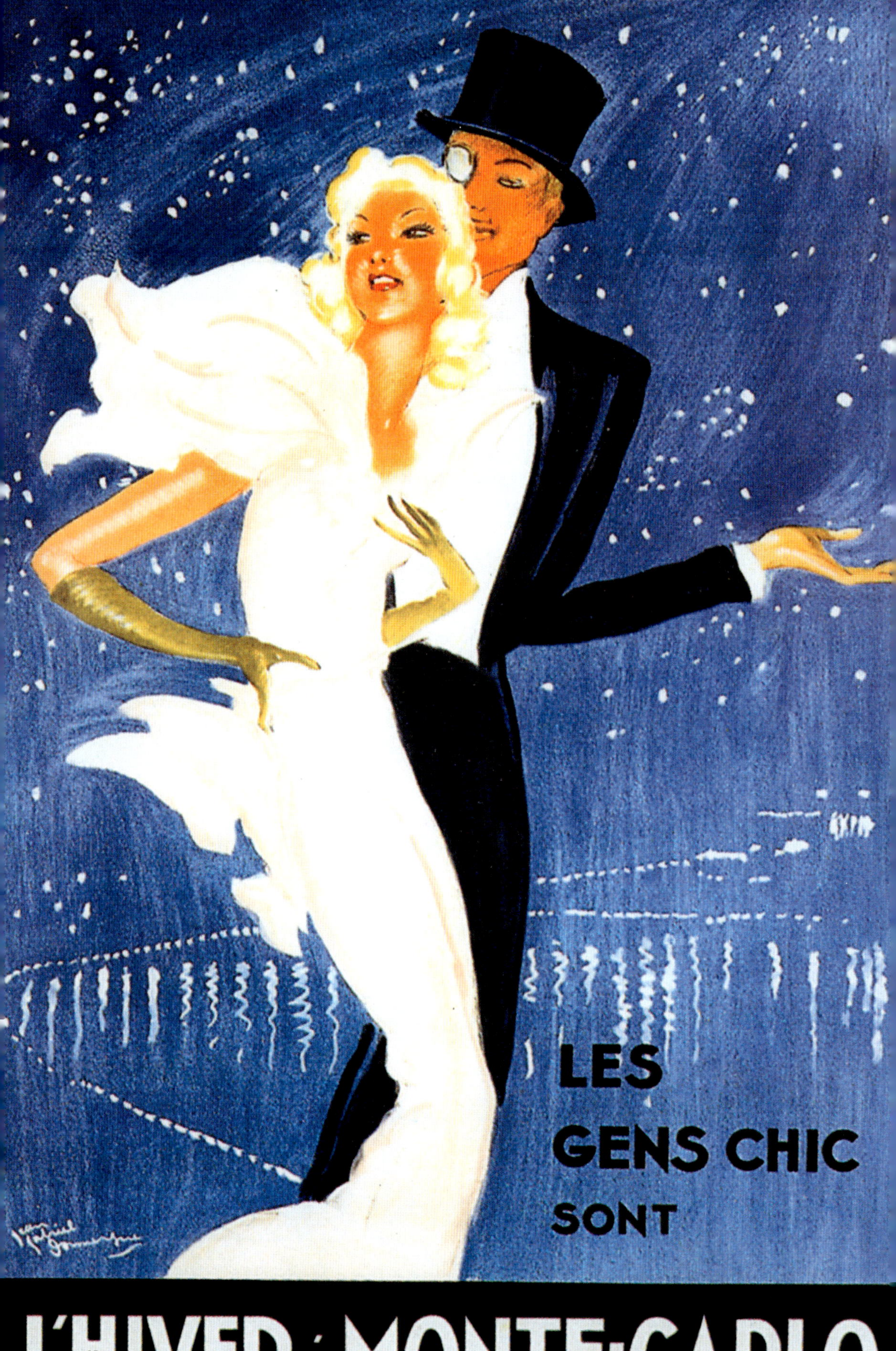

L'HIVER À MONTE-CARLO

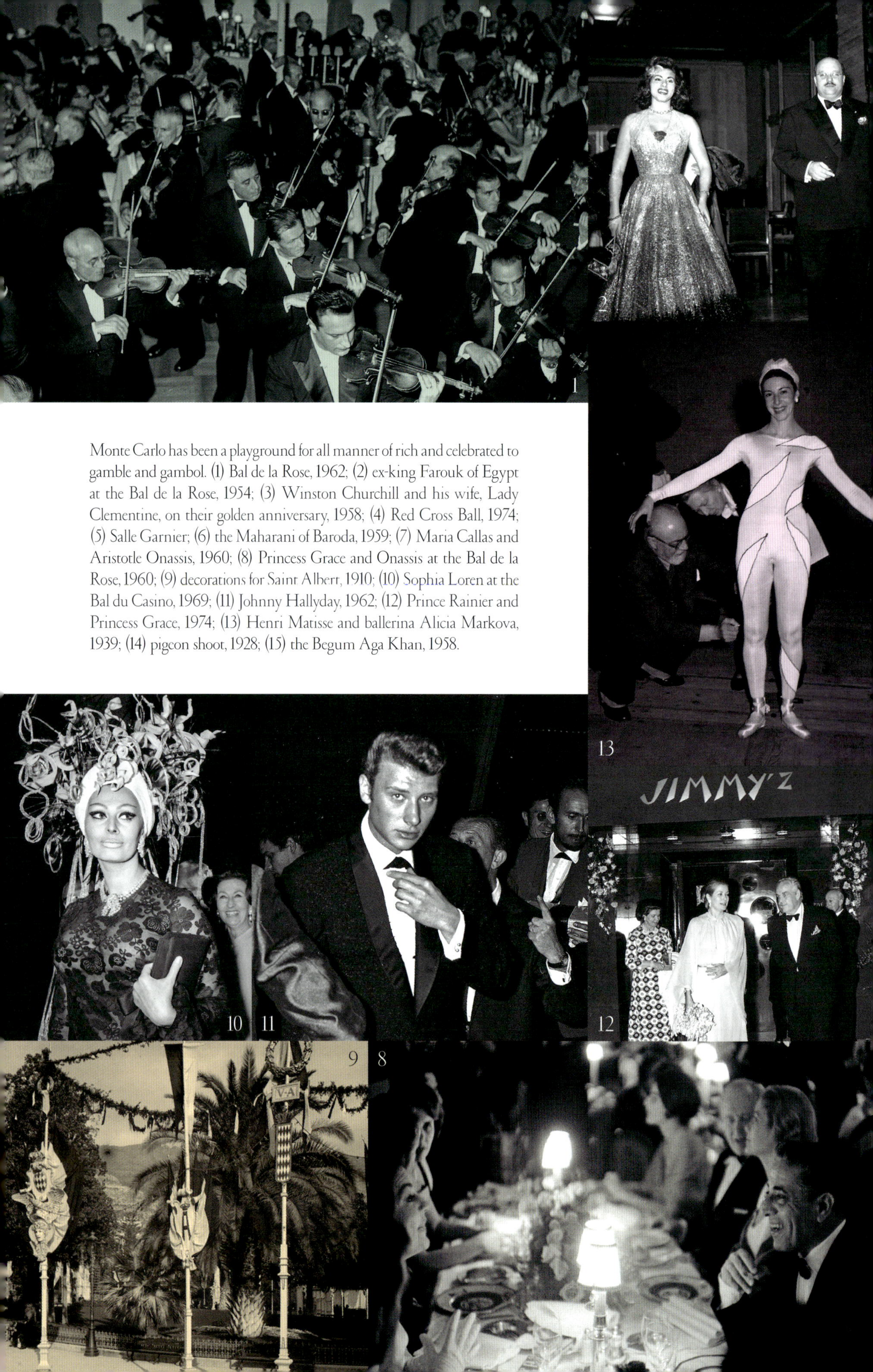

Monte Carlo has been a playground for all manner of rich and celebrated to gamble and gambol. (1) Bal de la Rose, 1962; (2) ex-king Farouk of Egypt at the Bal de la Rose, 1954; (3) Winston Churchill and his wife, Lady Clementine, on their golden anniversary, 1958; (4) Red Cross Ball, 1974; (5) Salle Garnier; (6) the Maharani of Baroda, 1959; (7) Maria Callas and Aristotle Onassis, 1960; (8) Princess Grace and Onassis at the Bal de la Rose, 1960; (9) decorations for Saint Albert, 1910; (10) Sophia Loren at the Bal du Casino, 1969; (11) Johnny Hallyday, 1962; (12) Prince Rainier and Princess Grace, 1974; (13) Henri Matisse and ballerina Alicia Markova, 1939; (14) pigeon shoot, 1928; (15) the Begum Aga Khan, 1958.

1

2

13

10 11

12

9 8

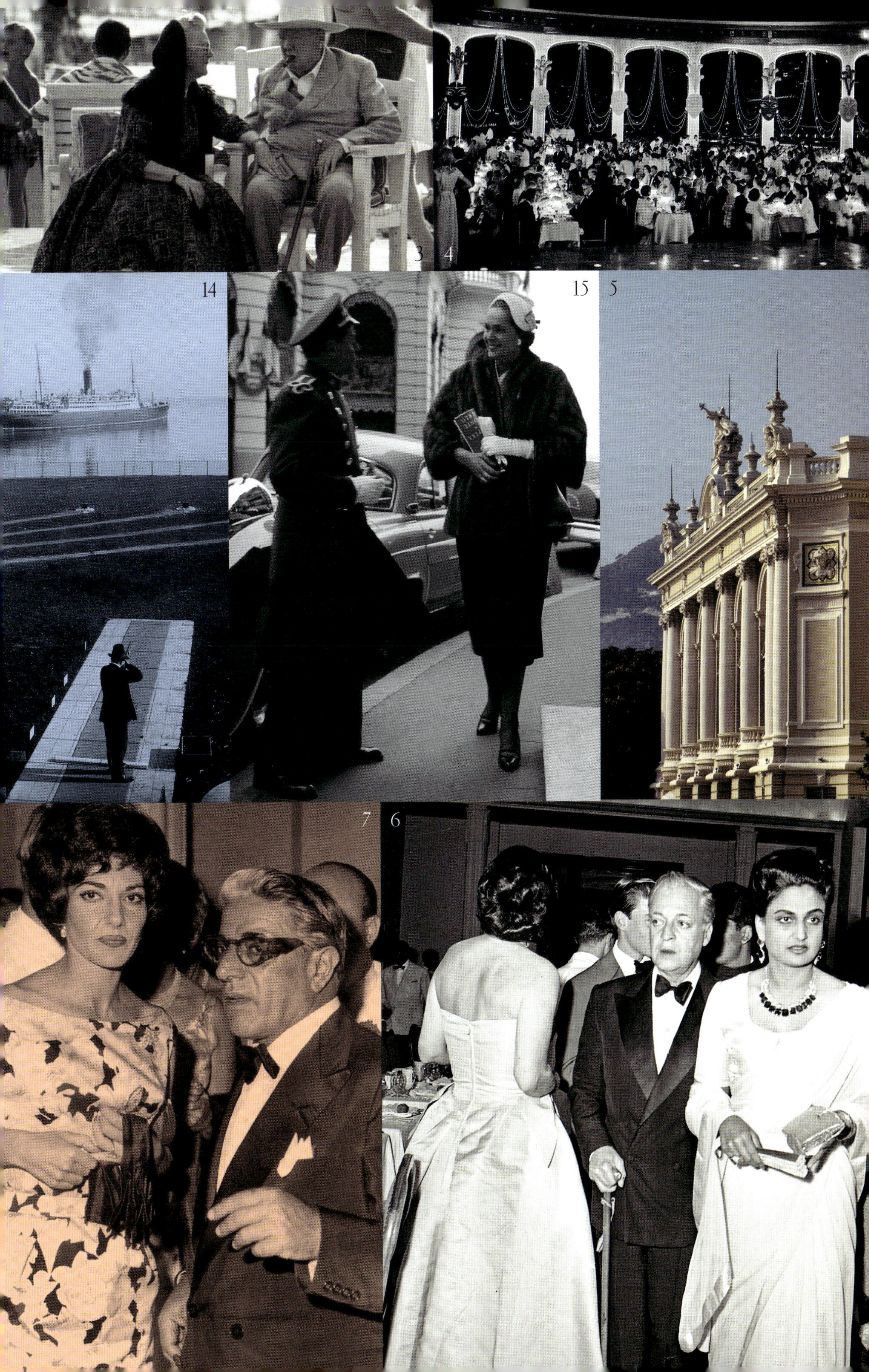
3
4
14
15
5
7
6

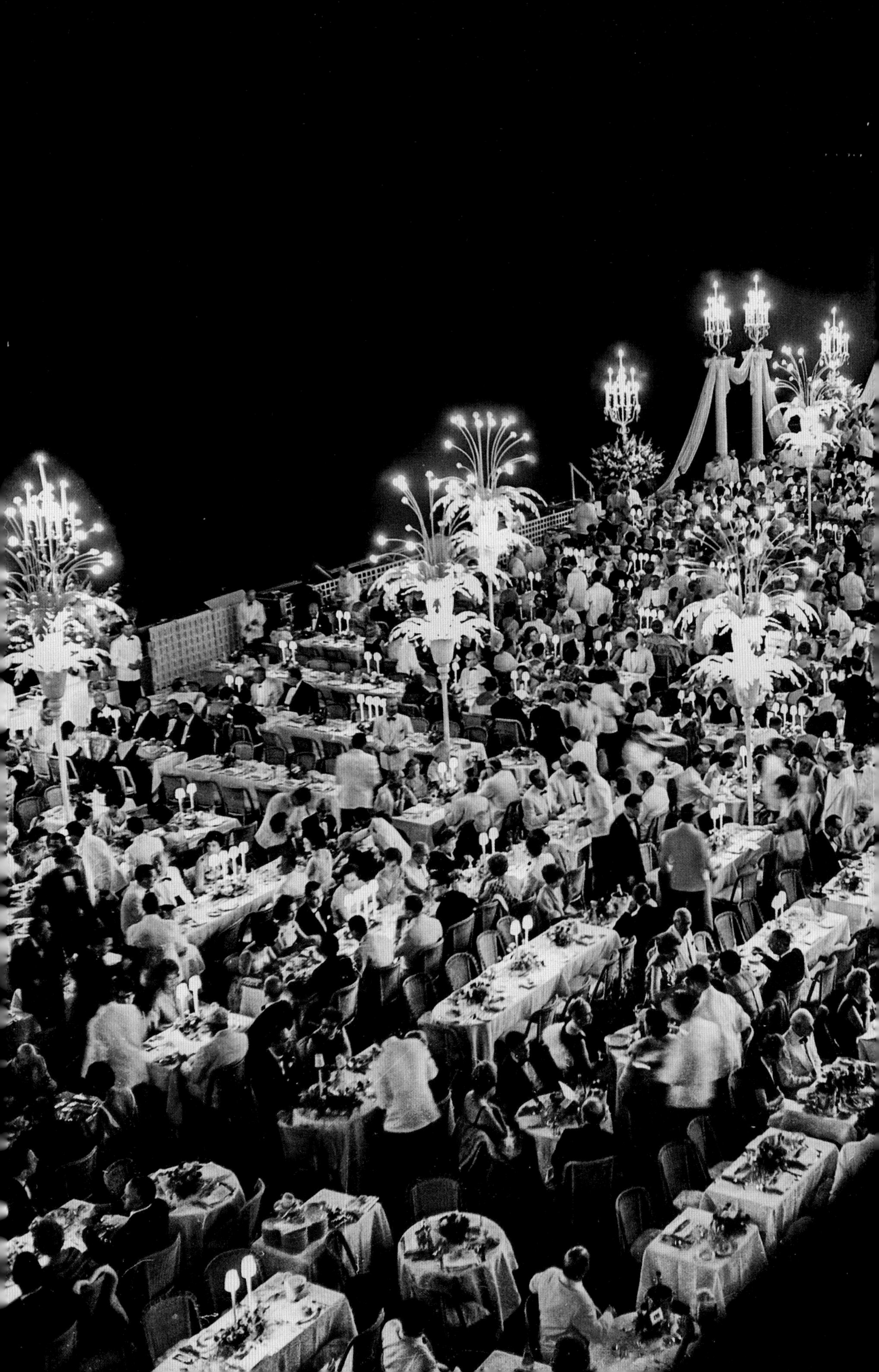

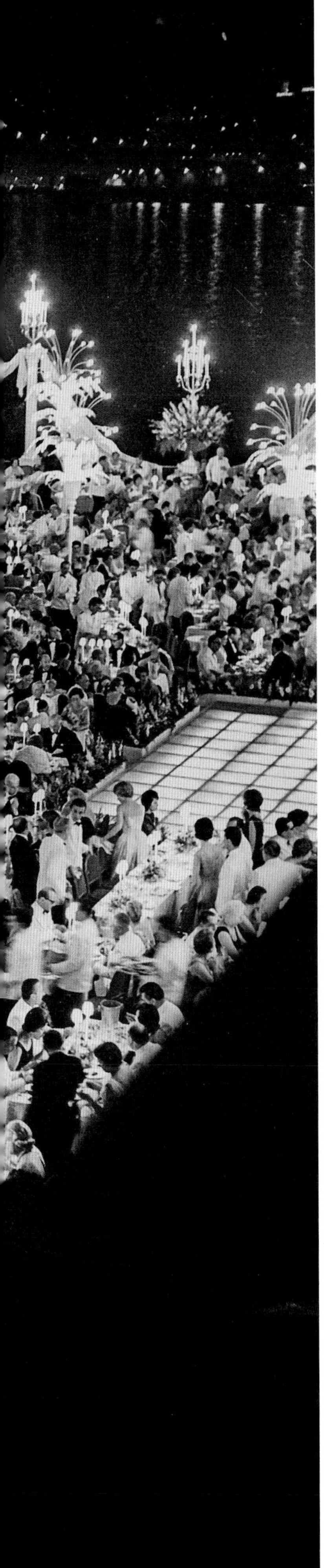

Apart from the gambling *salles,* or rooms, the building itself is majestic both inside and out, with ornately decorated ceilings and murals. The entrance has a graceful wrought-iron awning and two ceramic-covered domes. Several architects played a part in its Beaux Arts design, including Jules Dutrou and Garnier. In the twenty-first century, Las Vegas and Macao may make more money, but the Casino de Monte Carlo was and still is the most prestigious and most beautiful casino in the world, and so is its location.

The fortunes of Monte Carlo were not immune from European and world events, such as two major wars and severe economic downturns. It was in the late 1940s, a period of sluggish recovery, that Aristotle Onassis set his sights on Monte Carlo by stealthily acquiring a majority stake in the SBM and taking up residence. His enormous yacht was audaciously anchored in the harbor, as if thumbing its nose at the Principality. The press referred to Onassis as the "king of Monaco," which obviously didn't go down well with Prince Rainier. The two disagreed vehemently about Monte Carlo's future: Onassis wanted it to be a retreat for the rich; the Prince had visions of Las Vegas. In the end, the Prince prevailed. Onassis sold his stake back to Rainier for $9.5 million.

Losing SBM was a humiliating defeat for a man who had for more than a decade been the powerhouse of the Principality. In *Nemesis,* a searing portrait of Onassis, author Peter Evans describes the tycoon's last night in Monte Carlo: He "dined on the terrace of his beloved Hôtel de Paris with his children Alexander and Christina, and a few old friends. He knew he was part of the show as he sipped vintage Taittinger Comtes de Champagne, his beautiful yacht waiting in the harbor below to bear him off like a departing king." (HarperCollins, 2004)

A romantic gala at the Sporting Club in 1961.
Following pages: Port Hercule, the main harbor, aglow at night.

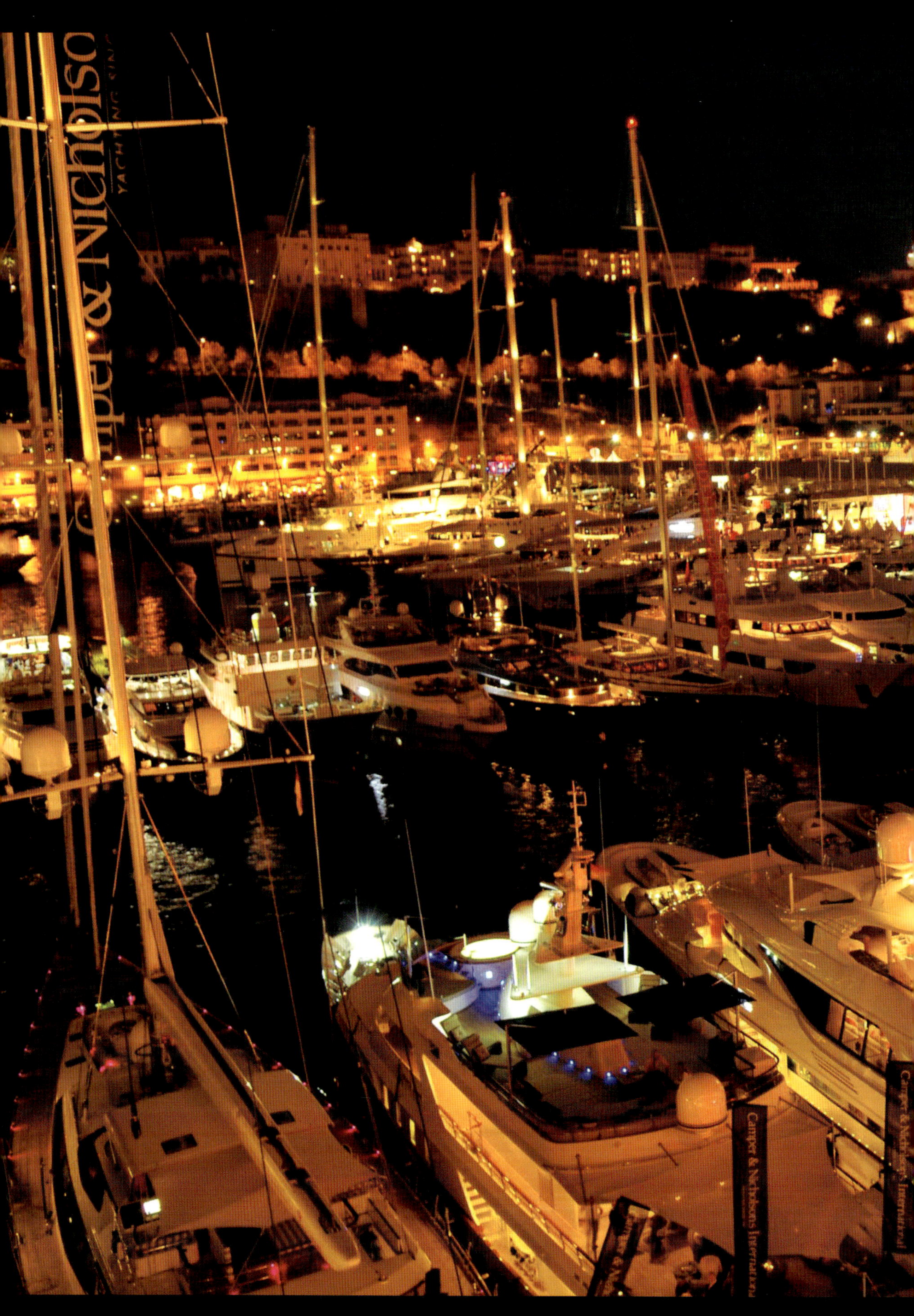
Camper & Nicholsons International

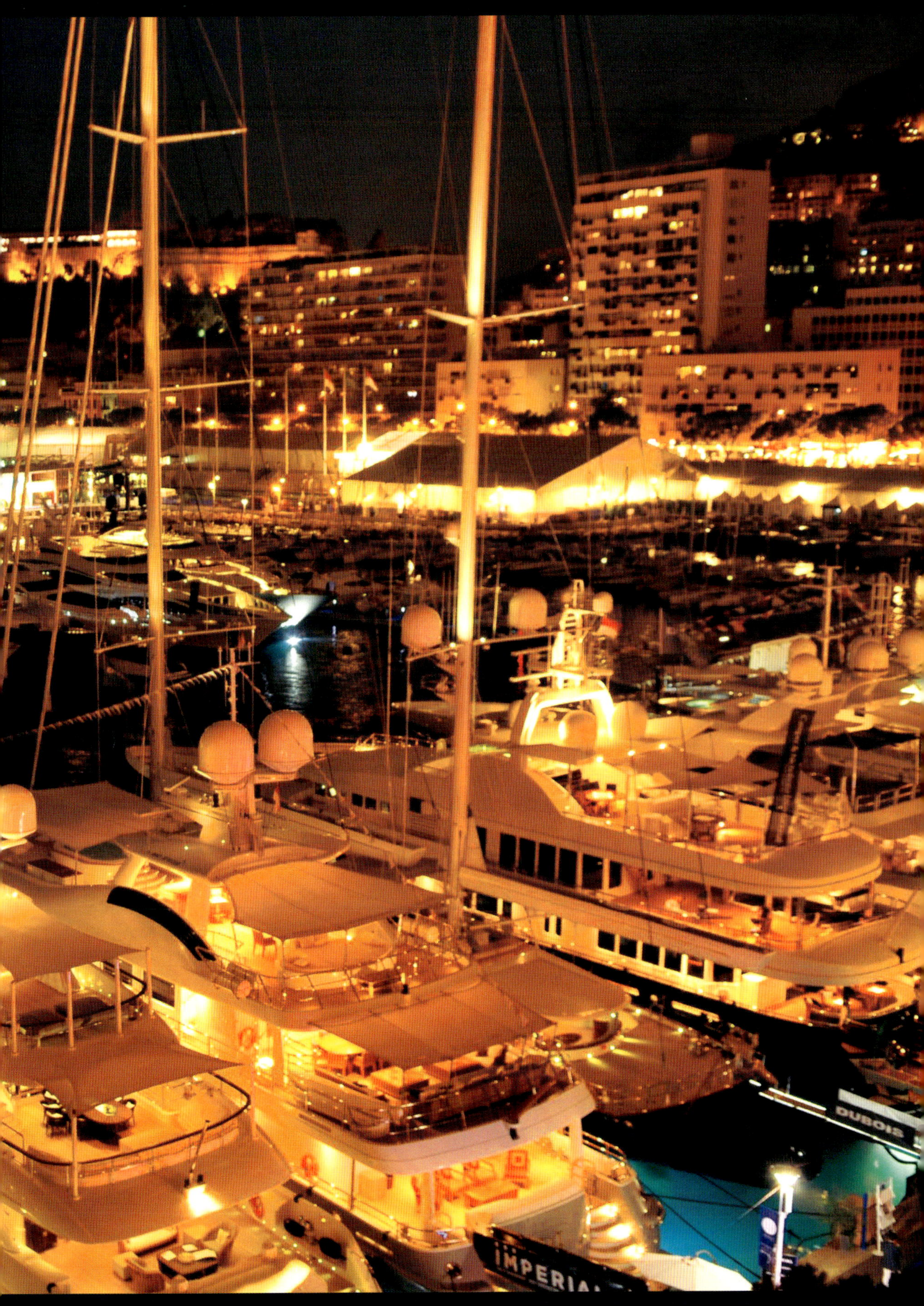
DUBOIS
IMPERIAL

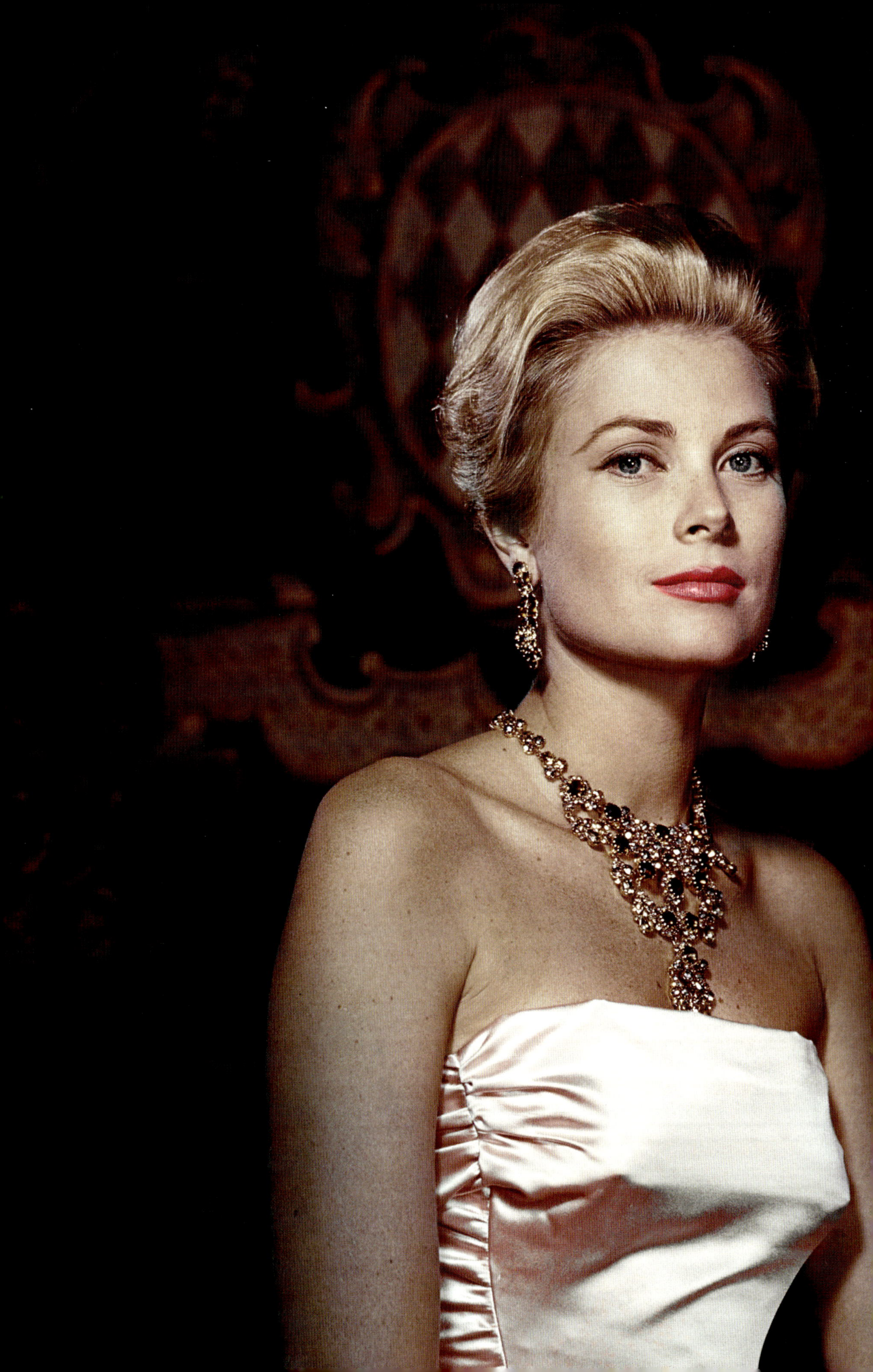

Grace Personified

"I believe that she will be remembered for her compassion and for her beautiful dignified way. It is amazing that she touched so many people's lives, so many people she never met."

—Prince Albert II of Monaco

Grace Kelly starred in only eleven films, between 1951 and 1956. In that brief period, she left a lasting impression on the movie-going public, one that persists to this day. In her most memorable films—*Rear Window*, *To Catch a Thief*, *Dial M for Murder*, and *High Society*—she played to her type: elegant, remote, ravishing. But it was her 1954 role in *The Country Girl*, as the dowdy, long-suffering wife of a washed-up musical star, played by Bing Crosby, which won her an Oscar.

Hollywood didn't hold on to Kelly for long. To everyone's astonishment, in 1956 she said goodbye to all that to play the role of a lifetime: that of Princess of Monaco. For the next twenty-six years, as wife of Prince Rainier III, she lived a life that contrasted with her freewheeling, independent days as an actress. As Her Serene Highness Princess Grace, she spent most of her time behind palace walls, protected by her ladies-in-waiting, existing in a bubble. Rather than live by her wits, she abided by ritual and protocol. But it was a role she chose and a challenge to which she rose with

A bejeweled Princess Grace, the embodiment of elegance and refinement, 1963.

a magnificence that may have surprised many who knew her, including her own family.

Grace Patricia Kelly was born in Philadelphia on November 12, 1929. The Kellys were often compared to the Kennedys of Massachusetts; both were big, wealthy Irish-Catholic clans whose money was made by ambitious, arrogant, and dynamic patriarchs. Whereas Joseph Kennedy made his fortune in the stock market, in Hollywood deals and, it has been speculated, bootlegging, Jack Kelly made his as a builder. And although the children in both families included daughters as well as sons, it was the boys who were favored and upon whom their fathers pinned their hopes.

It was hard to know whom the Kellys pictured as a perfect match for their second-eldest daughter. She had romances with many of her leading men—Ray Milland, William Holden, and Bing Crosby—and was involved with fashion designer Oleg Cassini. But none of them seemed suitable. The man closest to their ideal was the then senator from Massachusetts, John Fitzgerald Kennedy, but his father had other plans for his son and they didn't include marrying a budding Hollywood actress (even through, paradoxically, Joe Kennedy had had a longtime affair with Gloria Swanson).

In May 1955 Grace Kelly attended the Cannes Film Festival, just after winning her Oscar. Seizing an opportunity, the *Paris Match* movie editor, Pierre Galante, arranged for a meeting between Kelly and Prince Rainier

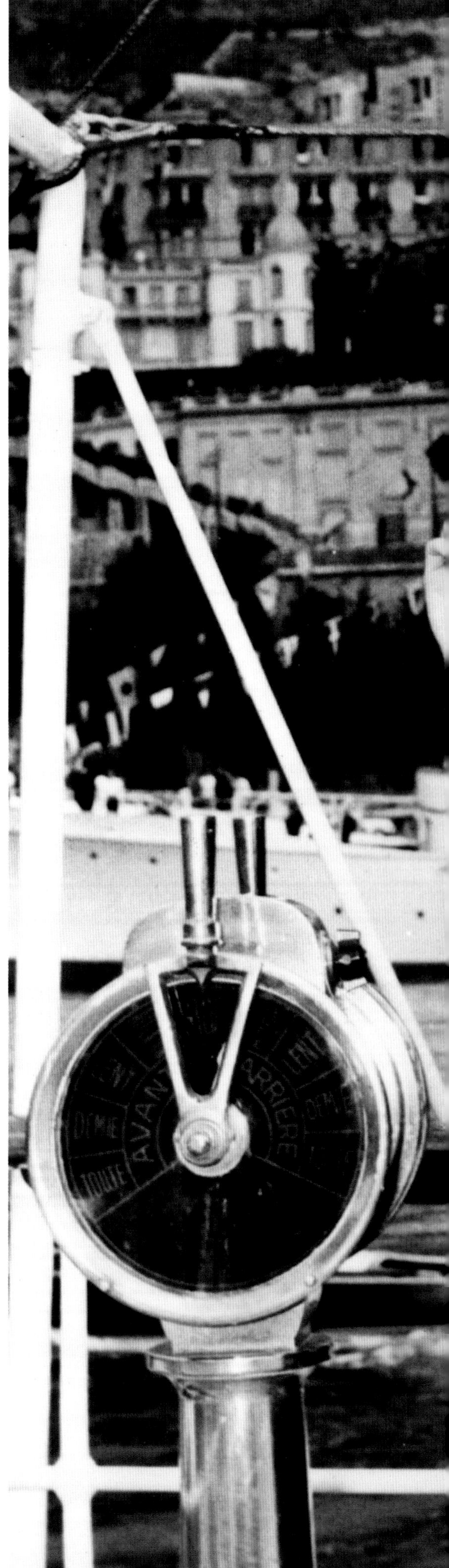

Prince Rainier and Princess Grace arriving at Port Hercule in 1956.

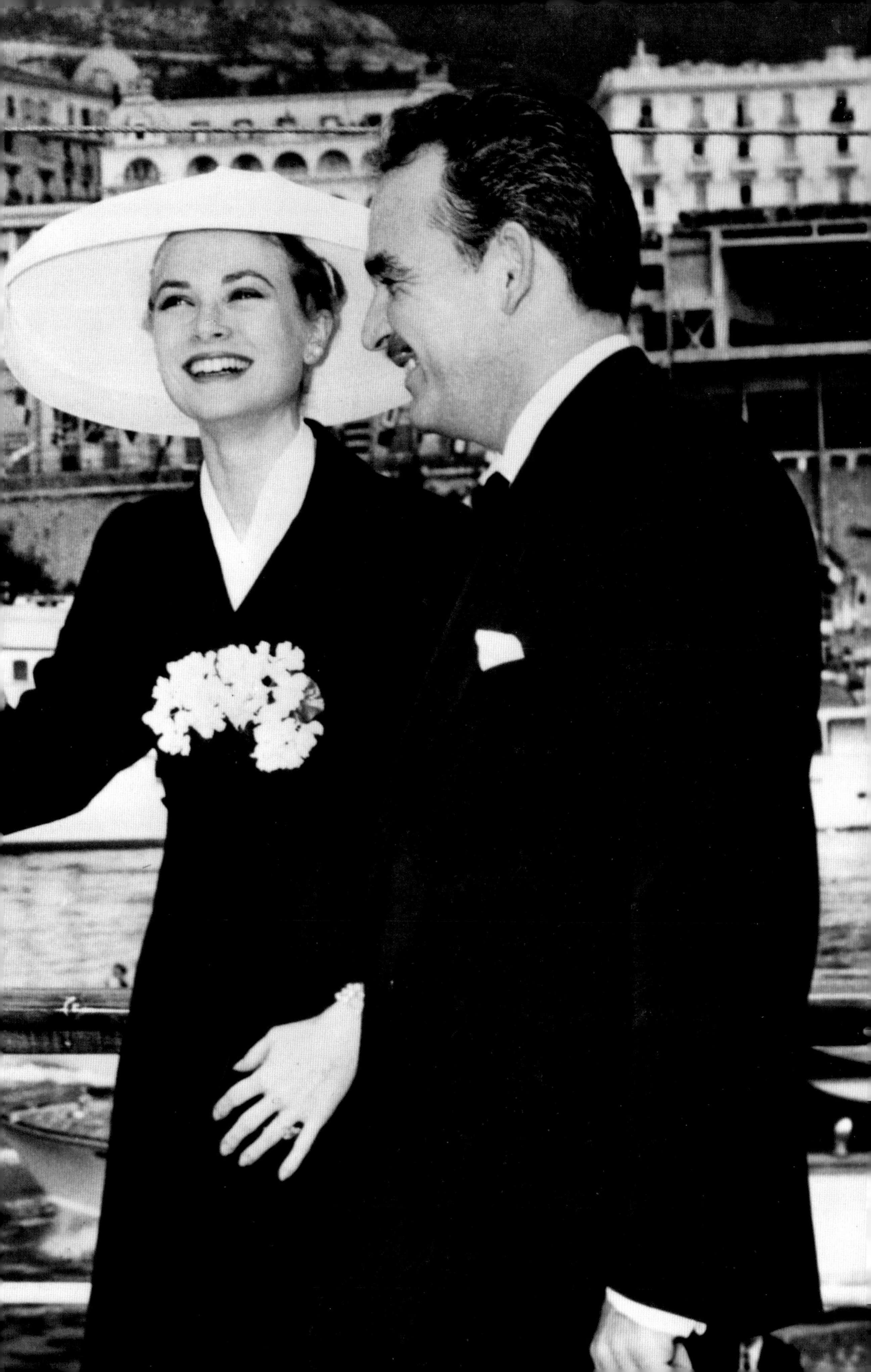

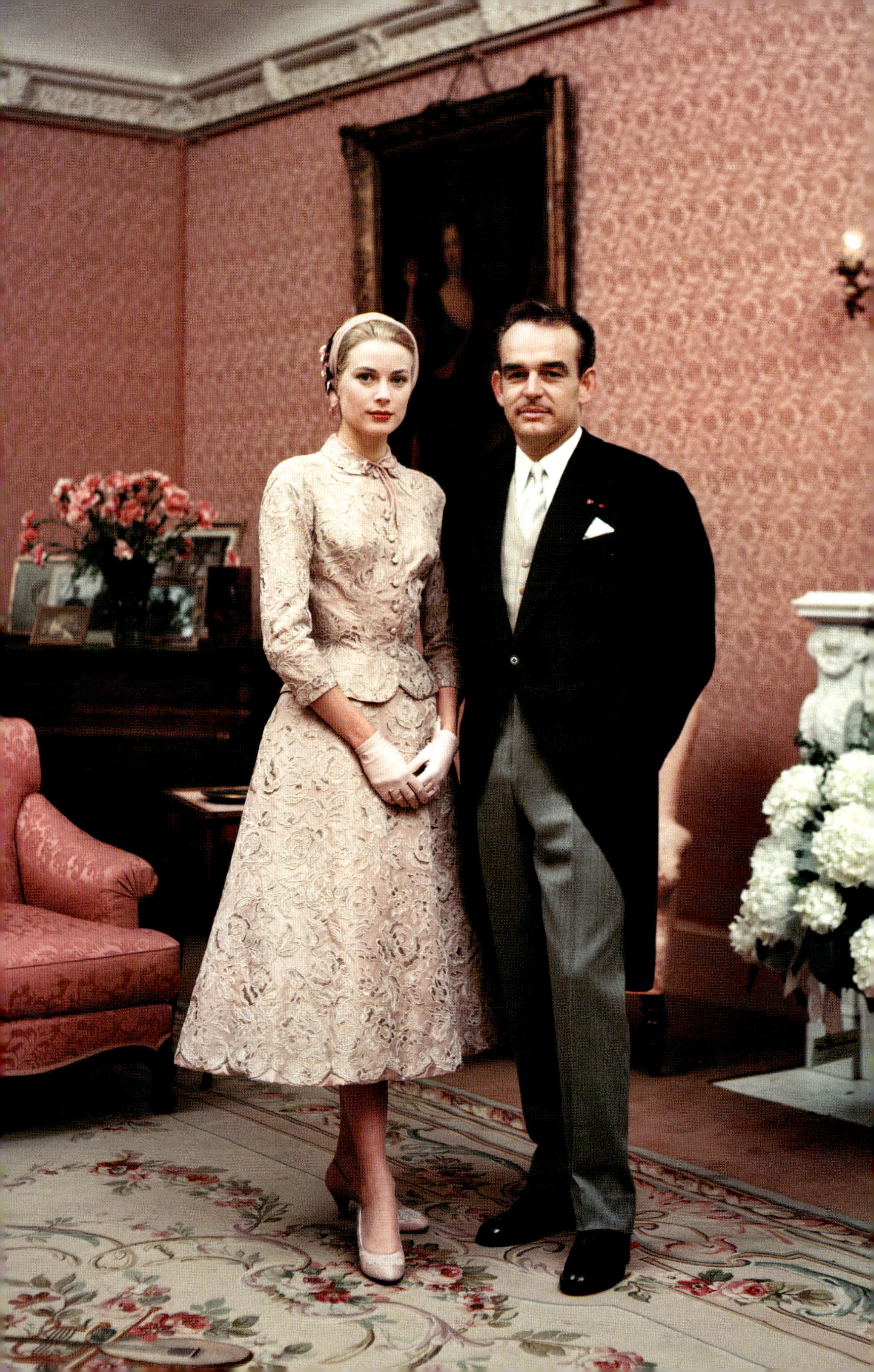

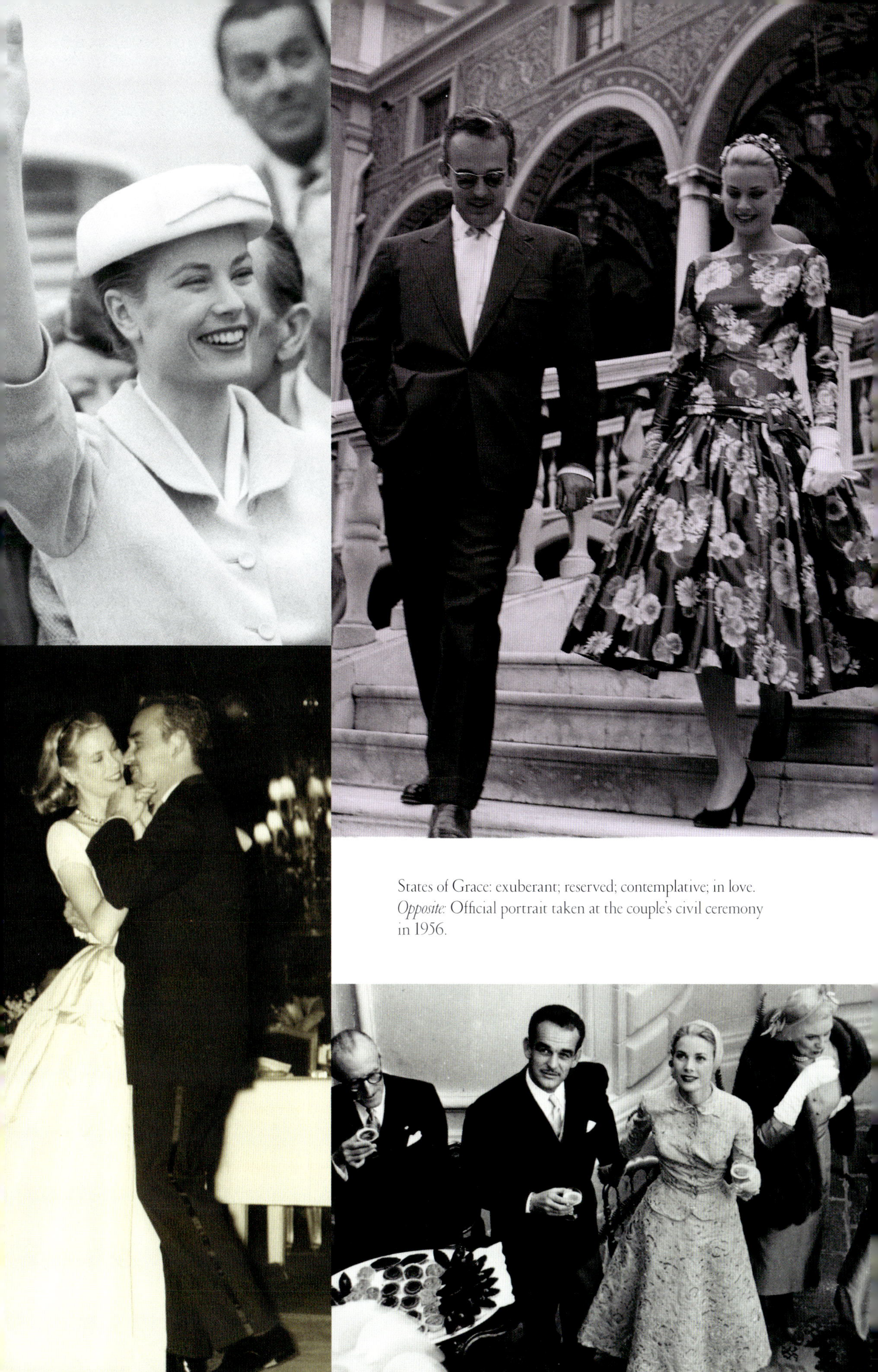

States of Grace: exuberant; reserved; contemplative; in love.
Opposite: Official portrait taken at the couple's civil ceremony in 1956.

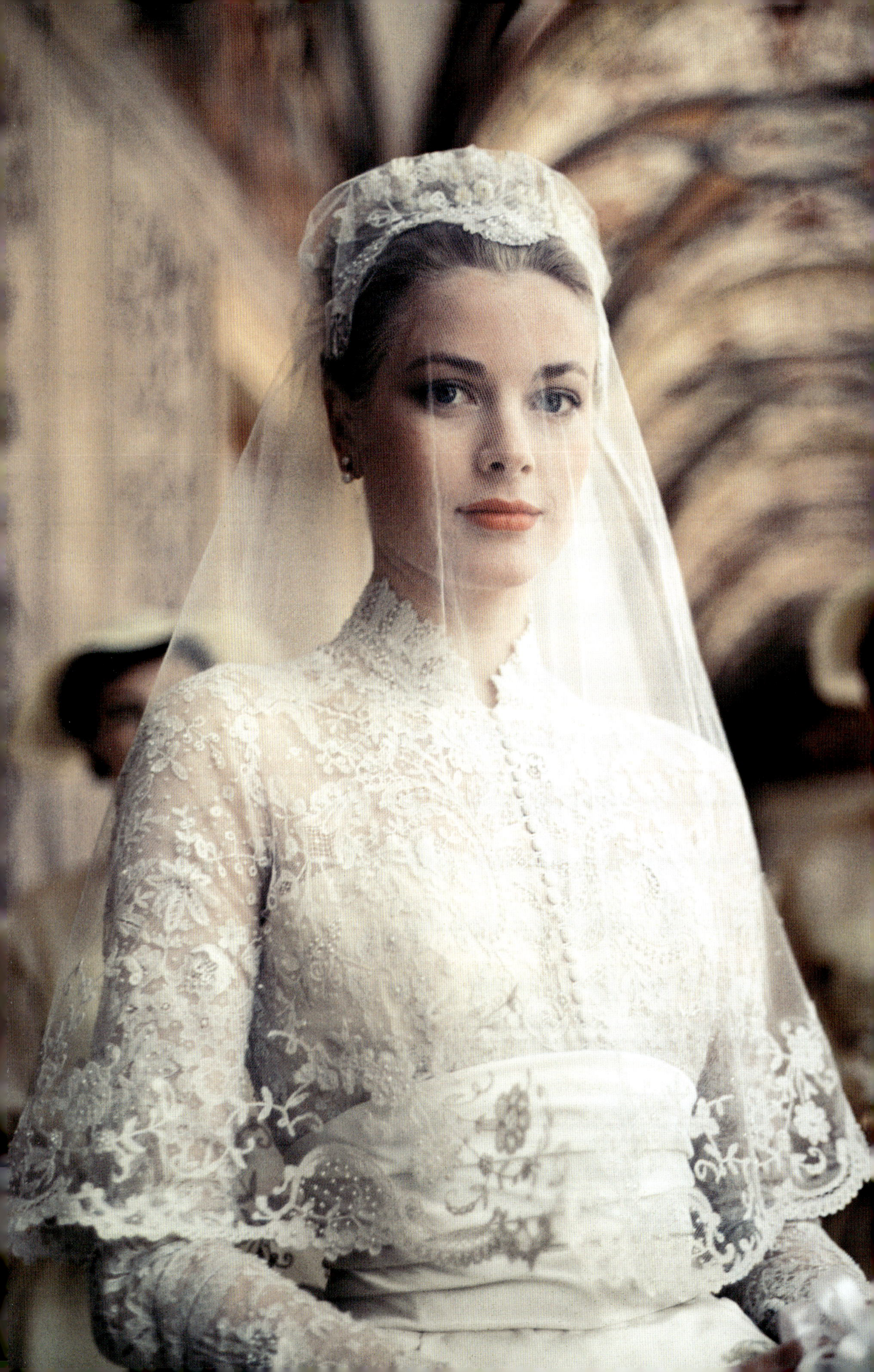

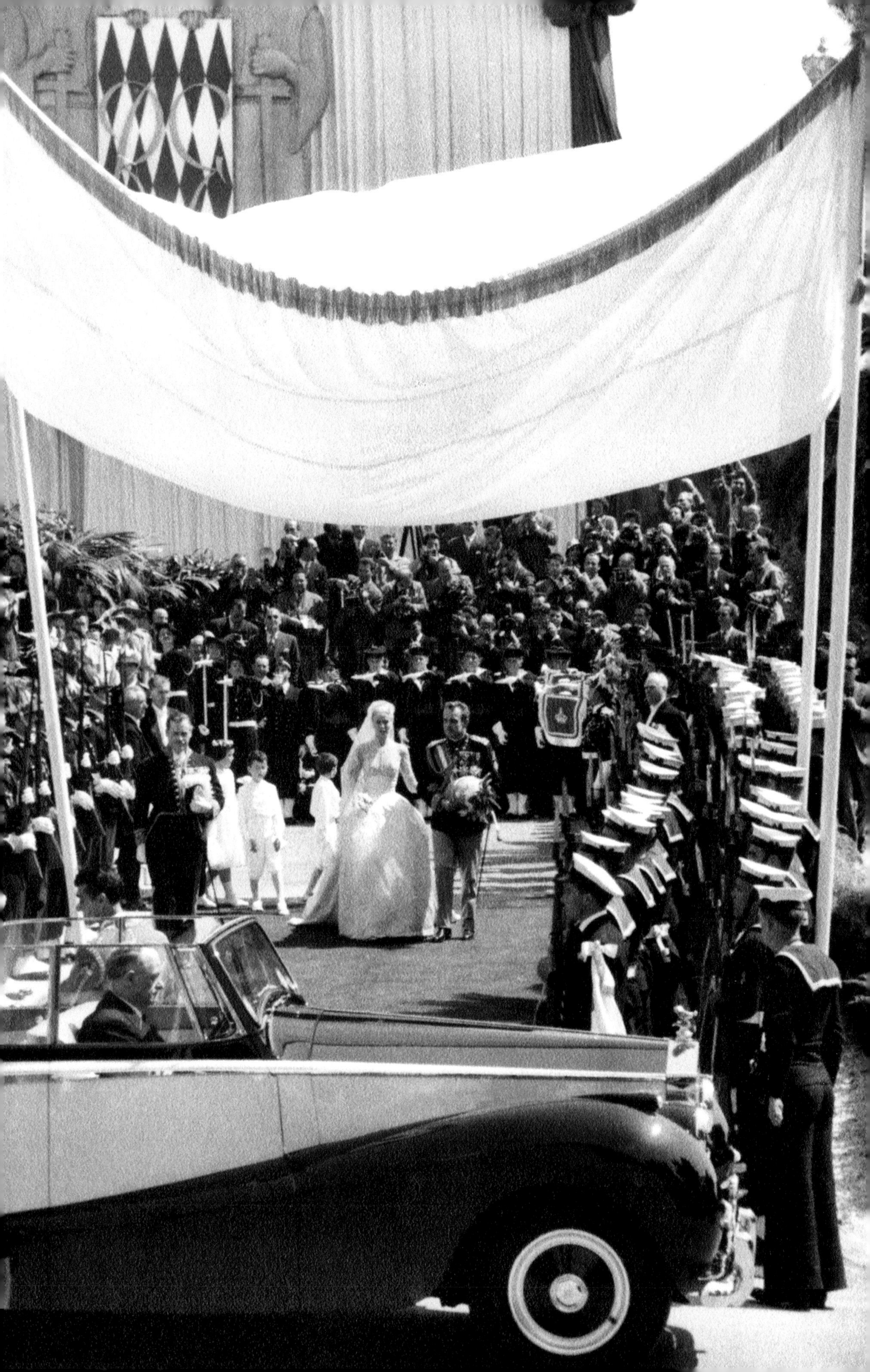

as a publicity stunt, nothing more. But when the two met in the palace gardens, sparks flew and a courtship began.

After they married in Monaco in 1956, Grace Kelly never made another movie—nor were any of her films shown publicly in Monaco—and settled into her new life as Princess. It was not an easy adjustment. She didn't speak French, the country's language (eventually she learned but never mastered it), and many Monegasques regarded her as an outsider. It took some time to win them over, but eventually she did. She devoted herself to being a wife and mother of three children and took on her official role with the same dedication that she had brought to her craft as an actress.

While her most significant contributions were in the arts, she also raised two annual charity events—the Bal de la Croix Rouge (Red Cross Ball) and the Bal de la Rose—to international prominence. In 1964 she founded the Fondation Princesse Grace to assist those with special needs that were not covered by ordinary social services. Today Princess Caroline is its president, and it is devoted to funding pediatric research and aiding families of handicapped children in France and developing nations. The Princess Grace Foundation–USA was established in 1982 to carry on her legacy of supporting the performing arts in America; to date, more than 700 artists have received support to help launch their careers in theater, dance, and film.

Being the wife of a prince wasn't always easy. The good-looking and charming Rainier was a Mediterranean man through and through. There were times when he went his own way, no questions asked—or expected. Whether Princess Grace tacitly accepted this arrangement is anyone's guess, but she was a devoted wife and adored being a mother and raising her children, Caroline, Albert, and Stéphanie. As they grew older and less dependent on her, she had to cope with their attempts to express themselves, sometimes rebelliously, but Princess Grace always stuck by them.

Every so often, acting offers would come her way. She turned them down, even though one—a starring role in *Marnie*, a film that came out in 1964, would have reunited her with Alfred Hitchcock, her favorite director—was tempting. But when it was revealed that the part was of a wayward woman, and that the movie included a scene in which she was to kiss her leading man (Sean Connery), the citizens of Monaco objected.

By this time, the Princess had become thoroughly enmeshed with the Principality and had endeared herself to the Monegasques. She was *their* princess, so she turned down the role. She took on local charity work and helped put Monaco and Monte Carlo back on the map after the Onassis era.

Princess Grace's biographers—and there have been several—have all written that her later years were lonely, leavened only by her visits to America and by a series of poetry readings outside of

Portrait of a royal family: Princess Caroline, Princess Grace, Prince Rainier, and Prince Albert pose for the official Christmas card, 1963.
Previous pages: On Her Serene Highness Princess Grace's wedding day, 1956.

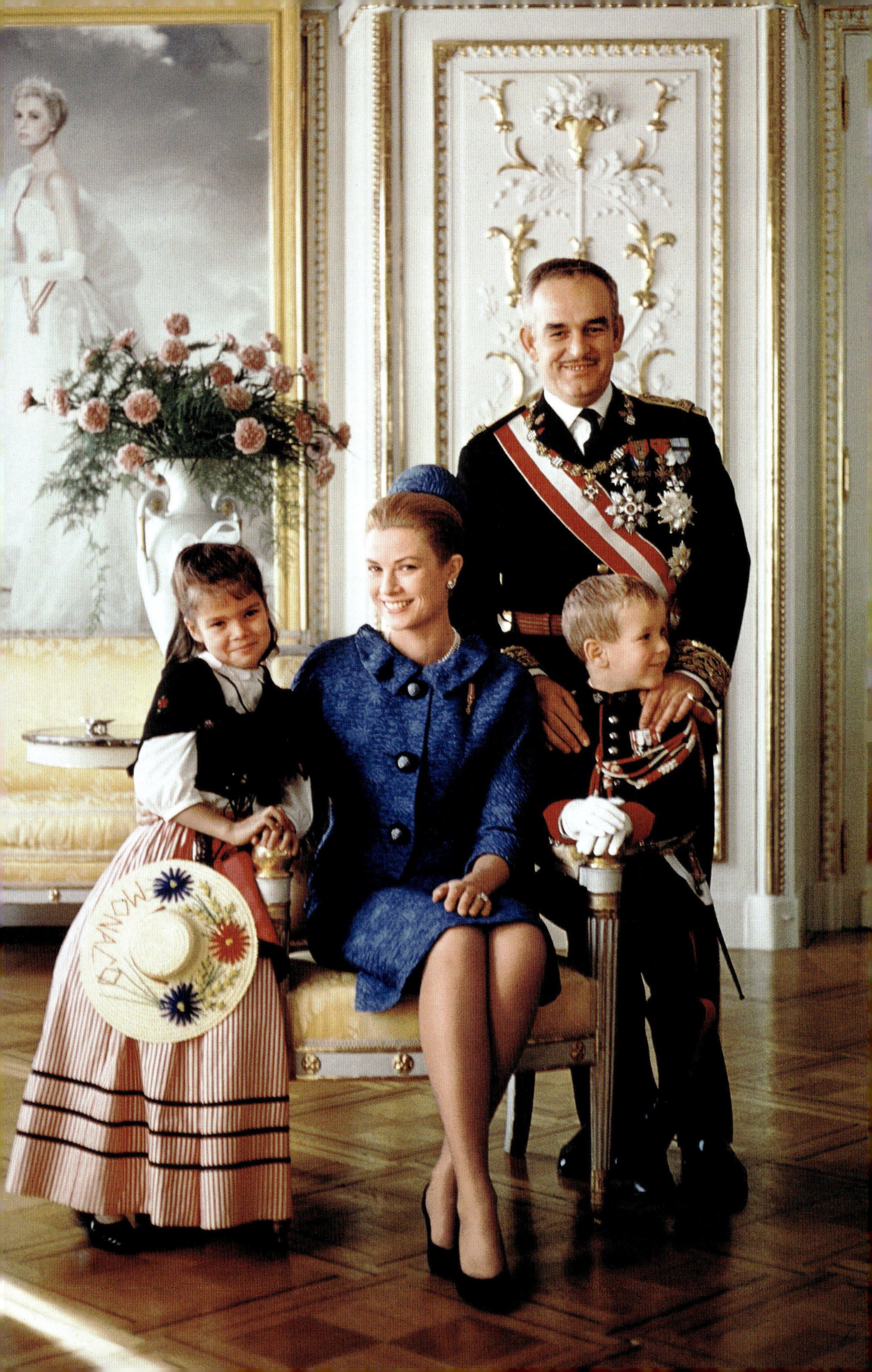
MONACO

> *Walt Disney World is nearly 30,000 acres, or 48 square miles. That is more than 80 times the size of Monaco. Grace Kelly would have been queen of a larger and wealthier kingdom if she'd married Uncle Walt instead of Prince Rainier.*
>
> EVE ZIBART

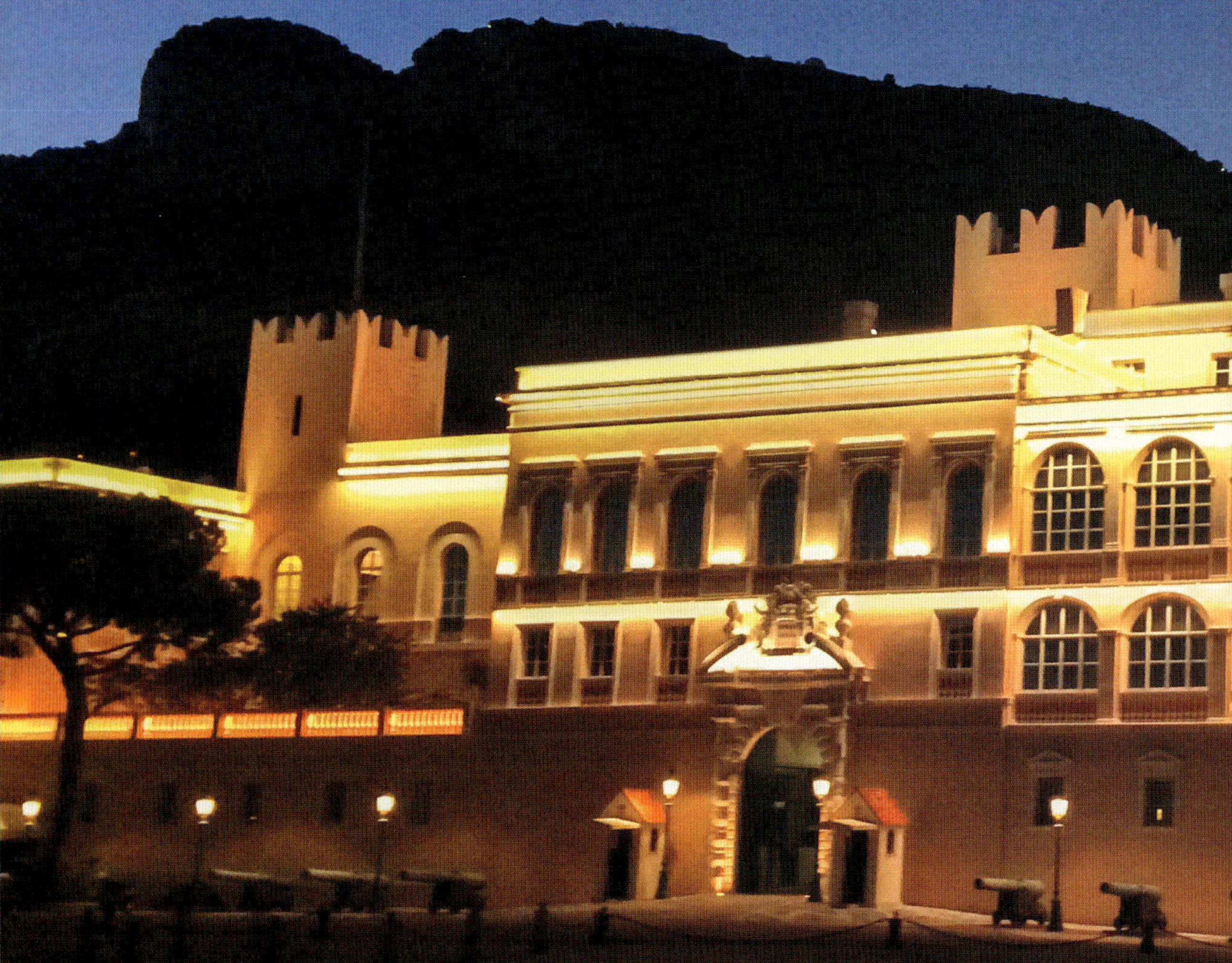

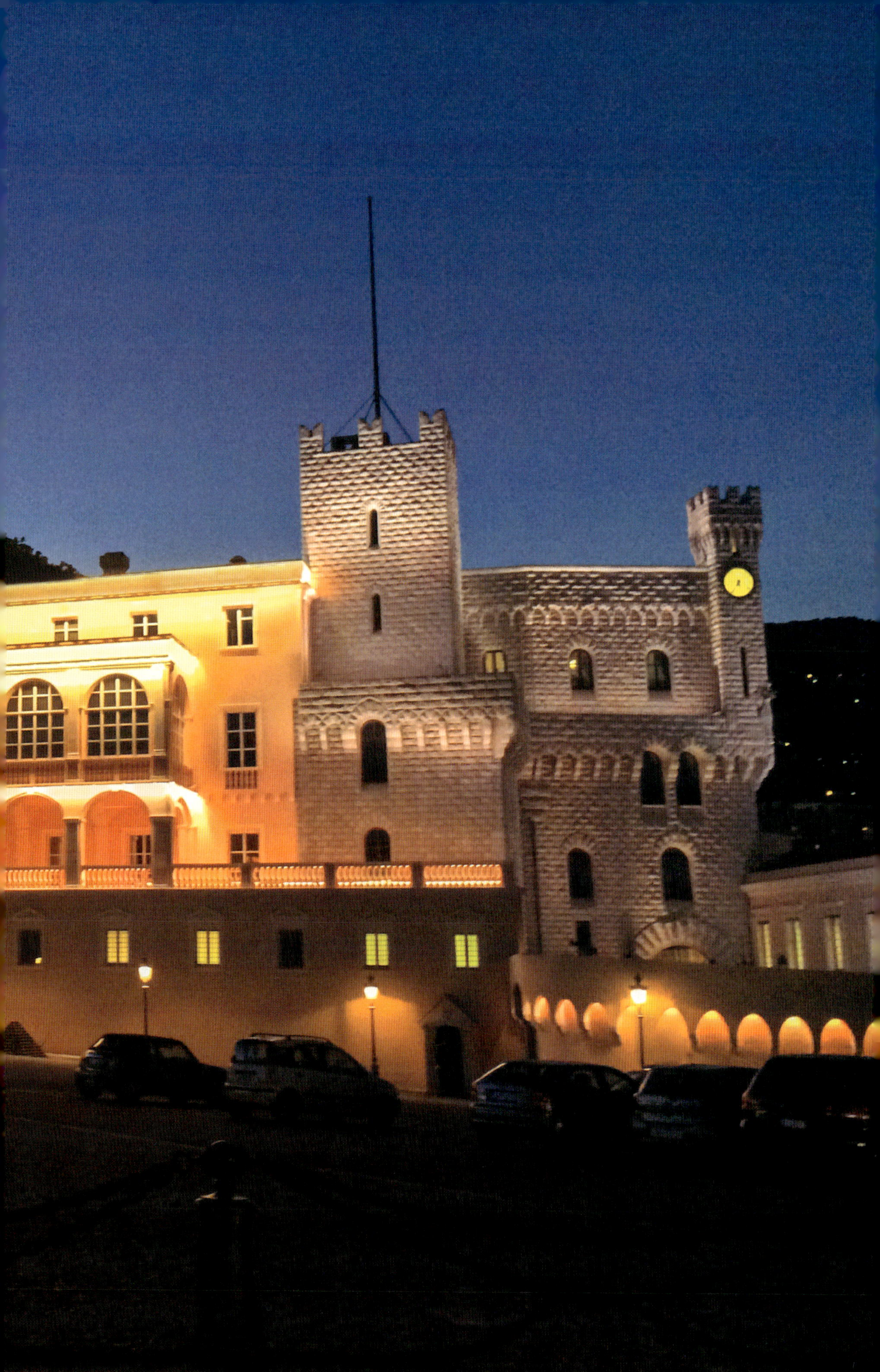

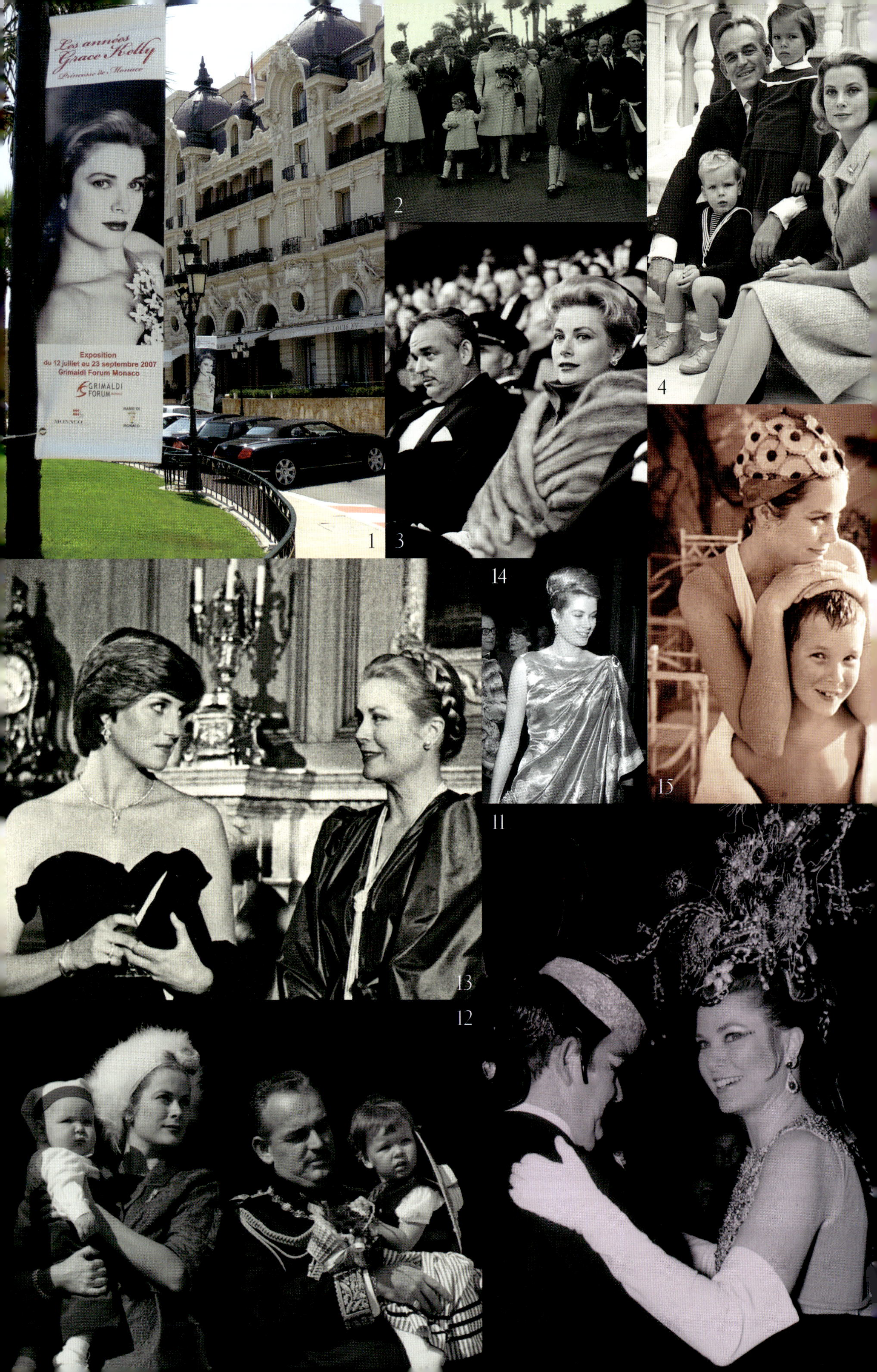
Les années
Grace Kelly
Princesse de Monaco
Exposition
du 12 juillet au 23 septembre 2007
Grimaldi Forum Monaco
GRIMALDI
FORUM
MONACO
MONACO
1
2
3
4
14
15
11
13
12

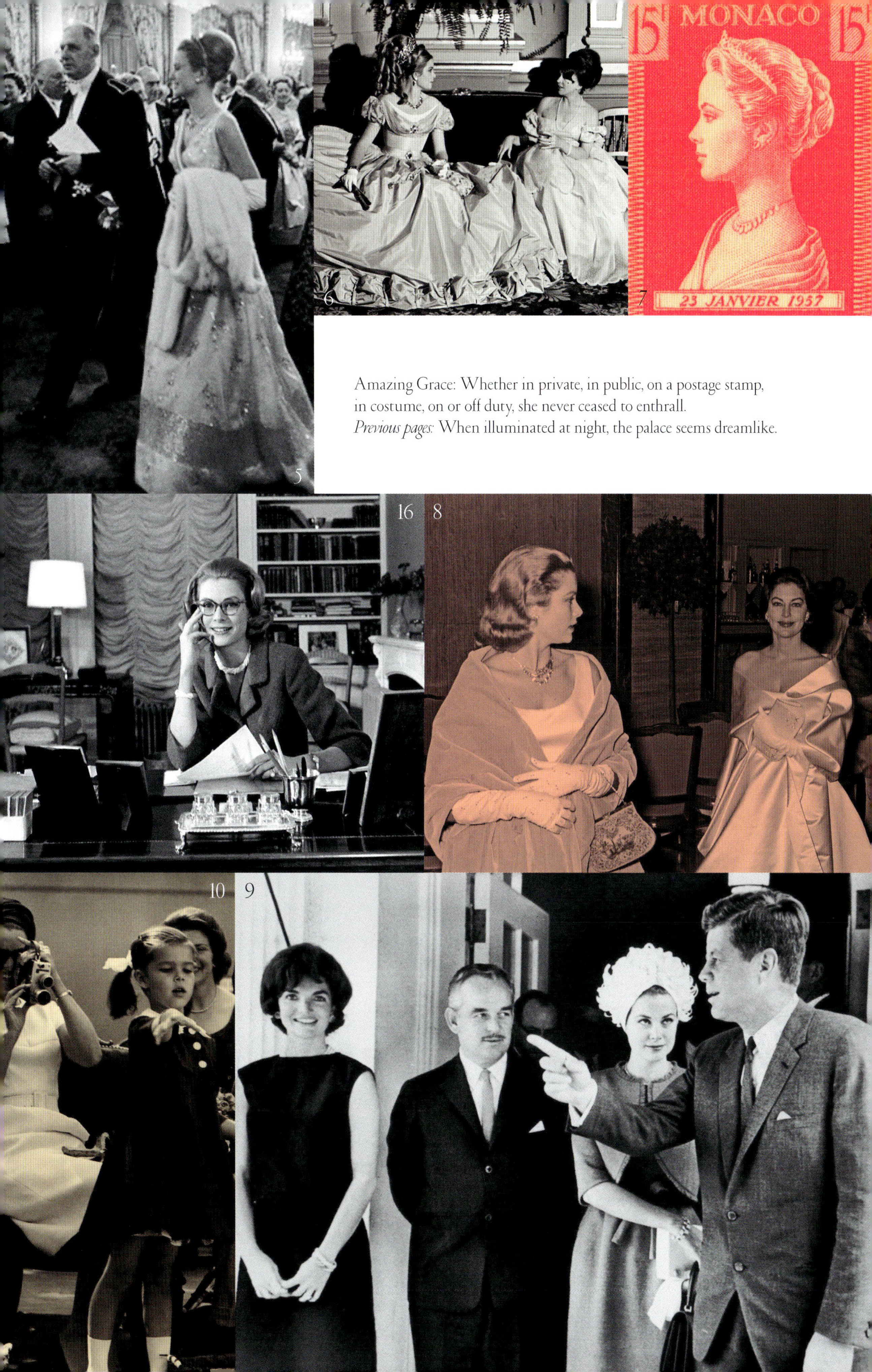

5 6 7

Amazing Grace: Whether in private, in public, on a postage stamp, in costume, on or off duty, she never ceased to enthrall.
Previous pages: When illuminated at night, the palace seems dreamlike.

16 8 10 9

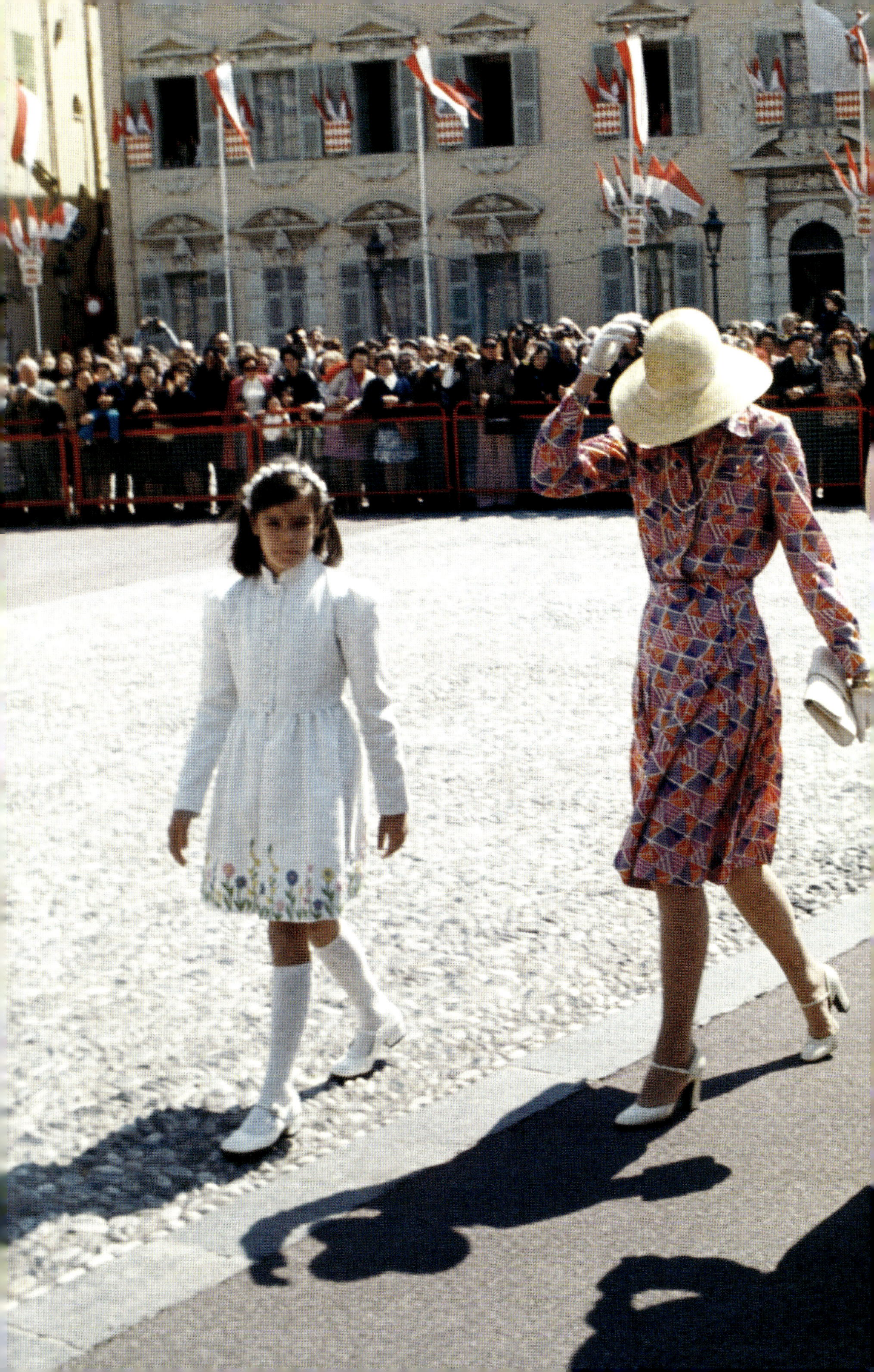

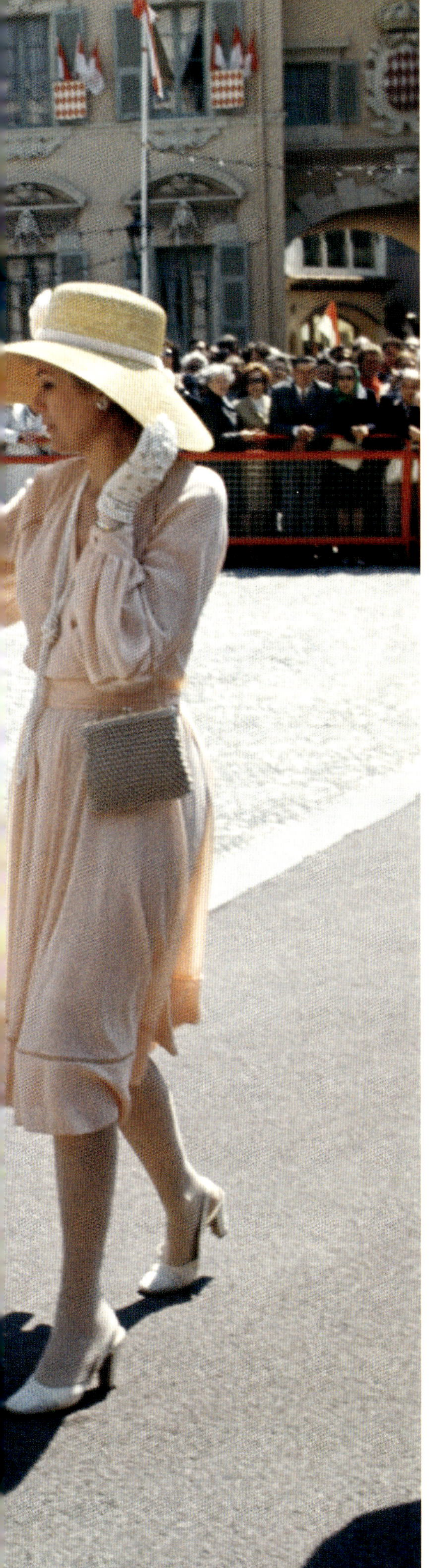

Monaco, which gave her great satisfaction. It is said (and written) that in the last months of her life she was not in good spirits or good health. She had gained some weight and was generally not feeling her best. The Princess made what was to be her final trip to the States in the summer of 1982.

Shortly after her return, on the morning of September 13, Princess Grace left the family's private residence, Roc Agel, in the mountains above Monaco, with seventeen-year-old Princess Stéphanie. They were to leave for Paris that night, but before departing Princess Grace had an appointment with her couturier in Monaco.

The road along the Côte d'Azur is among the most scenic on earth, but is also treacherous, full of twisting, hairpin turns. In a tragic irony, it was along a particularly perilous stretch of the very same road that she was filmed driving with Cary Grant in the 1955 movie *To Catch a Thief* that Princess Grace suffered a mild stroke, according to the investigation. Grace was in the driver's seat, Stéphanie in the passenger's seat. The seizure presumably happened just before their Rover swerved off the road and plunged over a cliff. Both women were injured and taken in separate ambulances to Princess Grace Hospital. Stéphanie recovered, but the Princess fell into a coma and never emerged. She died on September 14, 1982, at only fifty-three. How could this happen? Fairy tales are supposed to have happy endings.

Monaco's fair ladies: Princesses Stéphanie, Caroline, and Grace celebrate the 25th anniversary of Prince Rainier's reign. *Following pages:* Prince Rainier and Princess Grace relax at Roc Agel, the royal retreat above Monaco, 1980.

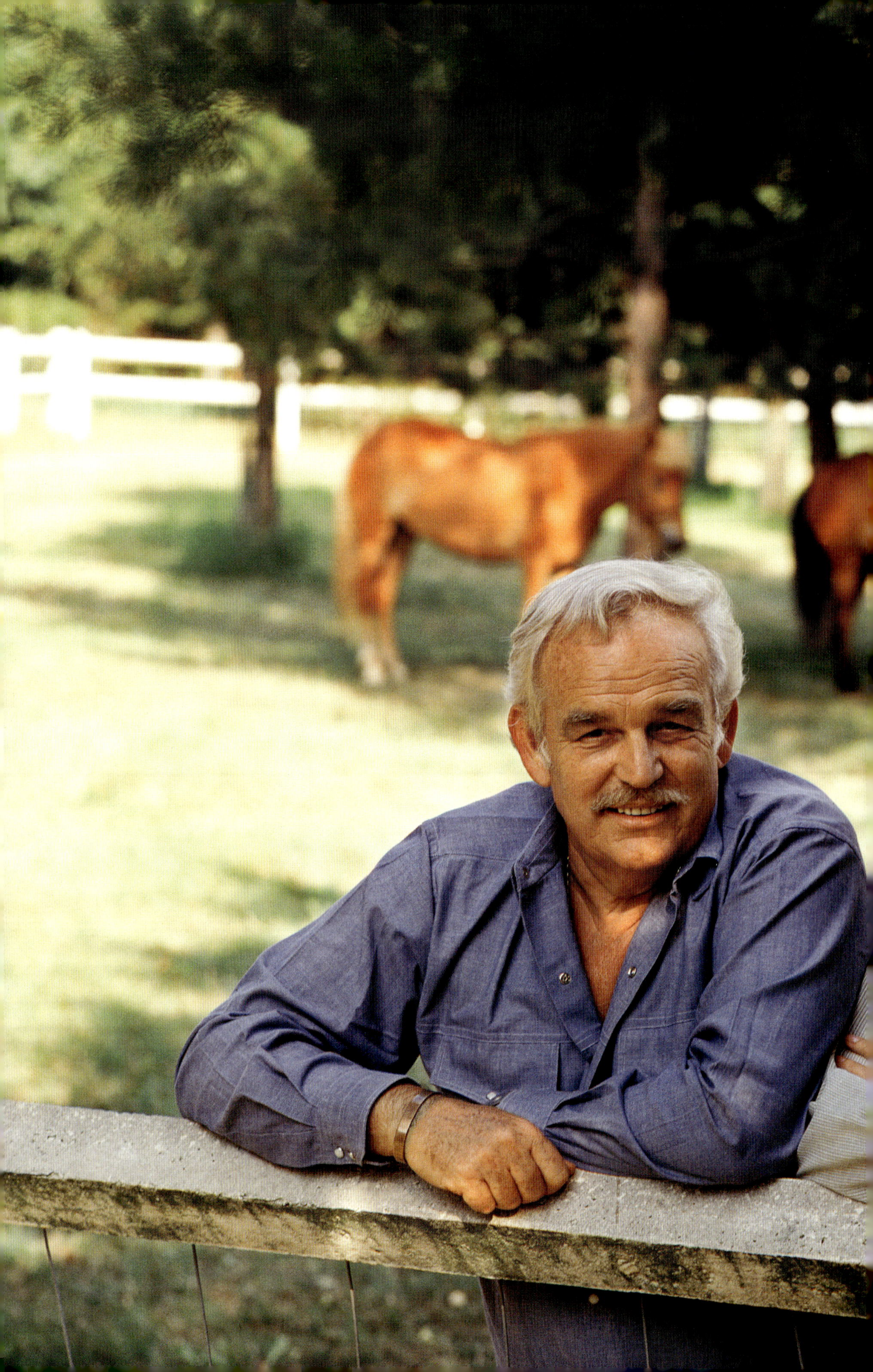

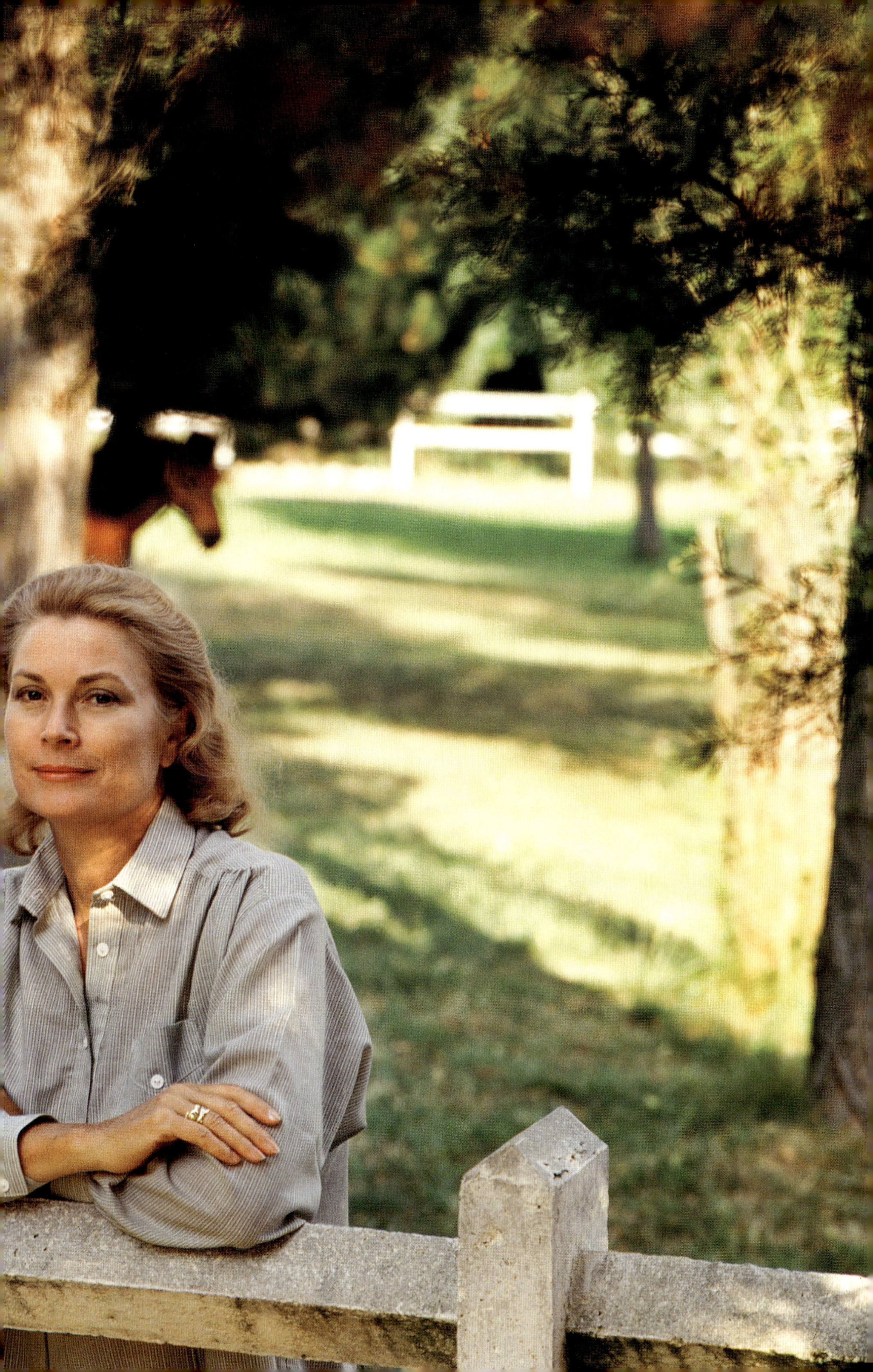

The Glamour Quotient

"The most start-studded, most glamorous and richest place on earth."
—Piers Morgan

The Princess Grace years were indeed star-studded. Her Hollywood connection brought movie stars like Cary Grant, Gregory Peck, Sophia Loren, Frank Sinatra, Bing Crosby, Ava Gardner, and her Cap Ferrat neighbor, David Niven. They came to perform, to attend the Rose Ball and the Red Cross Ball, to gamble, and to visit their beautiful friend—and when they did, they added their incomparable luster. But while there's no question that Princess Grace brought back glamour to the Principality and to Monte Carlo in particular, the fact is this minuscule piece of turf has always been synonymous with luxury and glamour. This is exactly what the Blancs envisioned it to be and what it has been throughout most—though not quite all—of its history. Wars and depressions may have intervened, but somehow Monte

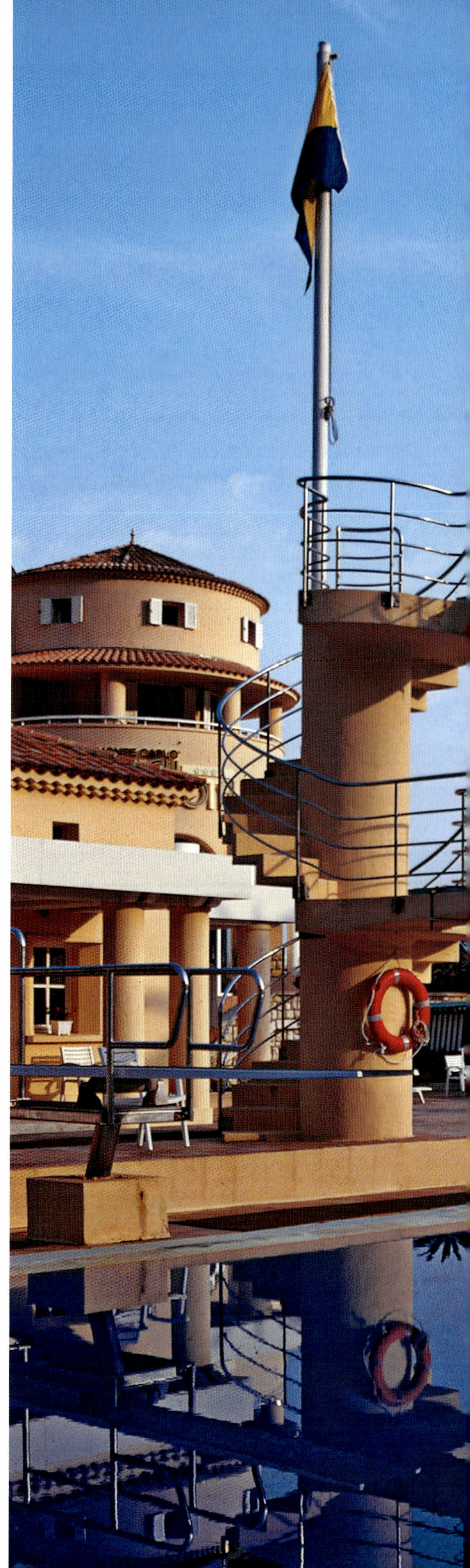

The pristine swimming pool at the Monte-Carlo Beach hotel, 1992.

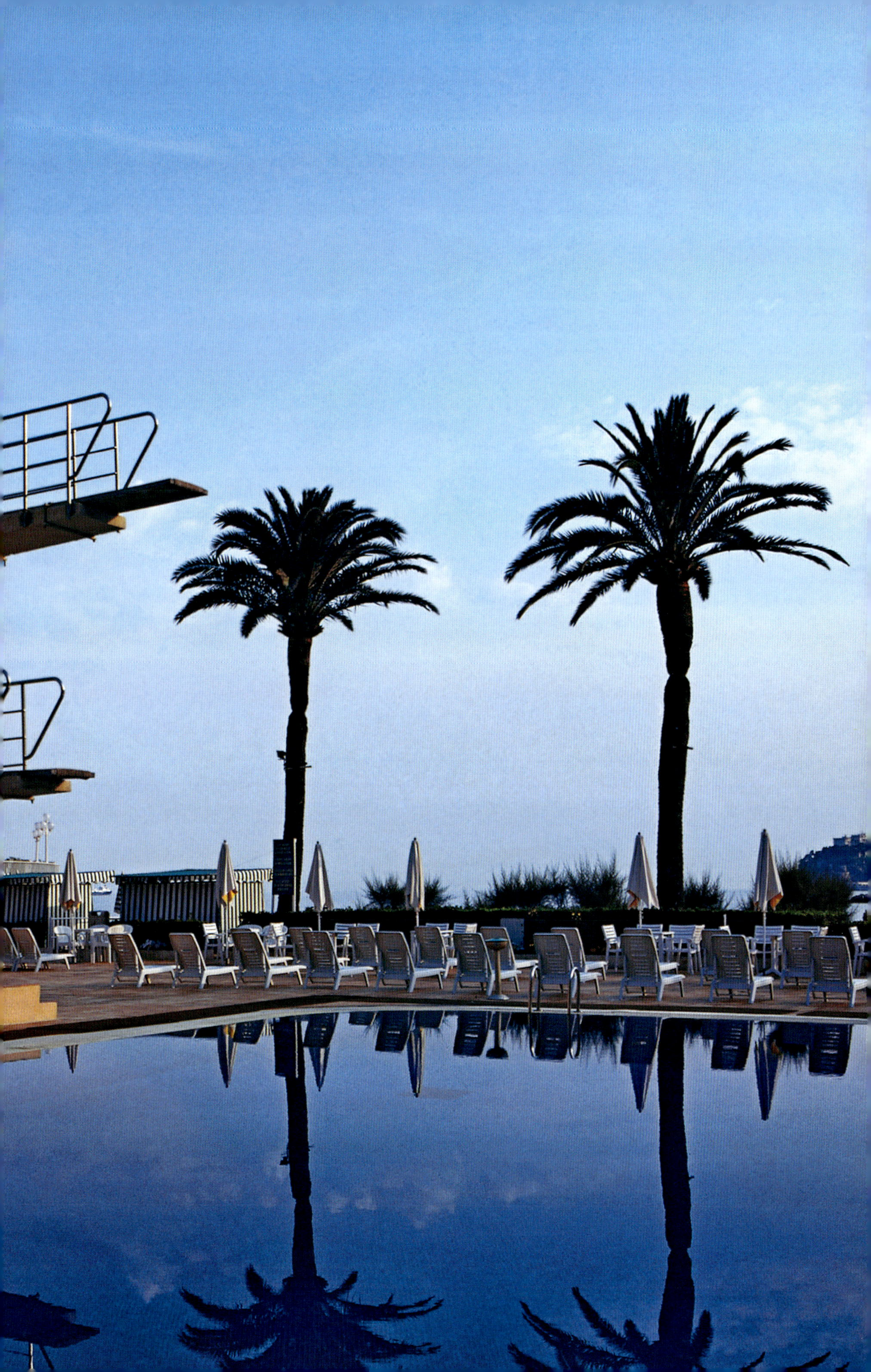

Carlo always made a remarkable recovery.

One of the first aristocratic groups to descend upon Monte Carlo were the White Russians. They first went to Nice, Cannes, and other parts of the Riviera, but once the road to Monte Carlo opened up, they couldn't get there fast enough. In *Mission to Monte Carlo,* Barbara Cartland describes their effect: "Once a year they would gravitate like migrating birds to Monte Carlo where they built themselves magnificently ornate villas, pursued the most beautiful women, whom they hung with emeralds and pearls, and gambled astronomical sums in the Casino to the immense satisfaction of the authorities."

The Place du Casino was a microcosm of all that any sophisticated person since the beginning of the twentieth century could possibly desire: a casino to play in; a performing arts theater in which to soak up culture; a deluxe hotel in which to sleep at night and to gather in full sight and in full regalia during the day; and an outdoor café at which to observe the stylish parade of passersby. Moreover, the square was a relatively small space from which everything could easily be reached on foot. Such proximity is still one of its drawing cards, although now there are other hotels near the square and alongside Larvotto Beach, such as the Monte Carlo Bay and the legendary Monte Carlo Beach hotels, both SBM properties.

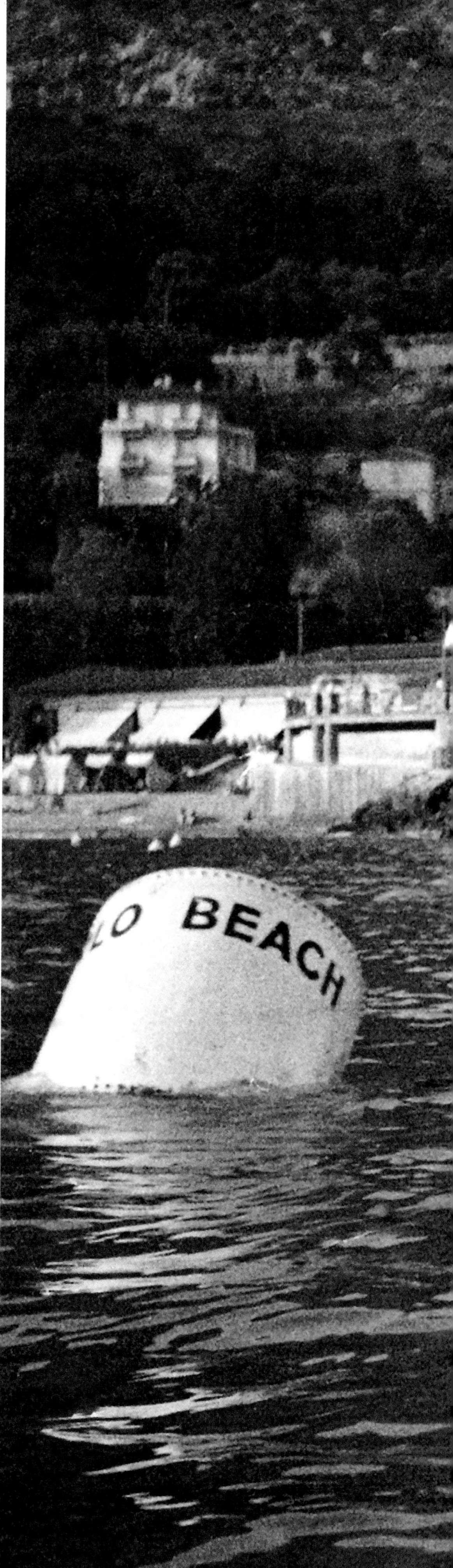

Sunbathing on a pontoon platform at the Monte-Carlo Beach hotel, 1937.

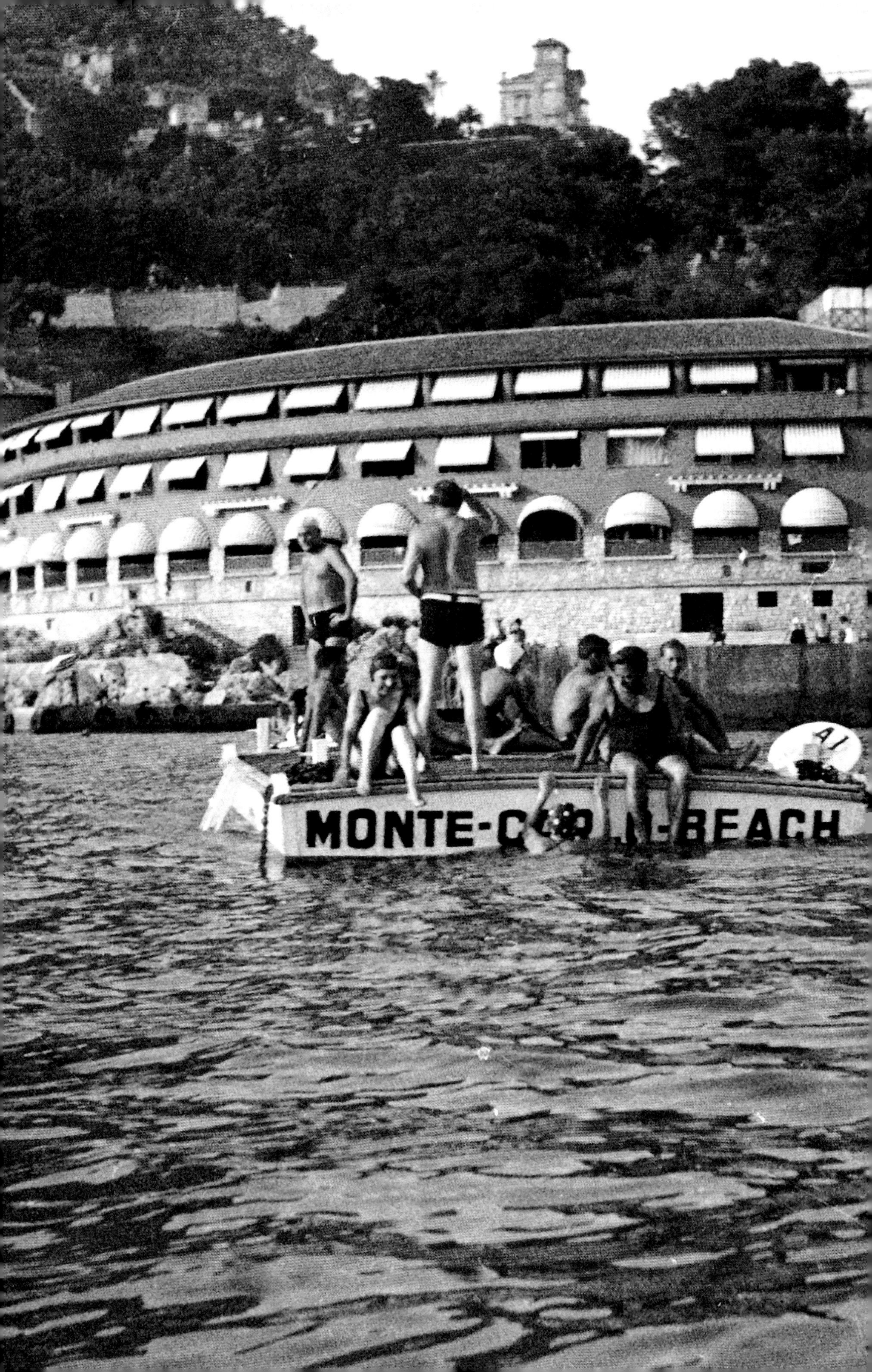
MONTE-C
BEACH

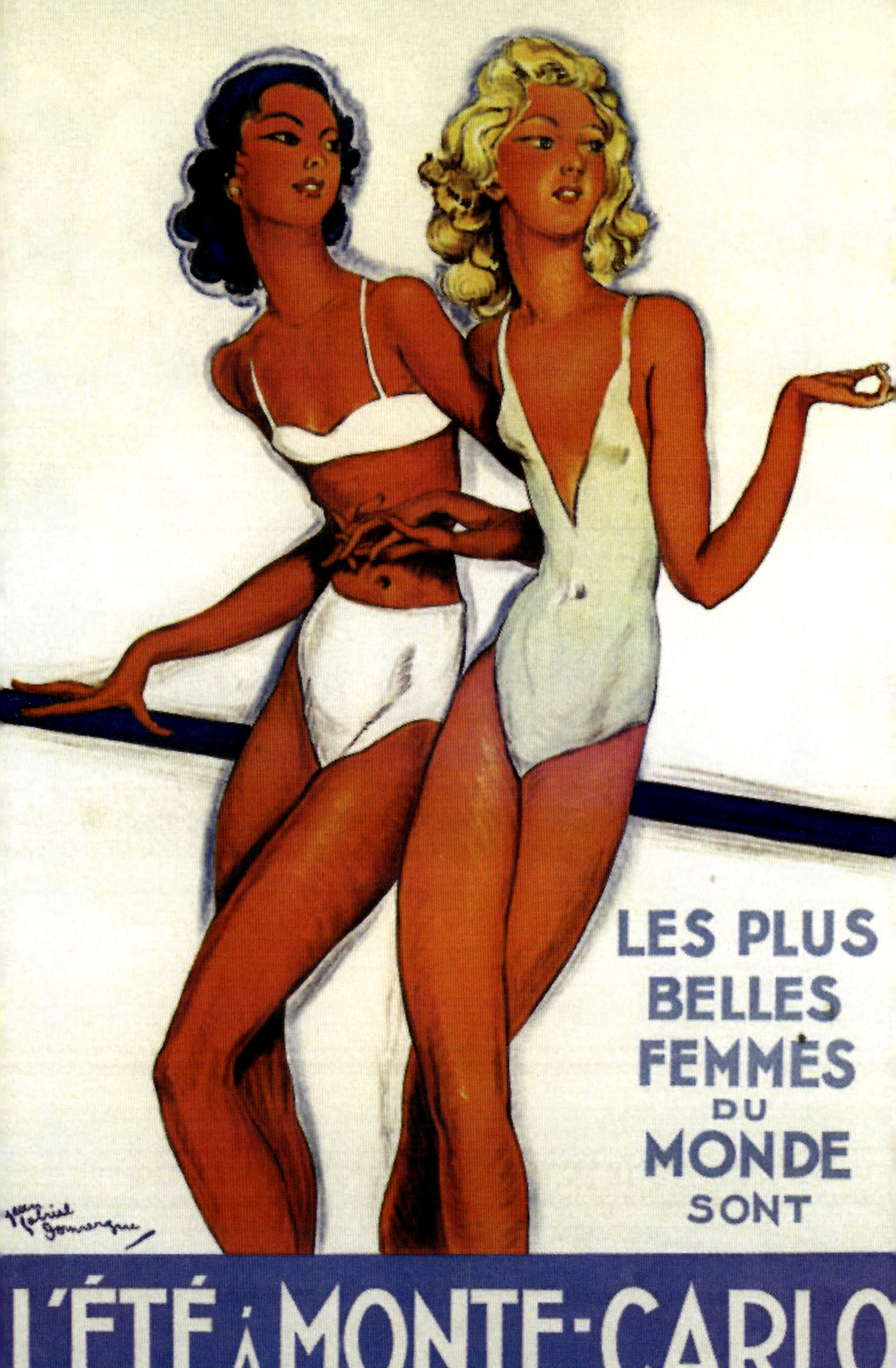
LES PLUS
BELLES
FEMMES
DU
MONDE
SONT
L'ÉTÉ À MONTE-CARLO

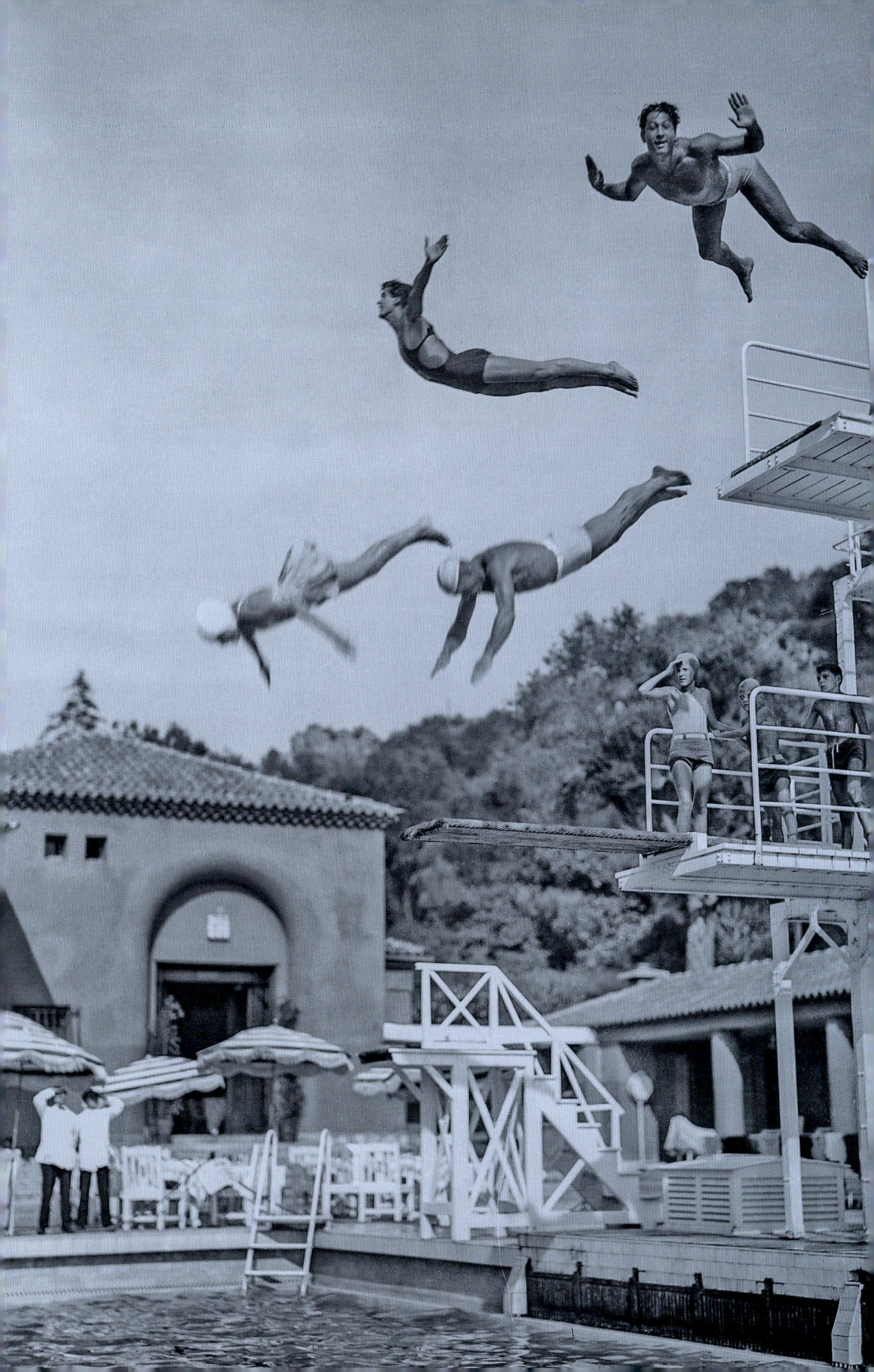

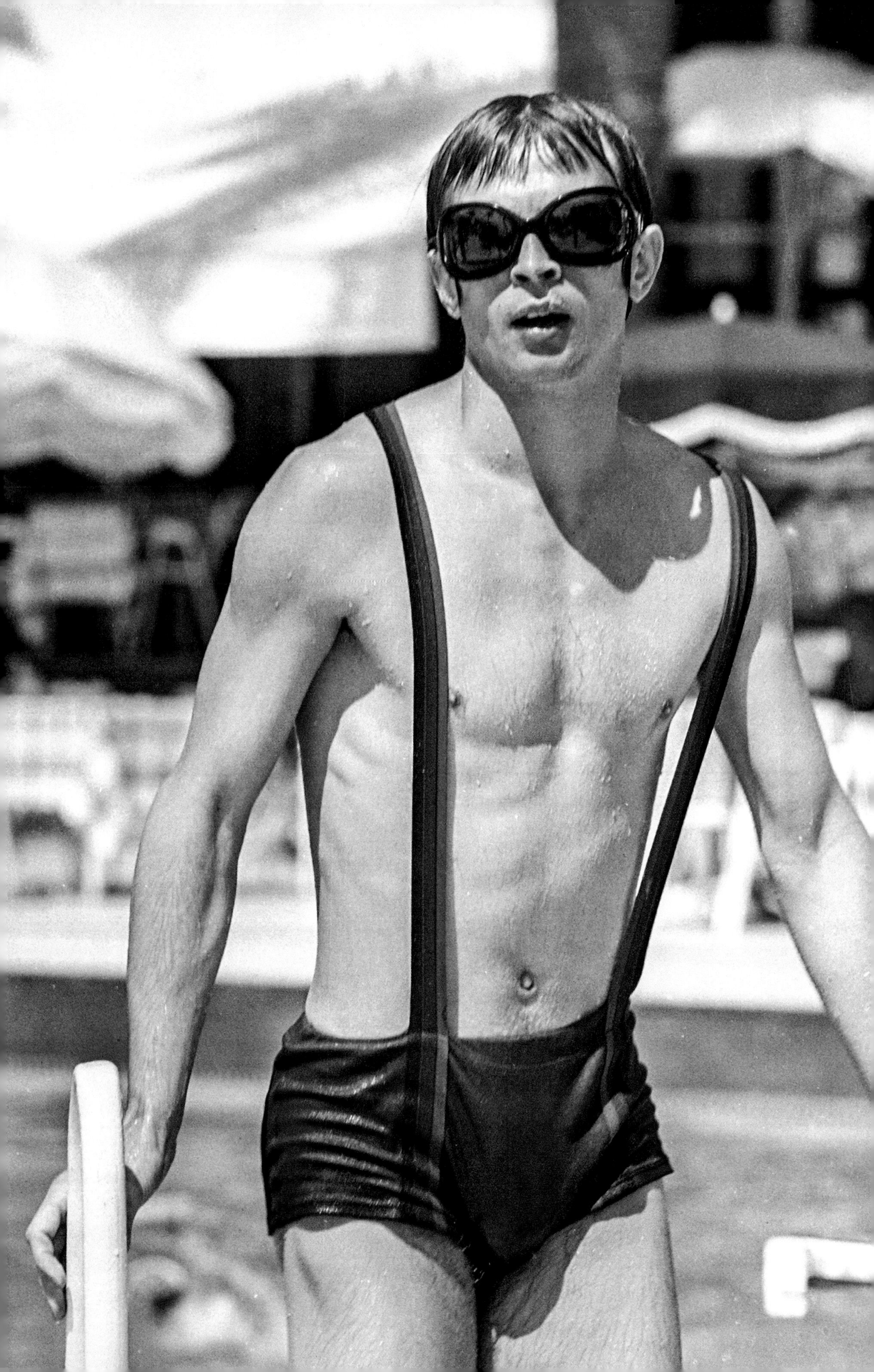

The Hôtel de Paris was Monte Carlo's epicenter and was the backdrop for many films, including the opening scene of Alfred Hitchcock's *Rebecca.* Sir Winston Churchill spent so much time there that the suite he stayed in bears his name. He was known to sit in the lobby like the Grand Pooh-Bah, puffing on his Havana cigars and sipping vintage port from the hotel's famous wine cellar. Next to him might have been the King of Sweden, another habitué. In 1952, it was the setting for the wedding of Hollywood's swashbuckler, Errol Flynn. As grand hotels go, the Hôtel de Paris was and remains one of the grandest.

Its sister hotel, the Hermitage, comes a close second. Located just behind the Hôtel de Paris, the Hermitage was designed as a Belle Époque confection complete with a winter garden whose ceiling was created by one of Gustave Eiffel's disciples and overseen by the great man himself. There have been modernizations, but the famous atrium is exquisitely intact.

A completely different hotel experience is the Monte Carlo Beach on avenue Princesse Grace. Its heyday was during the 1930s, following the period that Gerald and Sarah Murphy settled in Villa America in Cap d'Antibes. The Murphys (who inspired the characters of Nick and Nicole Diver in F. Scott Fitzgerald's Jazz Age novel *Tender Is the Night*) were known for lavish parties and a tony circle of friends such as Cole Porter, Pablo Picasso, Jean Cocteau, Fernand Léger, Ernest Hemingway, and, of course, Zelda and F. Scott Fitzgerald. When they weren't entertaining at Villa America, the Murphys were hobnobbing at the luxe Hôtel du Cap and its Eden Roc bathing pavilion.

René Léon, who was head of the Société des Bains de Mer, took notice and decided that what Monte Carlo needed was a hotel overlooking the beach, à la Eden Roc. Commissioning architect Roger Séassal to build it, then hiring American Elsa Maxwell, high society's high-spending doyenne, to use her connections to attract a high-flying crowd, Léon created an entirely new attraction to the Monte Carlo landscape: that of a posh resort hotel on the beach with an Olympic-size swimming pool where guests could preen and be seen. There the good life was lived to the hilt.

Even more than swimming, tennis became the sport du jour. Flamboyant French champions such as Suzanne Lenglen (who scandalized everyone when she began wearing sleeveless knee-length dresses that bared her athletic physique) and René Lacoste (who invented the tennis ball–launching machine and the metal-frame racket, not to mention the famous crocodile-logo knit shirts!) dominated the world tennis scene in the 1910s, '20s, and '30s. Professional tennis is still prominent in Monaco today, with the annual Monte Carlo Masters tournament (which actually began in 1897) one of the biggest in the run-up to the French Open, drawing not only the star players but also celeb spectators like Bono, Tommy Hilfiger, and Athina Onassis (Aristotle's granddaughter) to the Monte-Carlo Country Club.

Rudolph Nureyev takes a dip at the Monte-Carlo Beach hotel pool, 1966.
Previous pages, from left: A travel poster boasts that "The Most Beautiful Women in the World Are in Monte Carlo in the Summer," 1955; daring divers at the Monte-Carlo Beach hotel, 1932.

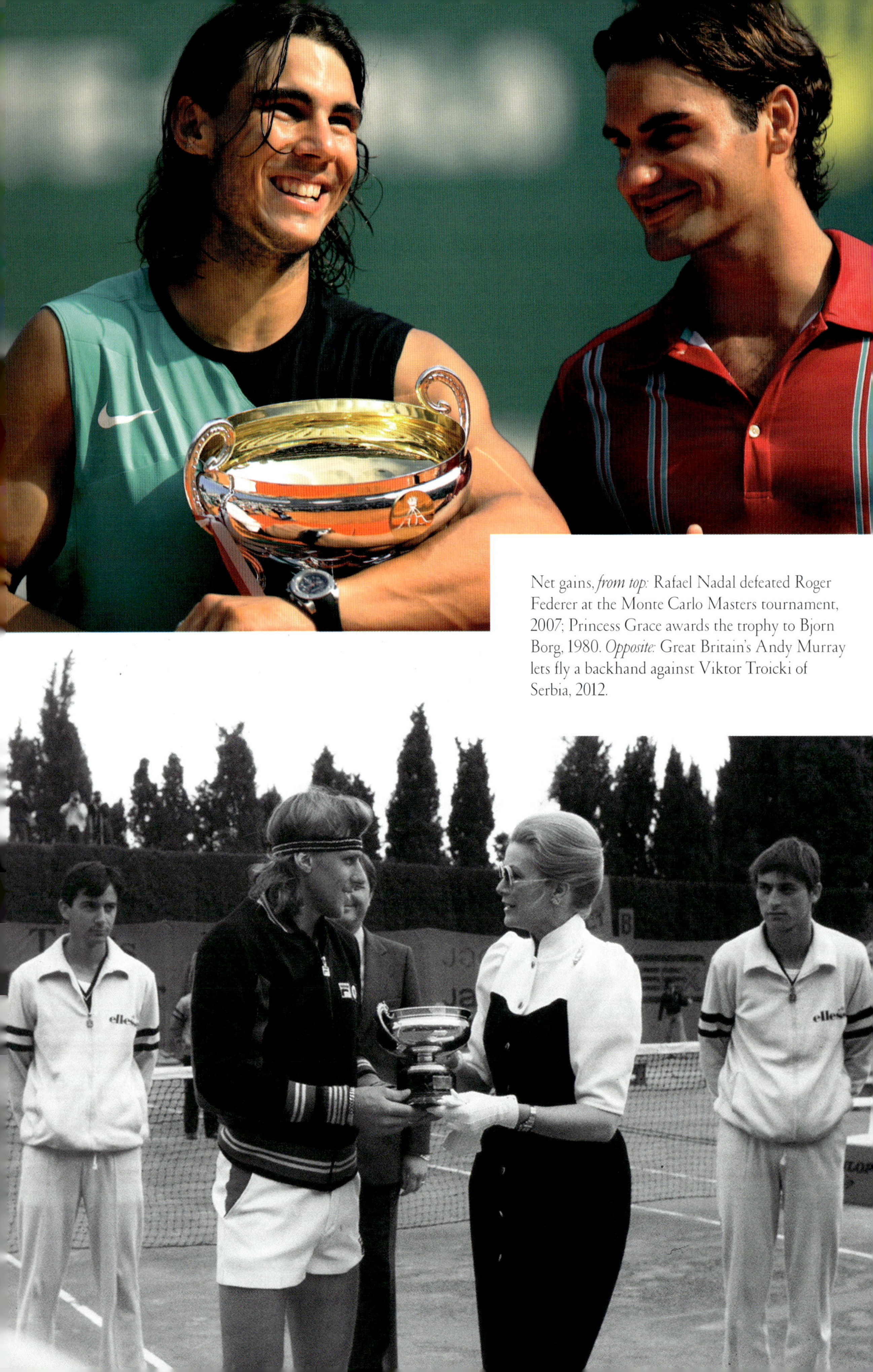

Net gains, *from top:* Rafael Nadal defeated Roger Federer at the Monte Carlo Masters tournament, 2007; Princess Grace awards the trophy to Bjorn Borg, 1980. *Opposite:* Great Britain's Andy Murray lets fly a backhand against Viktor Troicki of Serbia, 2012.

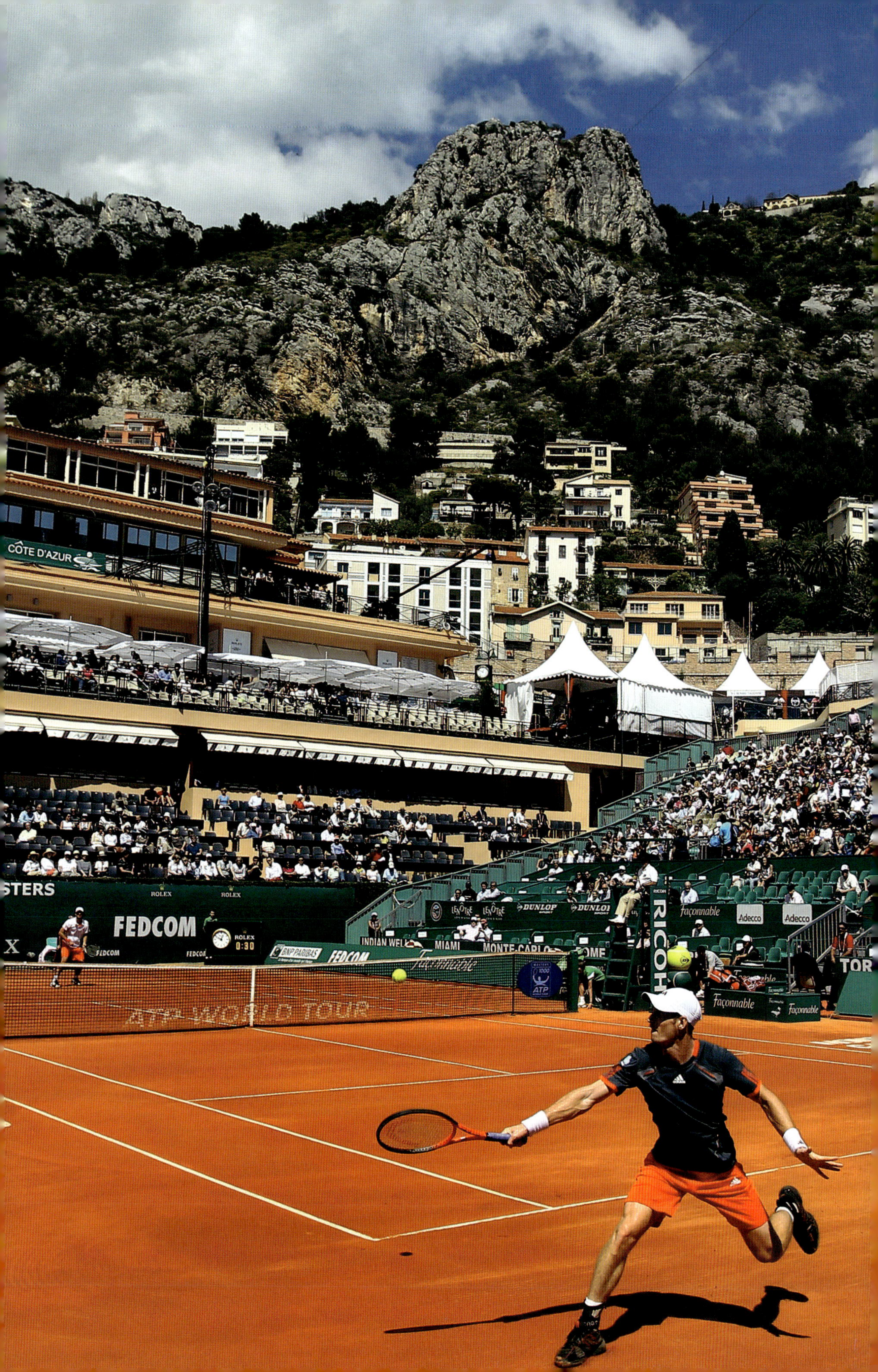
CÔTE D'AZUR
STERS
ROLEX
FEDCOM
BNP PARIBAS
DUNLOP
RICOH
Façonnable
Adecco
INDIAN WELLS
MIAMI
MONTE-CARLO
ATP
ATP WORLD TOUR

In the early part of the twentieth century, proper behavior was to avoid the sun, so women dressed accordingly, wearing wide-brimmed hats and usually carrying parasols. Coco Chanel, the Ballet Russe's Serge Lifar, and artist Jean Cocteau changed all that when they daringly shed their cover-ups and invented sunbathing. Suddenly it was deemed fashionable to enjoy outdoor sports and to seek the sun rather than avoid it. Except for the extremely fair-skinned, parasols went the way of the dodo bird, and swimsuits, sundresses, bare legs and espadrilles, and slacks (*mon dieu!*) for women became de rigueur on the Riviera.

Monte Carlo was no exception, although dressing to the nines at night was still customary. "There were robes of shimmering beads, robes of rich brocade, robes trimmed with gold and robes hung with lustrous sequins" was how Robert W. Service described the finery in his 1922 novel *The Poisoned Paradise.* The designs of the French couturier Frederick Worth were earlier in evidence and later replaced by those of Chanel and, to a certain extent, Balenciaga in the 1920s and 1930s.

The Jazz Age is usually associated with America in the 1920s, but it played out loudly and manically in certain European cities (Madrid, Paris, Berlin), on the Côte d'Azur, and most notably Monte Carlo. In *Monte Carlo: A Living Legend,* Frédéric Mitterrand brings the era tantalizingly to life: "Money spent as if there were no tomorrow... in the jewelry shops with convenient hours. Caviar consumed by the ladle-full, and champagne drunk by the magnum.... Banks of flowers, expensive clothes, and promises of eternal love, at least until the following night." Jay Gatsby would have been right at home—as at home as were Josephine Baker, Colette, Nijinsky, Barbara Hutton, Rudolph Valentino, and even Queen Victoria herself. Of course, "home" is a relative word. These were extravagant villas, Belle Époque estates, and the princely Palace itself.

World War II was a more sober and sobering time in Monte Carlo, but in postwar Europe it sprang to life again. Greek tycoons (Stavros Niarchos and, more significantly, Aristotle Onassis) claimed Monaco as their playground and moored their yachts there as a conspicuous reminder of their presence. A whole new set of international celebrities arrived—Romy Schneider and Alain Delon, Vittorio de Sica, Omar Sharif, Françoise Sagan, Maria Callas—and altered the social landscape. Monte Carlo was hopping.

In the early 1970s, "Queen of the Night" Régine, in collaboration with SBM, opened Jimmy'z, one of the most legendary nightspots on the planet. In 1975 it moved to its present site, smack in the middle of Monte Carlo. The very fact that Régine was behind the enterprise was enough to bring in jet-set revelers from America, France, Italy, and elsewhere. And they still come, although today you're more likely to see Rihanna, Leonardo DiCaprio, and Beyoncé. Régine is no longer involved (she lives in St. Tropez), but Jimmy'z prevails.

Following pages: Even swank sports cars are sheltered from the sun.

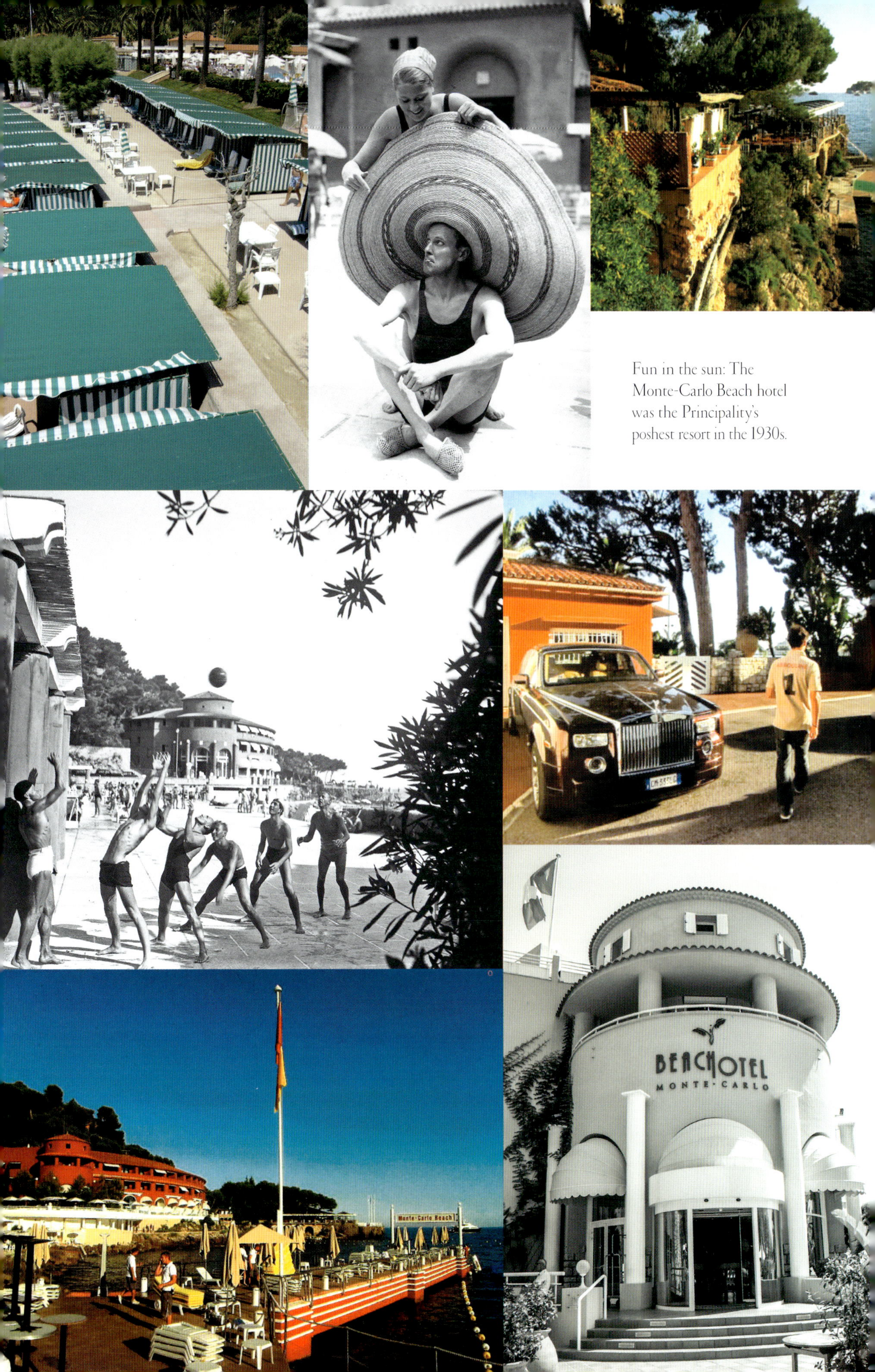

Fun in the sun: The Monte-Carlo Beach hotel was the Principality's poshest resort in the 1930s.

Living large is still the modus operandi of those who choose Monte Carlo and other towns in the Principality. Monaco attracts the rich and famous from all over the globe (it is sometimes referred to as "Money Carlo"), although the men are not nearly as nattily dressed or the women as festooned as they used to be. Nevertheless, as galas like the Bal de la Rose or the Red Cross Ball approach, the safes are unlocked and the jewels reappear, as dazzling as ever. The couture gowns are brought out of storage and impeccably prepped so not a wrinkle appears (ditto the faces of many who don them). On such festive occasions as these, Monte Carlo shines again like the brightest star in the firmament.

In the article he wrote for *Condé Nast Traveler* in May 2007, G. Y. Dryansky relates the almost visceral sensation of returning to Monte Carlo: "Each time I fly beyond the Bay of Angels on the helicopter from Nice toward Monte Carlo, I remember, shamelessly happy, that I am heading for the homeland of True Glitz—not some fool's gold rendition but the whole twenty-four-karat version of uninhibited, sybaritic luxury."

Nevertheless, there is still a high regard for privacy and a respect for decorum. A protective police force ensures the safety of its citizens. The paparazzi are more than unwelcome; they are not allowed. Much of the day-to-day is conducted quietly, rituals are strictly observed, and life seems blessedly serene. Jack Nicholson called it "Alcatraz for the rich."

To an outsider, Monte Carlo appears to be a picture-perfect Eden with not much going on. In the first scene of the 1932 classic *Grand Hotel*, the narrator stares into the camera with a straight face and says: "Grand Hotel. Always the same. People come. People go. Nothing ever happens." Sounds like Monte Carlo... at least on the surface.

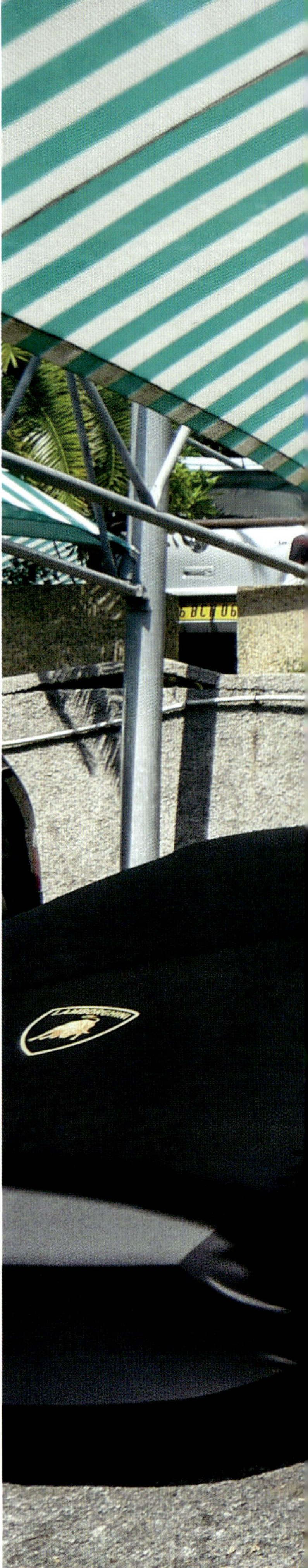

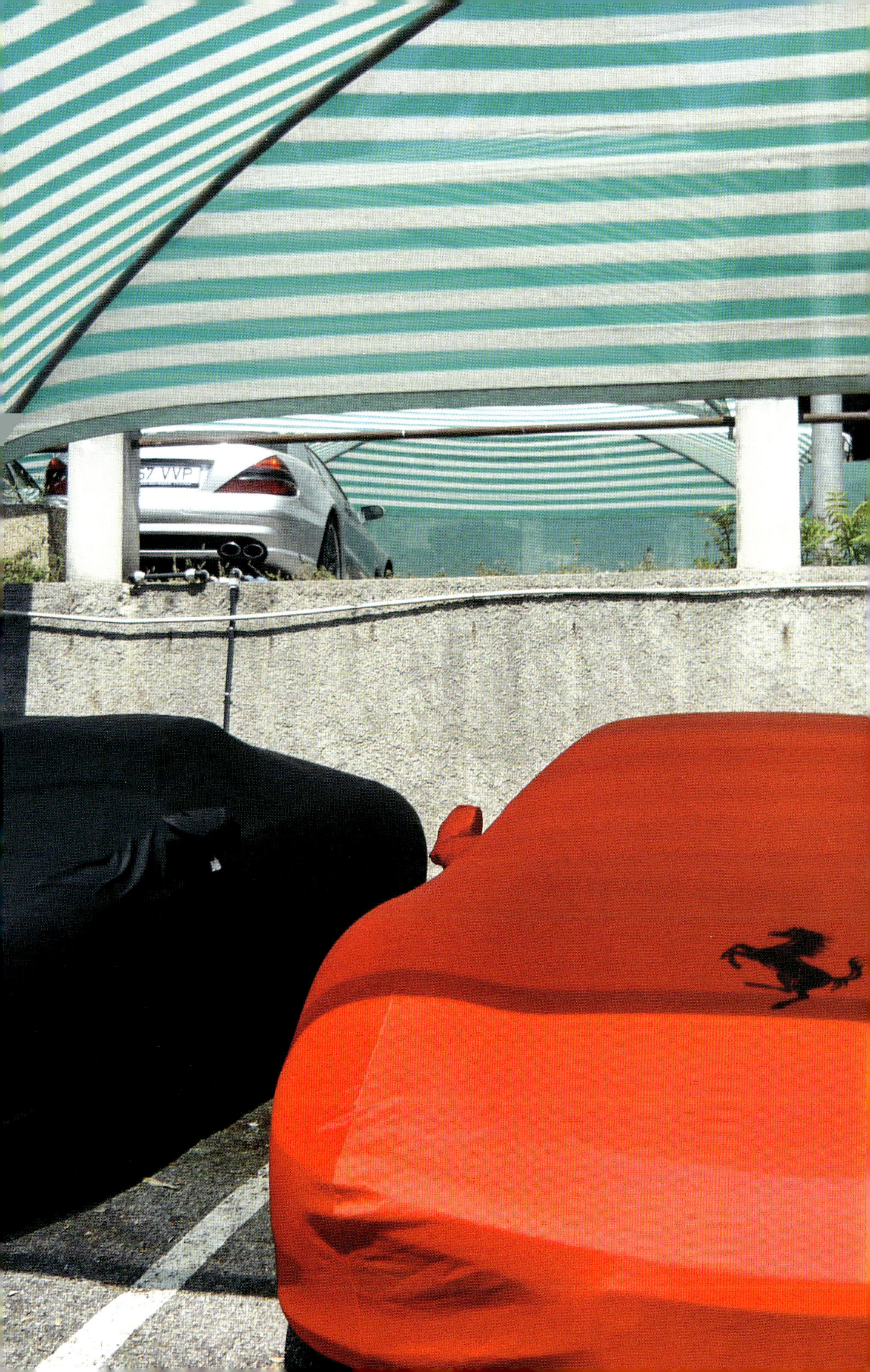

Cultural Magnet

"If the Paris Opera, on its opulent site in the Place de l'Opéra, is considered to be the chef d'oeuvre of Charles Garnier, its architect, then the Opera of Monte Carlo can be nominated as his dessert."

—Michael Powell and Emeric Pressburger,

The Red Shoes

The addition of the opera house, called the Salle Garnier, in 1879, ushered in a period of high culture that tied in neatly with Monte Carlo's high-stakes offerings as a gambling center. Built as part of the casino, the opera's only public entrance, even now, is through the casino's front door. Instead of turning to the left, where the casino is located, a theatergoer must turn to the right. The thinking is ingenious: Once inside, there is every probability that an attendee would pay a visit to the gaming rooms either before or after a performance or even during intermission. In this regard, the concept is no different from the Las Vegas model of positioning nightclubs and auditoriums

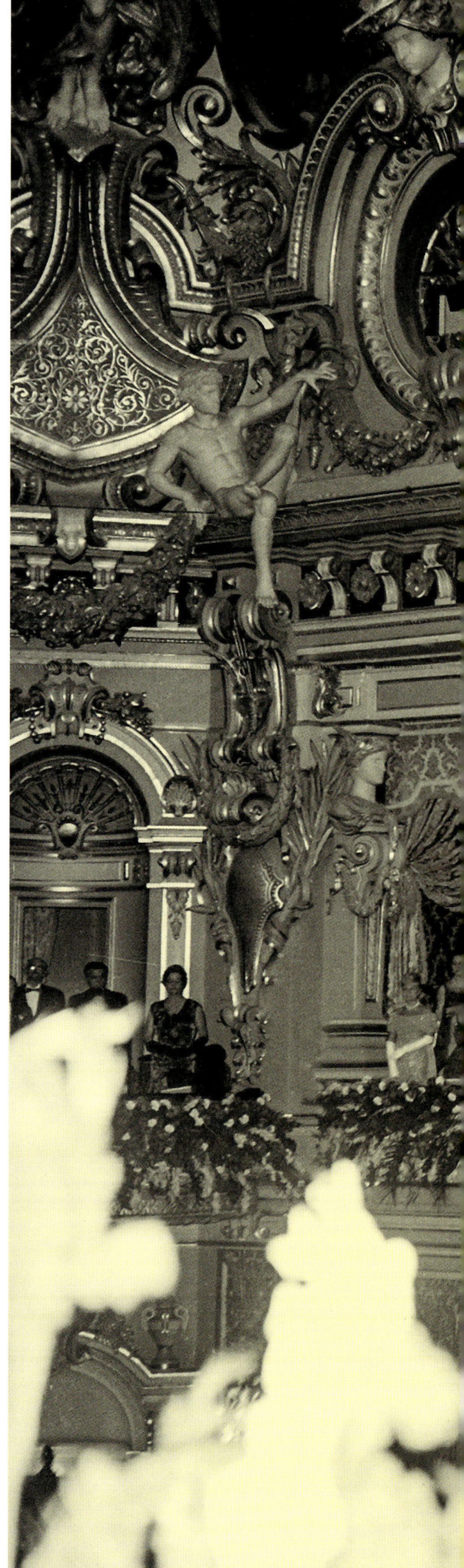

The gloriously ornate interior of the Salle Garnier opera house, named after its architect, Charles Garnier.

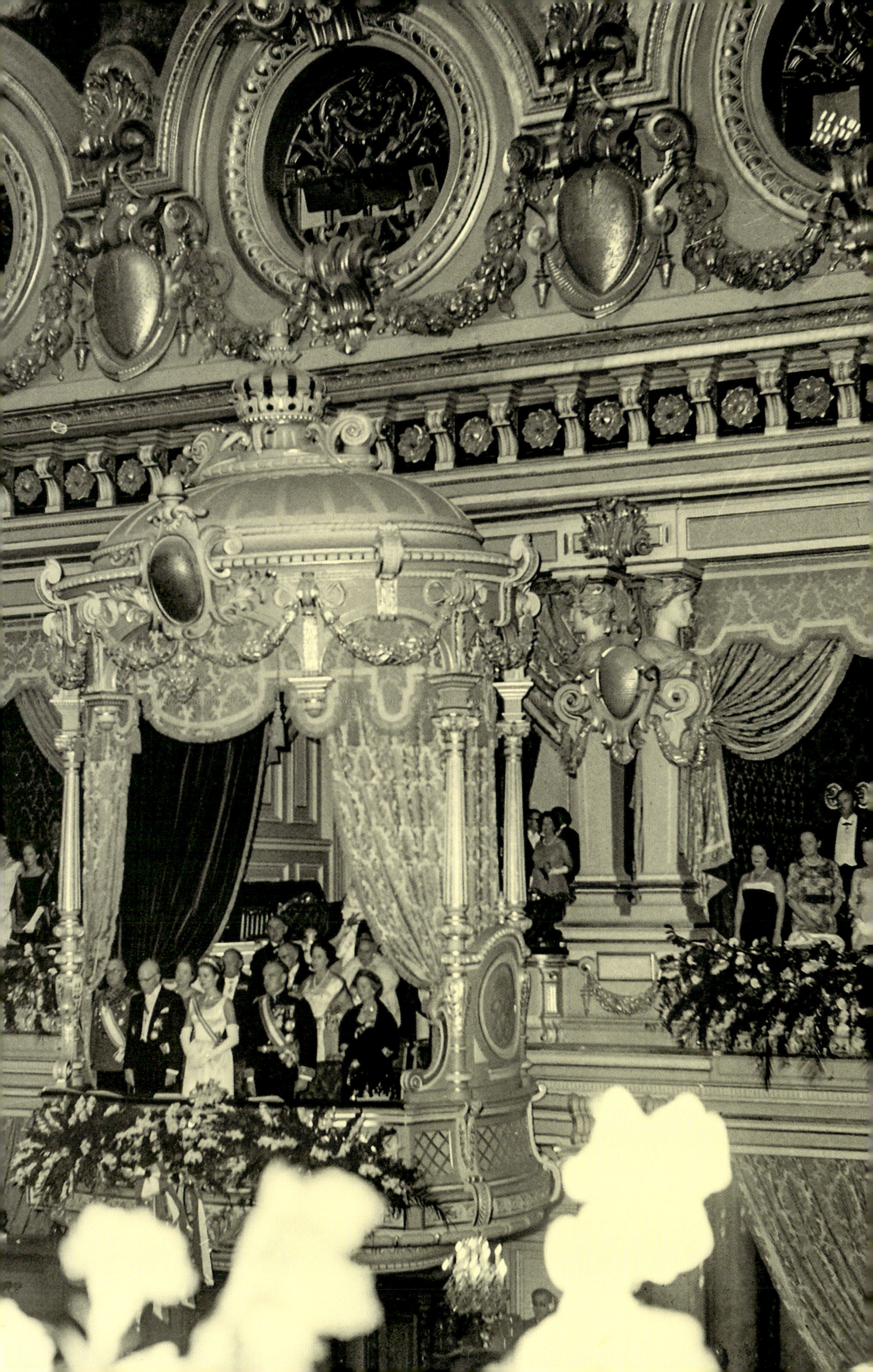

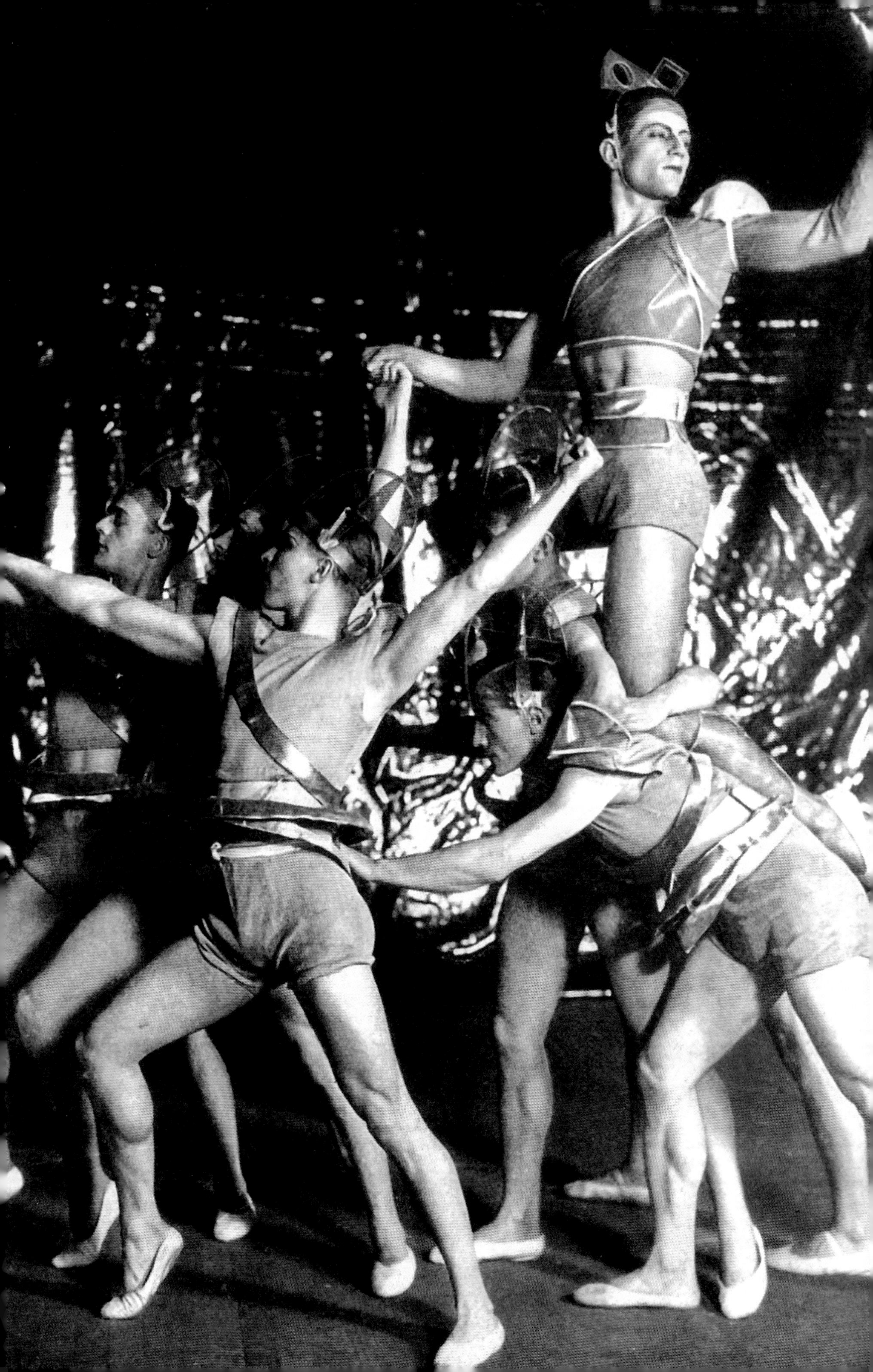

THEATRE DE MONTE-CARLO

SOIRÉE DU 19 AVRIL 1911

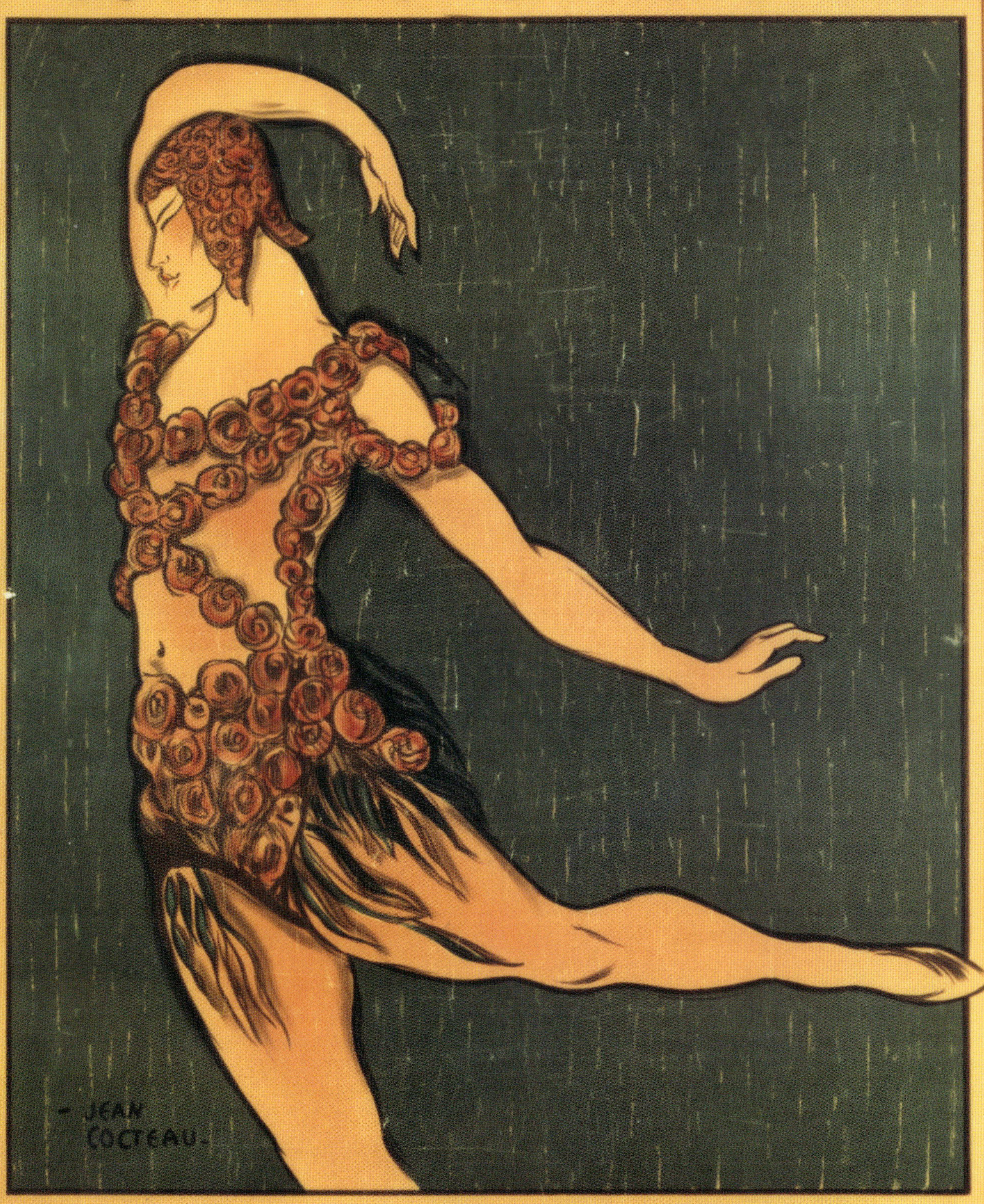

BALLET RUSSE

inside the casino to be within easy reach. The Royal family has its own private entrance, through a side door. Everyone else is thrown in the path of temptation—which was precisely the point. The Salle Garnier brought legitimacy to Monte Carlo while at the same time filling the coffers of the Principality with an entirely new constituency, and not a moment too soon.

On opening night, none other than the diva Sarah Bernhardt appeared in a nymph costume. Hector Berlioz's *The Damnation of Faust* made its debut in 1893. Much later, the hall featured such stars as Nellie Melba and Enrico Caruso (as Mimi and Rodolfo in *La Bohème*), Tito Schipa, Lily Pons, and the compositions of Massenet, Mascagni, and Saint-Saëns.

As popular as opera was ballet, particularly the offshoot of the avant-garde company Ballet Russe. Originally based in Paris, it toured Europe and North and South America to great acclaim. Its founder, the autocratic Sergei Diaghilev, commissioned Igor Stravinsky, Claude Debussy, and others to compose works and asked artists such as Picasso, Matisse, Dalí, André Derain, Joan Miró, Léon Bakst, Utrillo, and even Coco Chanel to design extravagant and sensational sets and costumes. Despite its name, the Ballet Russe never performed in Russia (a certain revolution got in the way). No ballet company before or since has had such an impact on dance—both because of its groundbreaking productions and its dancers and choreographers, including Anna Pavlova, Vaslav Nijinsky, Serge Lifar, Fokine, Petipa, Léonide Massine, and George Balanchine. When the Ballet Russe de Monte Carlo was formed, it was Massine who was its leader.

In the 1948 movie *The Red Shoes*, the most ravishing film about ballet ever made, the high-handed impresario Boris Lermontov is a thinly veiled Diaghilev. A good part of the movie takes place in Monte Carlo, where romantic love and love of art collide. A subsequent novelization of the *The Red Shoes* has a description of the opera house that is beyond compare: "Its exterior merges into the facade of the Casino, the triumph of sugar-plum architecture of which it is a component, but the interior of the theatre is a jeweled workbox. The auditorium, which seats not more than three hundred, is exquisite, a dream of white, gold and crimson, of looped curtains, shining chandeliers, glittering ornaments.... One can stroll from the lobby into the gaming room, and from the gaming rooms back into the lobby of the theatre, having become a few thousand dollar richer, or poorer, during the entr'acte."

The Ballet Russe is long gone, replaced in 1985 by a new company, formed by Princess Grace's eldest daughter, Caroline (formally known as Her Royal Highness the Princess of Hanover). Les Ballets de Monte-Carlo is now the official dance company of Monaco and stages works associated with classic opera, including the Ballet Russe, as well as new productions, all under the direction of Jean-Christophe Maillot. But the Salle Garnier, as glorious as ever, is still very much in evidence and in business.

Detail of elaborate moldings inside the Salle Garnier opera house.
Previous pages, from left: Ballet Russe dancers performing in *La Chatte*; an iconic poster from 1911, featuring an illustration by Jean Cocteau depicting Nijinsky in *Spectre de la Rose.*

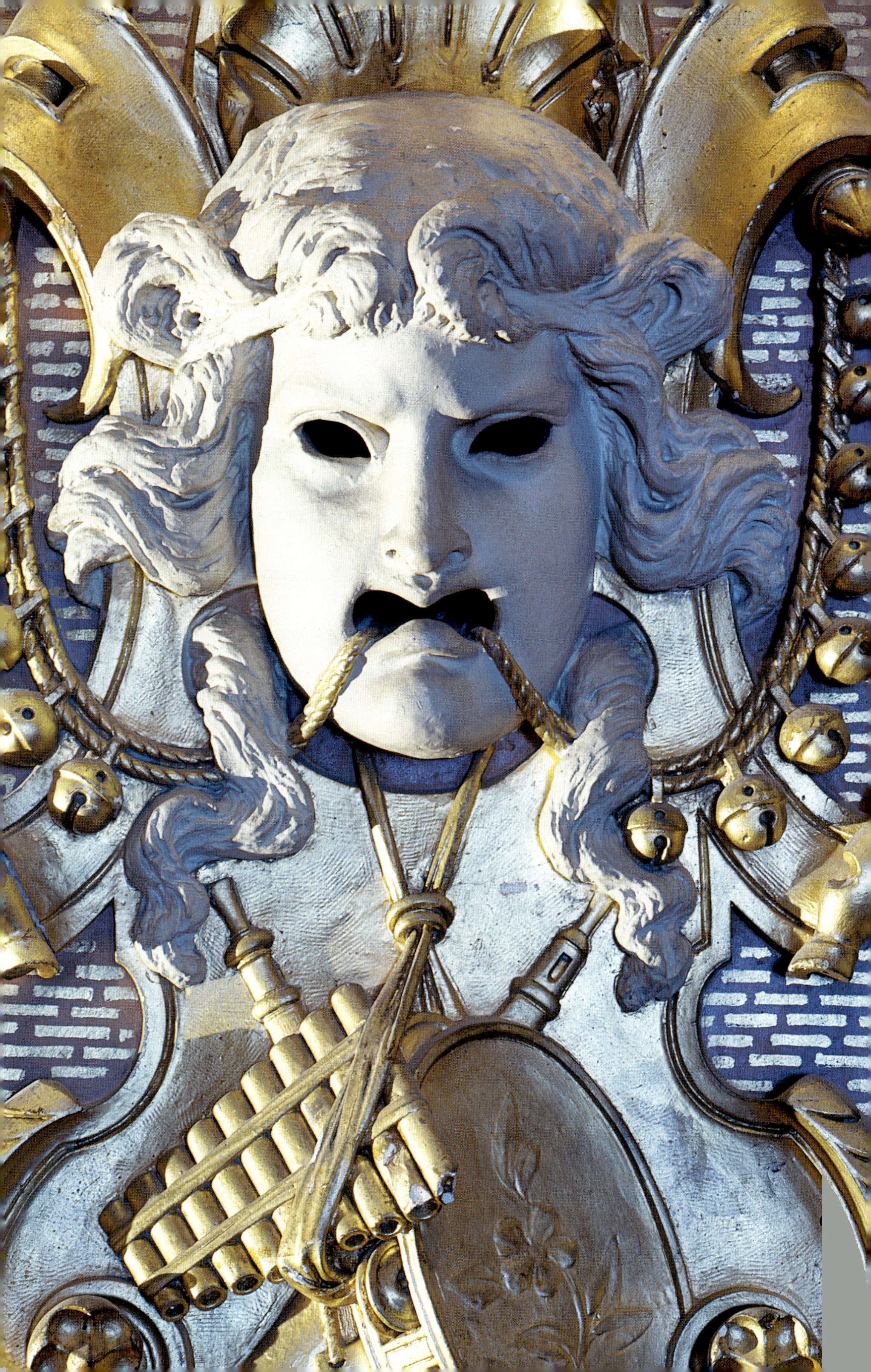

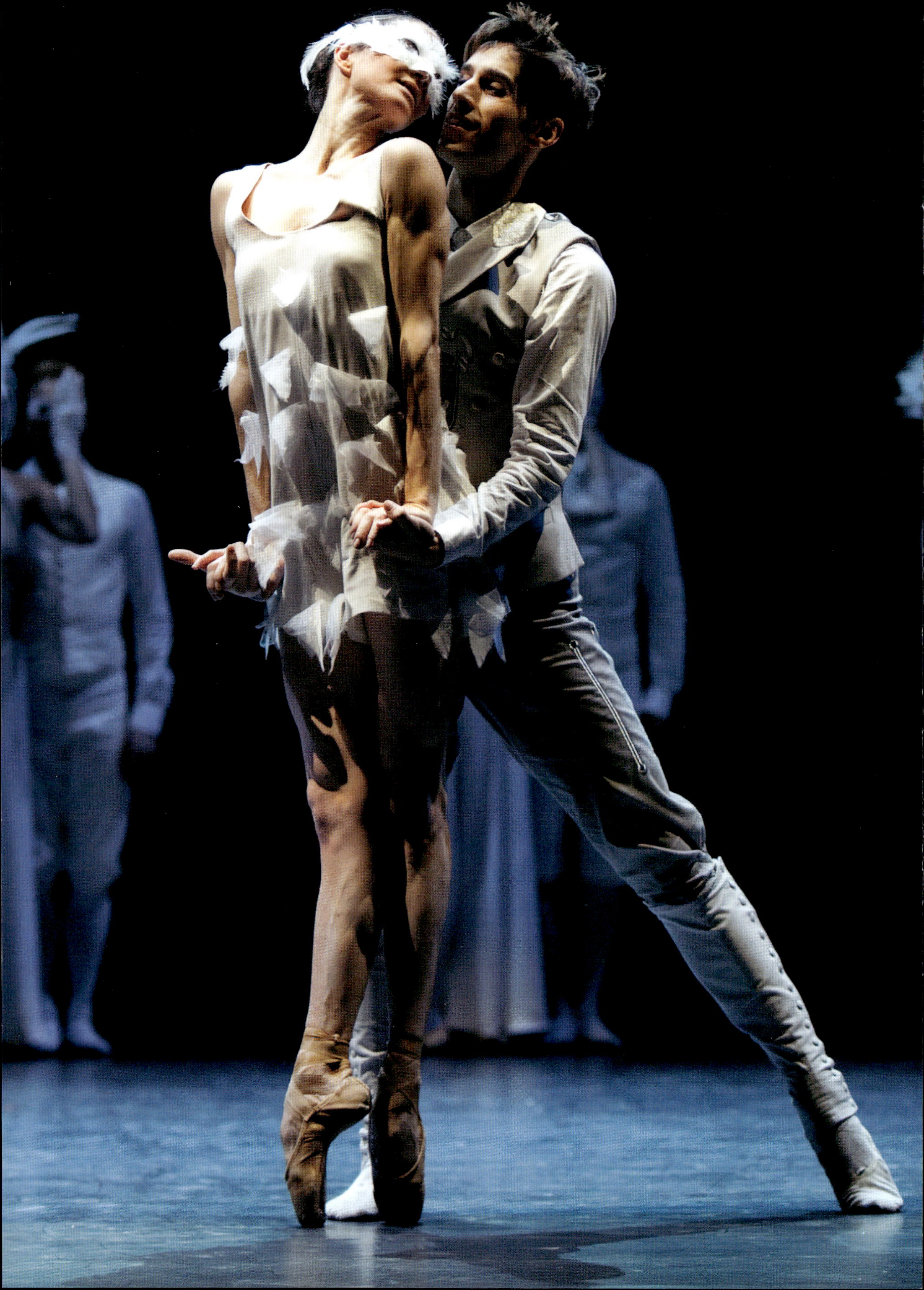

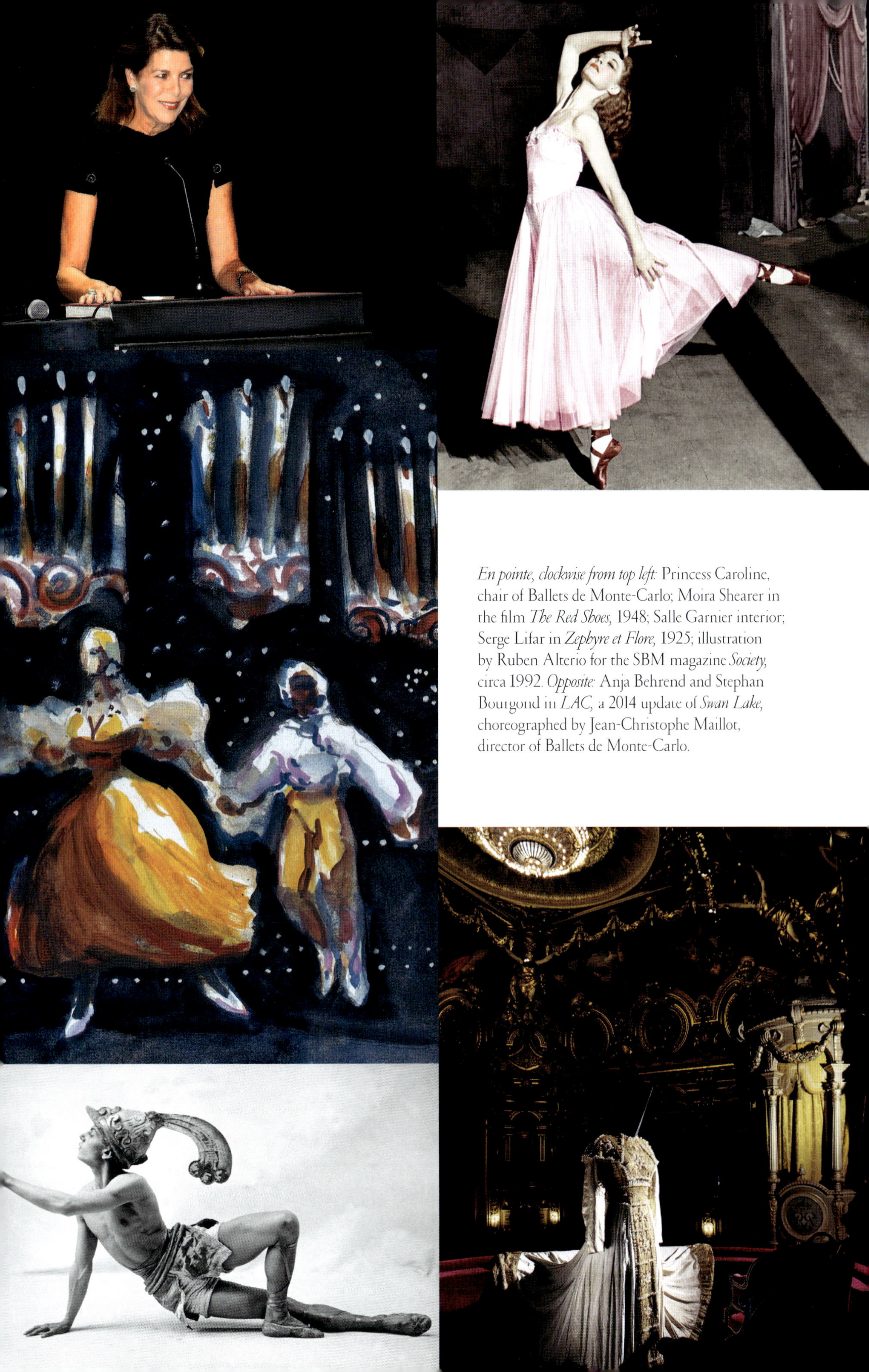

En pointe, clockwise from top left: Princess Caroline, chair of Ballets de Monte-Carlo; Moira Shearer in the film *The Red Shoes,* 1948; Salle Garnier interior; Serge Lifar in *Zephyre et Flore,* 1925; illustration by Ruben Alterio for the SBM magazine *Society,* circa 1992. *Opposite:* Anja Behrend and Stephan Bourgond in *LAC,* a 2014 update of *Swan Lake,* choreographed by Jean-Christophe Maillot, director of Ballets de Monte-Carlo.

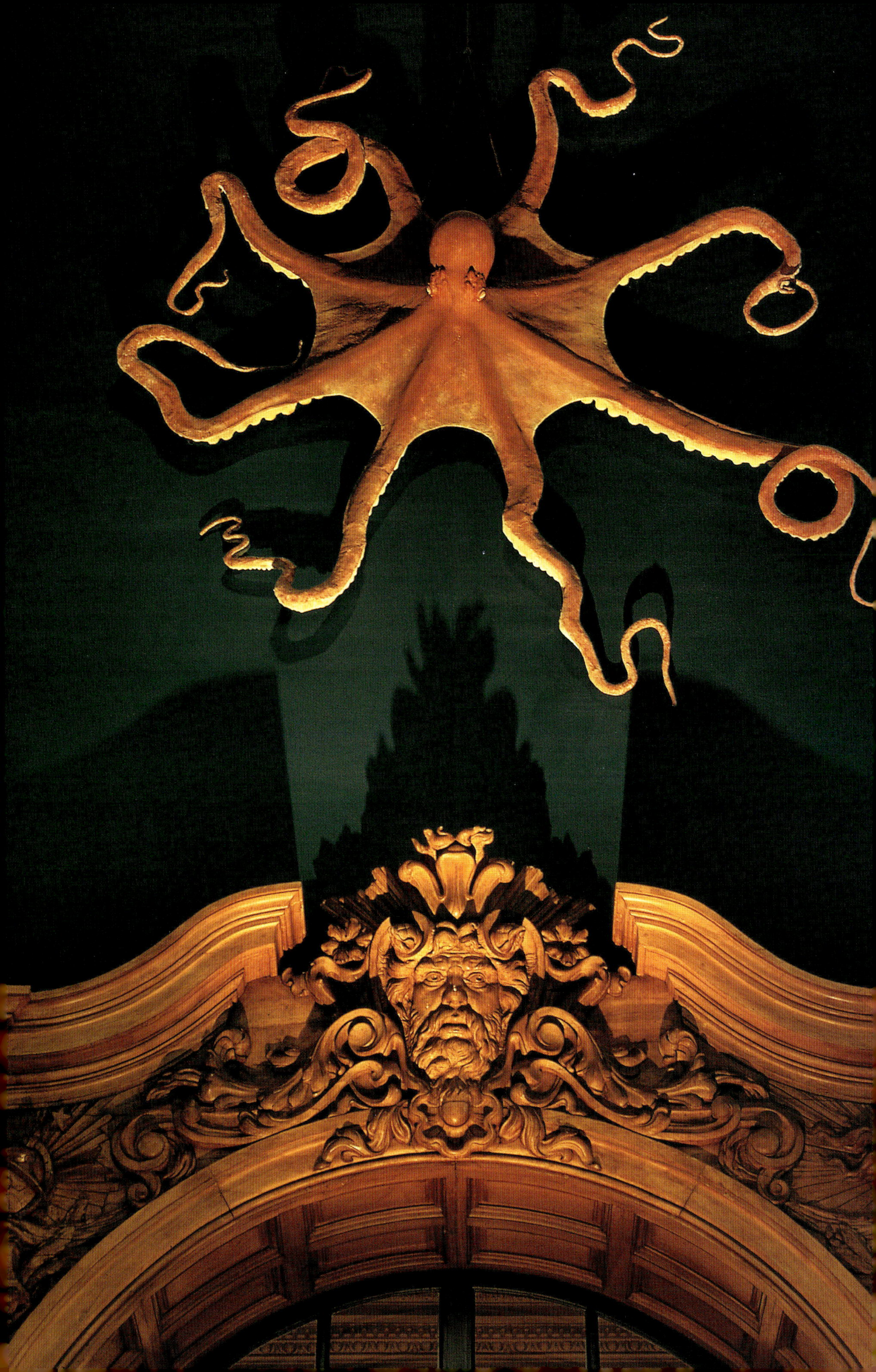

For those who are not operagoers or balletomanes, Monaco has several small museums. The New National Museum of Monaco (NMNM) is housed in two separate buildings: Villa Sauber, in Monte Carlo, and its younger sister, in the Villa Paloma, adjacent to the Jardin Exotique (Exotic Garden). Both specialize in contemporary art and have revolving installations.

The Musée Océanographique (Oceanographic Museum) describes itself as "a crossroads between art and science." Built on a promontory within walking distance of the Palace in Monaco Ville and overlooking the harbor, the museum was commissioned by sea-loving Prince Albert I. Designed by Paul Delefortrie, it opened on March 28, 1910, as a repository for all things related to the sea, as a laboratory for researchers, and as a way to introduce the wonders of ocean life to the public.

In his rhapsodic commemoration speech, Prince Albert addressed his remarks specifically to marine scientists: "When their thoughts wander from this monument over the blue waters which veil the mystery of our origin, they can sweep around the world, coming in contact with organisms which hand down to us the story of the ages. When they skirt the flank of our mountains, or rest in their caverns, or in the midst of remains of dead generations, they can plunge into dreams called forth by the history of the Earth. And if they mount to the summits which dominate all the horizon, they will easily reach the recesses of the universe, there to lose themselves in the secret of our destiny."

Aside from *A Sailor's Career,* a permanent exhibition based on the work of Prince Albert, the museum displays all manner of sea fauna—starfish, sea cucumbers, eels, rays, and shellfish of all shapes and sizes. And let's not forget sharks, the subject of its latest exhibition. Anyone who has longed to touch a shark can pet one in the *bassin caresse.* And anyone who doesn't can head the opposite direction.

The museum's most famous director was Jacques-Yves Cousteau, who based himself in Monaco from 1957 to 1988 (its overseer today is Robert Calcagno). His experiments on *Calypso,* his legendary vessel, served not only to bring attention to the study of oceanography but also to bring credibility to the museum.

Now it is up to Prince Albert II to follow in his great-grandfather's footsteps, which means treading lightly when it comes to the preservation and protection of marine life. Through his foundation, experiments and explorations are ongoing, with an acute awareness of the impact of pollution, erosion, and climate change as well as other threats to the seas, which, he is quick to remind, cover two-thirds of our planet.

Interior detail of the Oceanographic Museum.
Following pages: Skeletons of sea creatures at the Oceanographic Museum.
Pages 100-101: Commander Jean-Yves Cousteau with Prince Albert II and Prince Rainier III at the Oceanographic Museum.

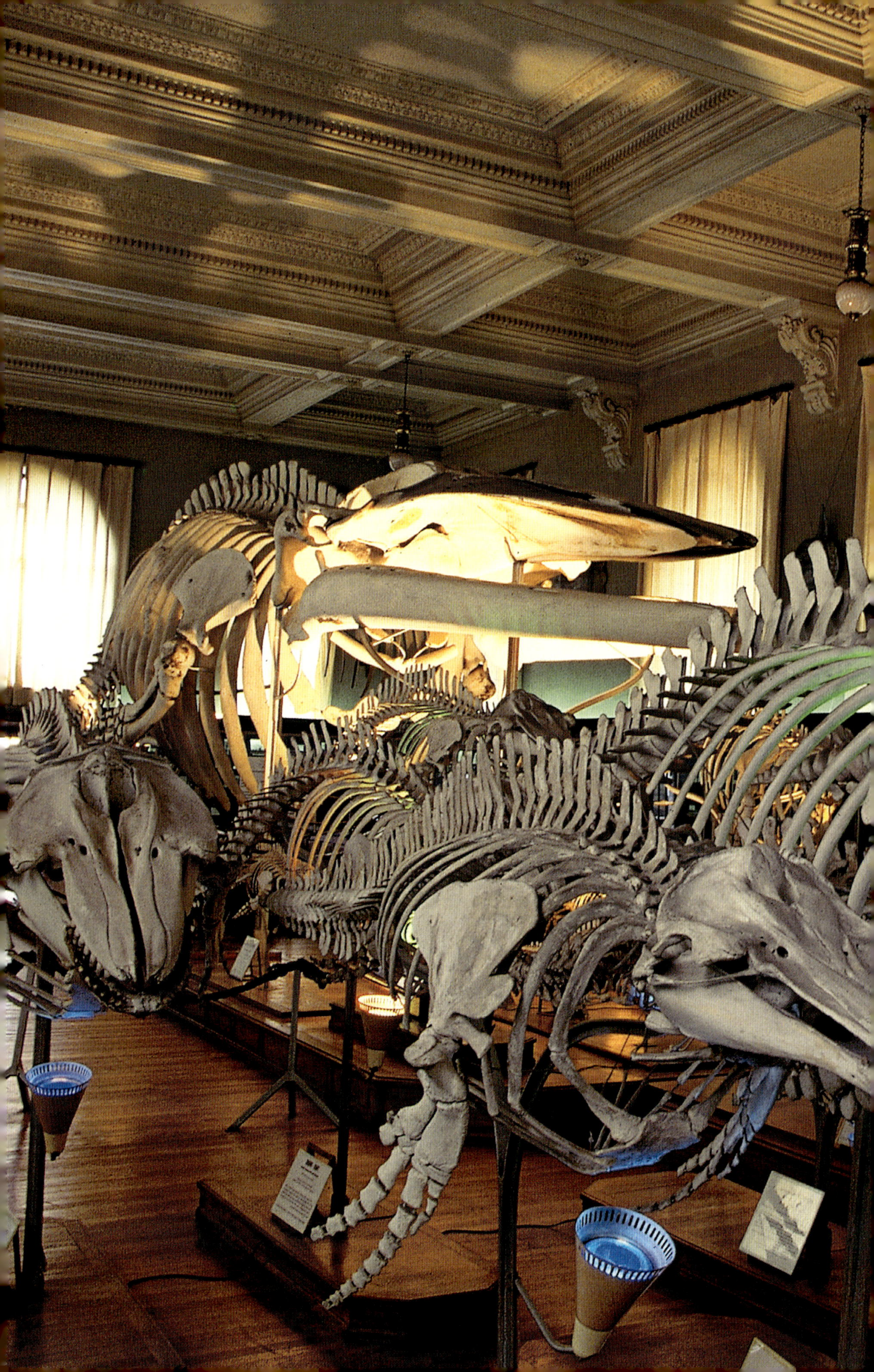

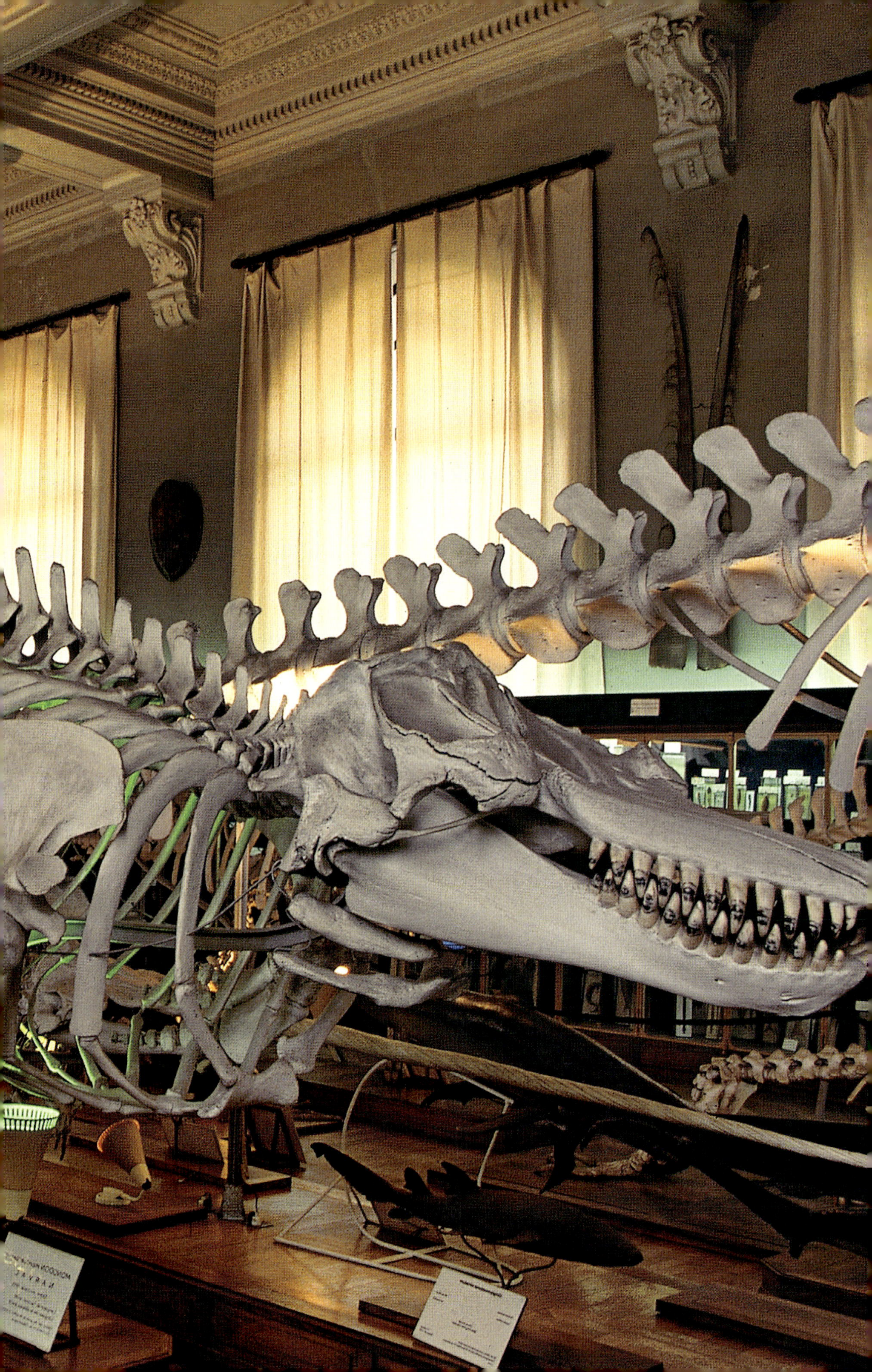

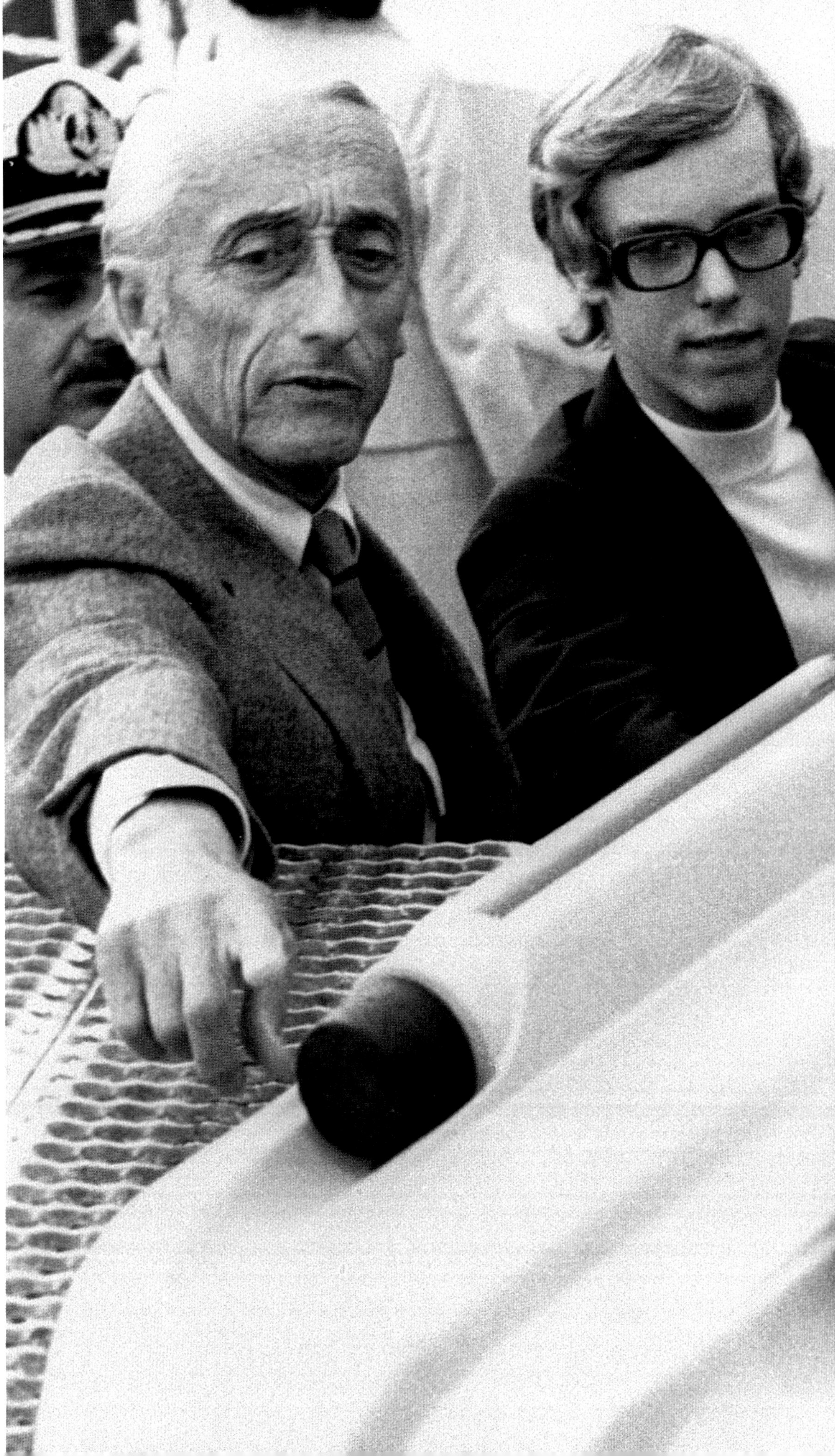

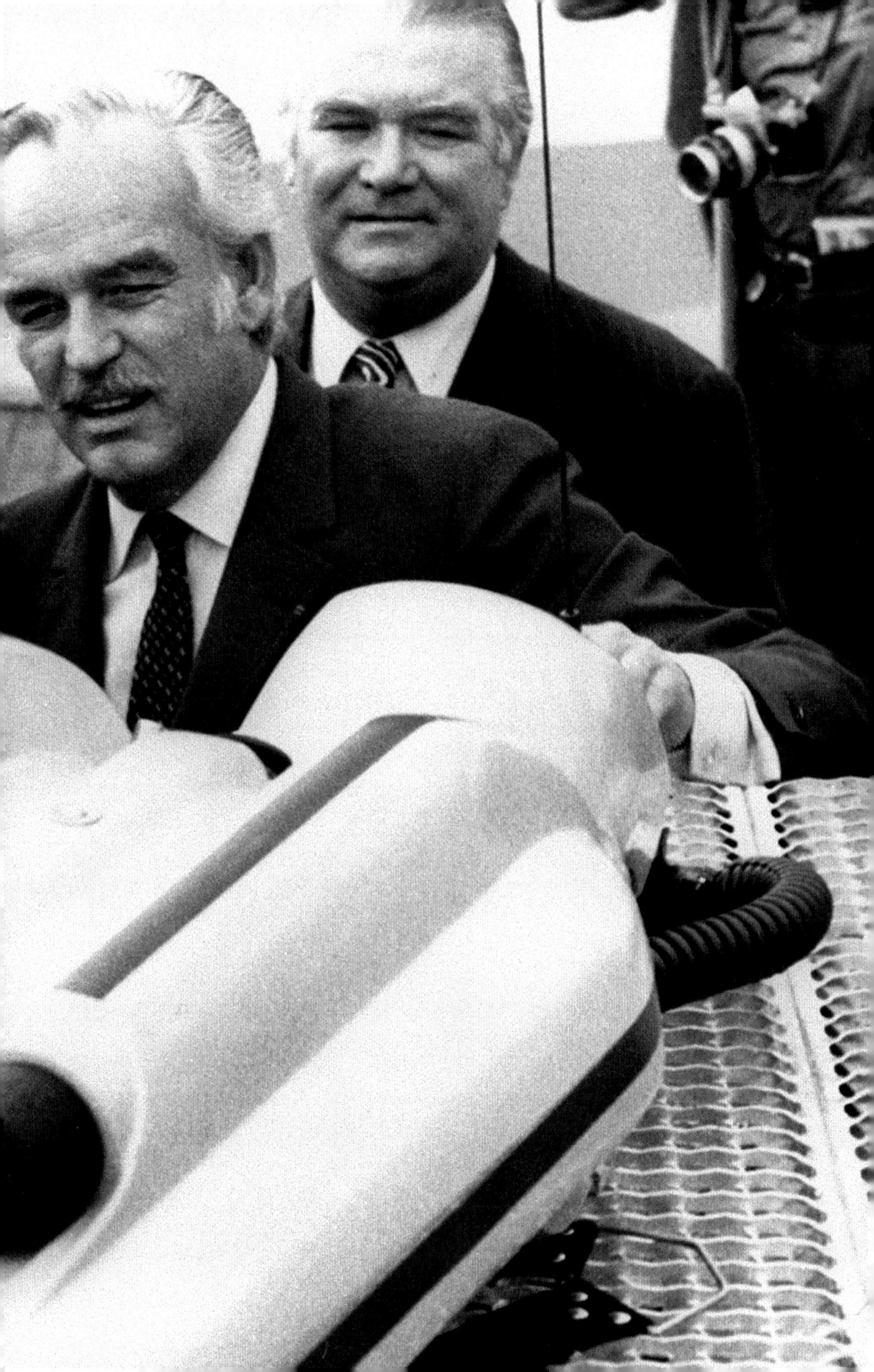

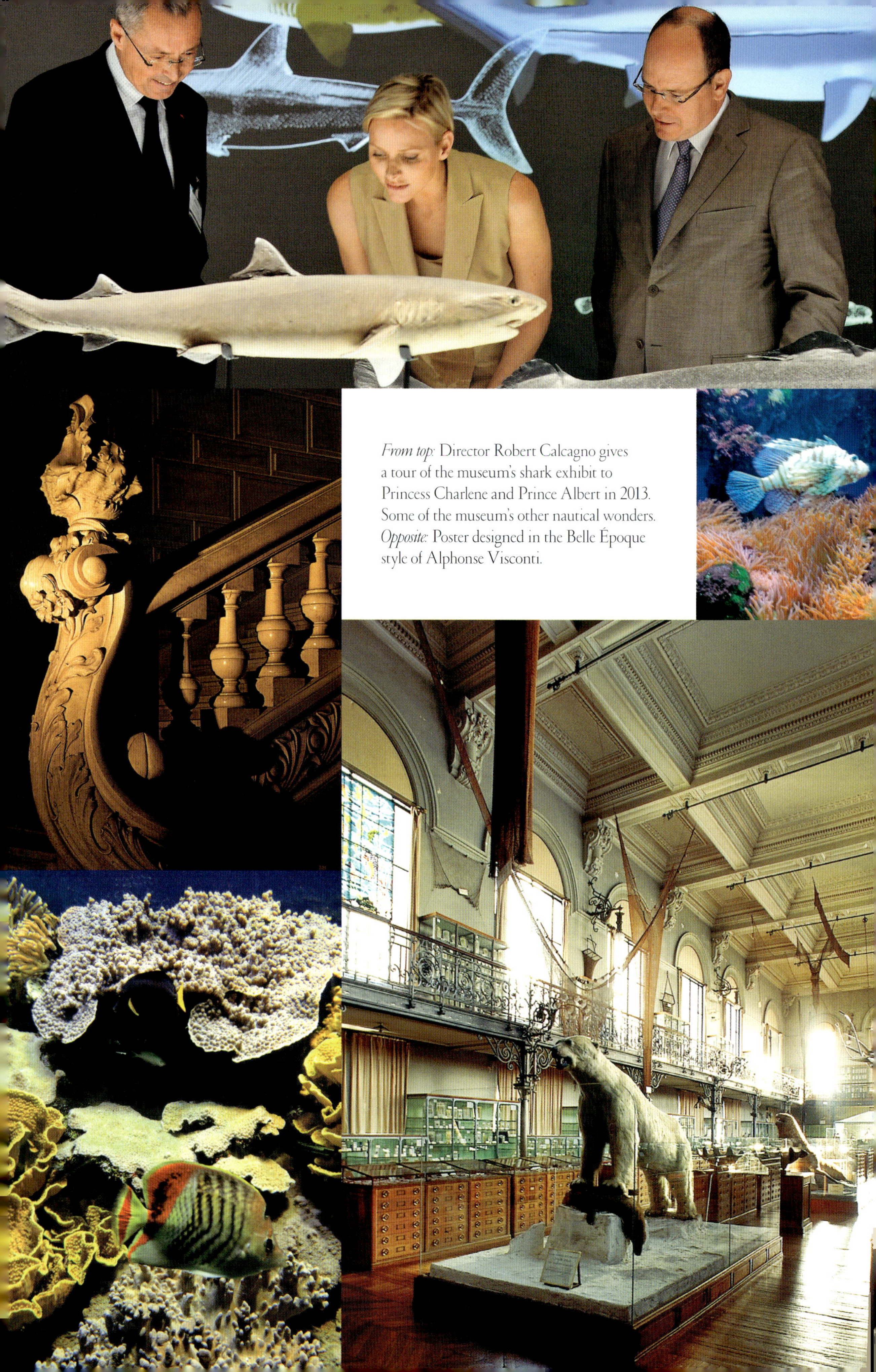

From top: Director Robert Calcagno gives a tour of the museum's shark exhibit to Princess Charlene and Prince Albert in 2013. Some of the museum's other nautical wonders. *Opposite:* Poster designed in the Belle Époque style of Alphonse Visconti.

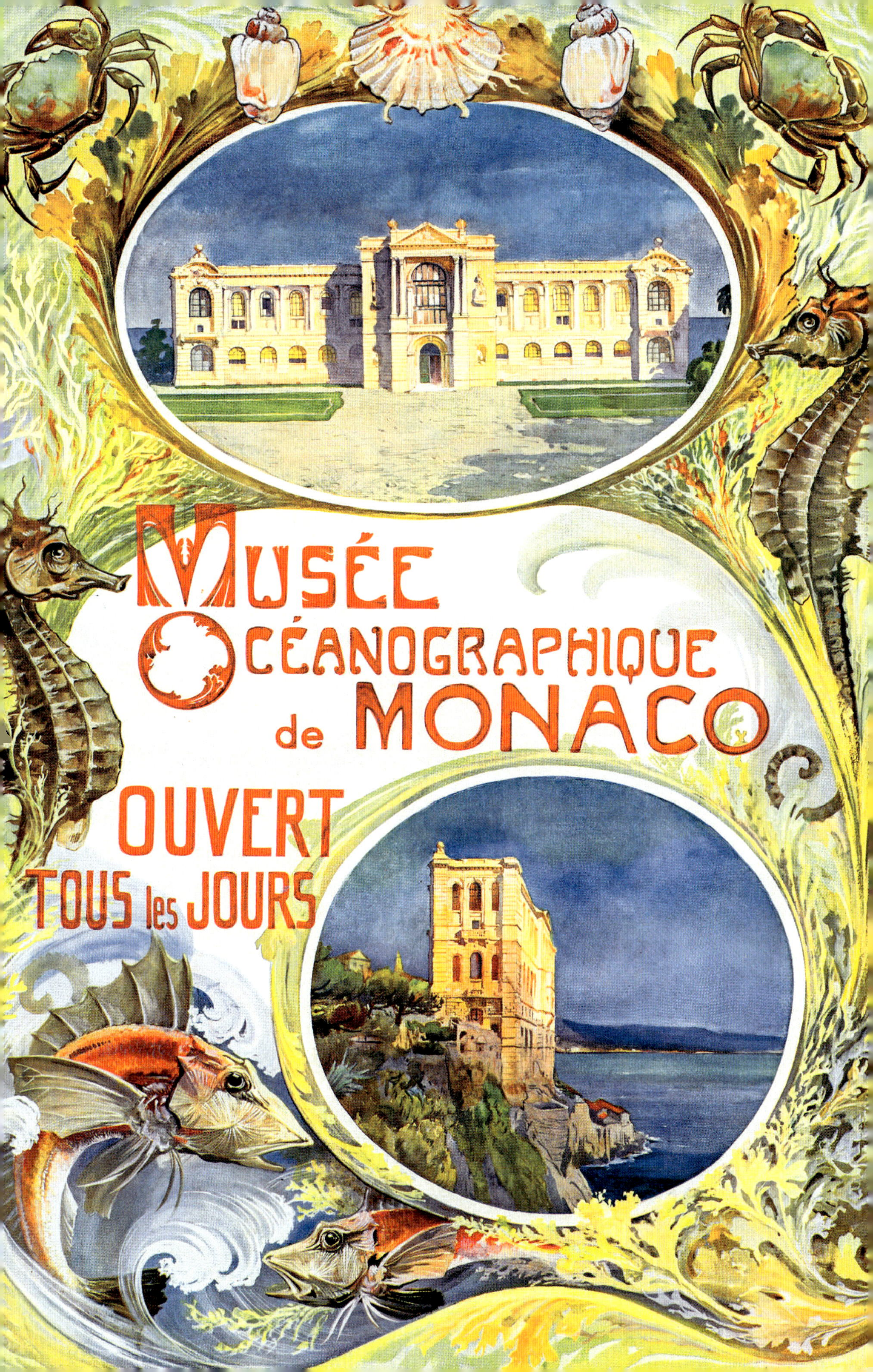

MUSÉE
OCÉANOGRAPHIQUE
de MONACO
OUVERT
TOUS les JOURS

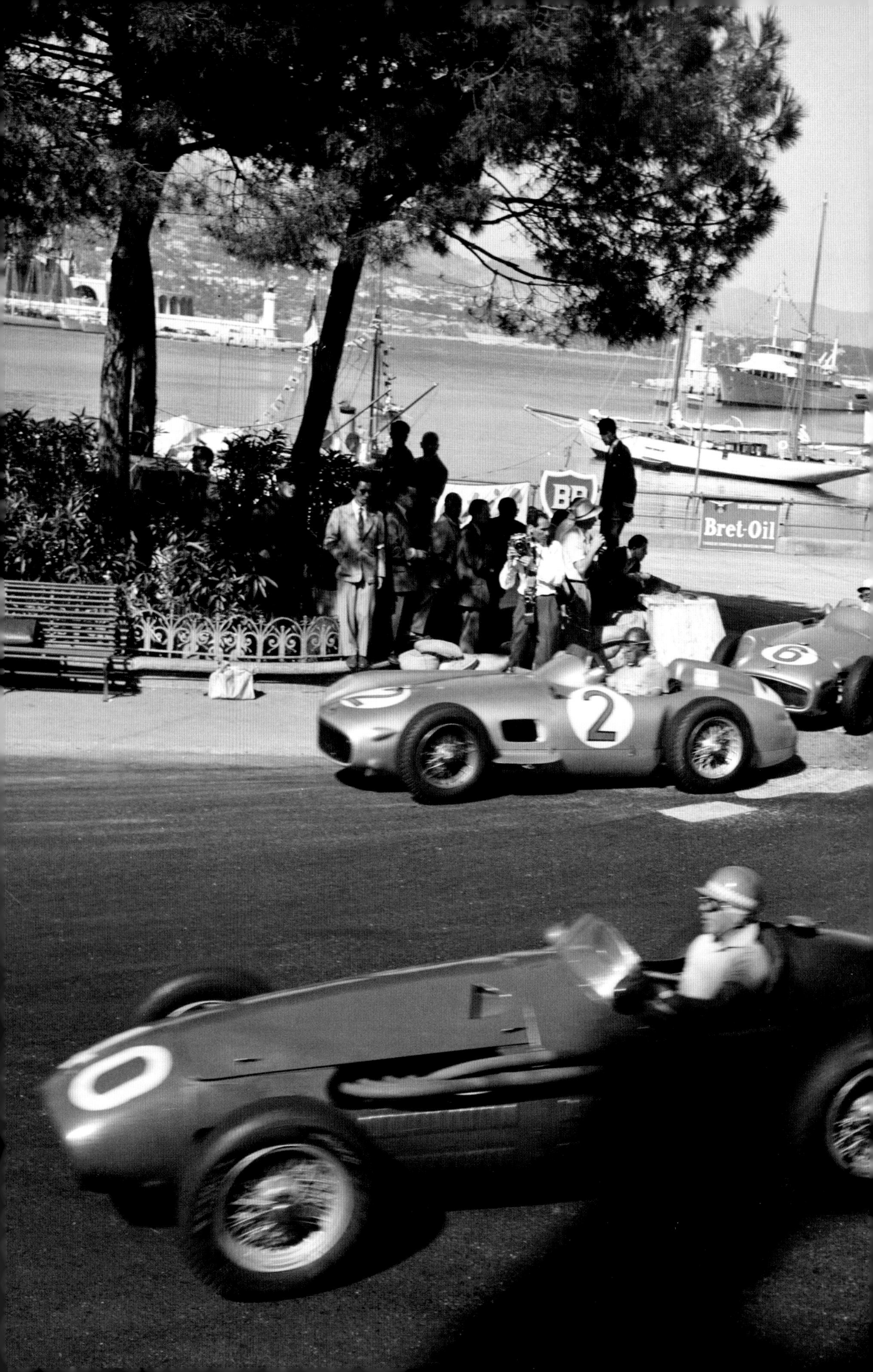

Bret-Oil
2
6

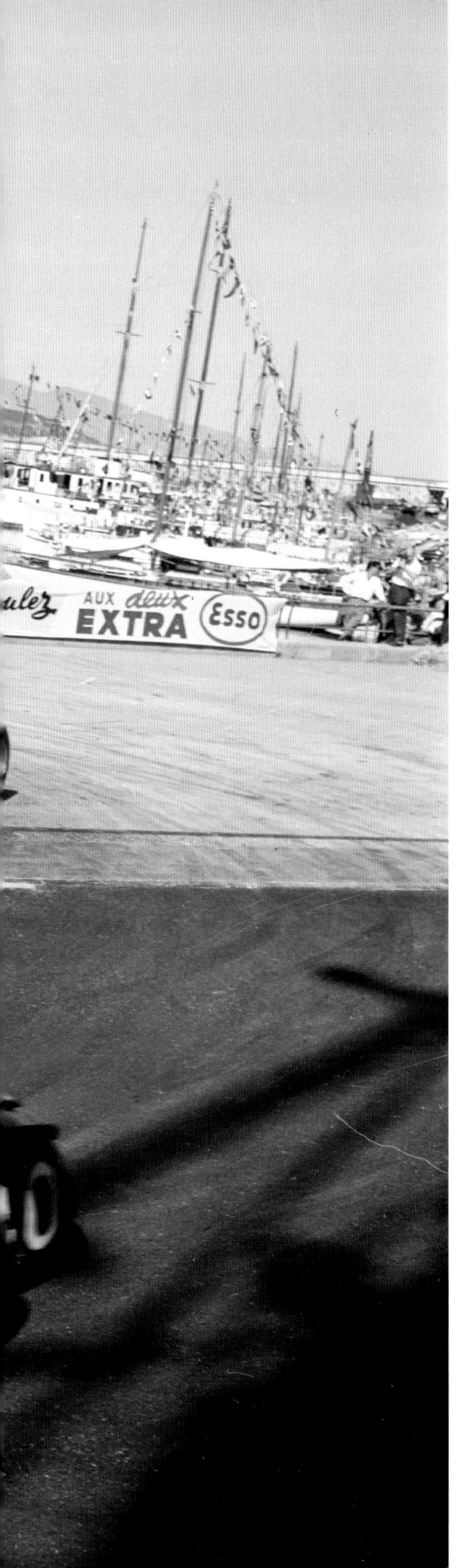

Vroom With a View

"But it's not just the track that makes Monaco special; it's the atmosphere as well. The grandstands are closer to the track than anywhere else... and that gives us a very close connection with the spectators."

—Sergio Pérez, Formula One driver

For most of the year Monaco is an unusually quiet and proper place—except, that is, for those several days when the auto races take place. The most prestigious is the Grand Prix, the ne plus ultra of all Formula One races, which occurs in the late spring. Then all hell breaks loose. The normally delicate air is spiked with noxious exhaust fumes. Race cars noisily careen around corners, twist and turn on roads precipitously close to the sea, speed through a dark tunnel (to which their eyes must adjust), and swirl around Monte Carlo's Casino Square like guided missiles as the thrill-seeking crowds cheer them on. But none are more thrill-seeking than the drivers themselves—those daredevils who tempt fate at every turn. Being at the wheel has been

Cesare Perdisa (No. 40), Juan Manuel Fangio (No. 2), and Stirling Moss (No. 6) during the Grand Prix of Monaco, 1955.

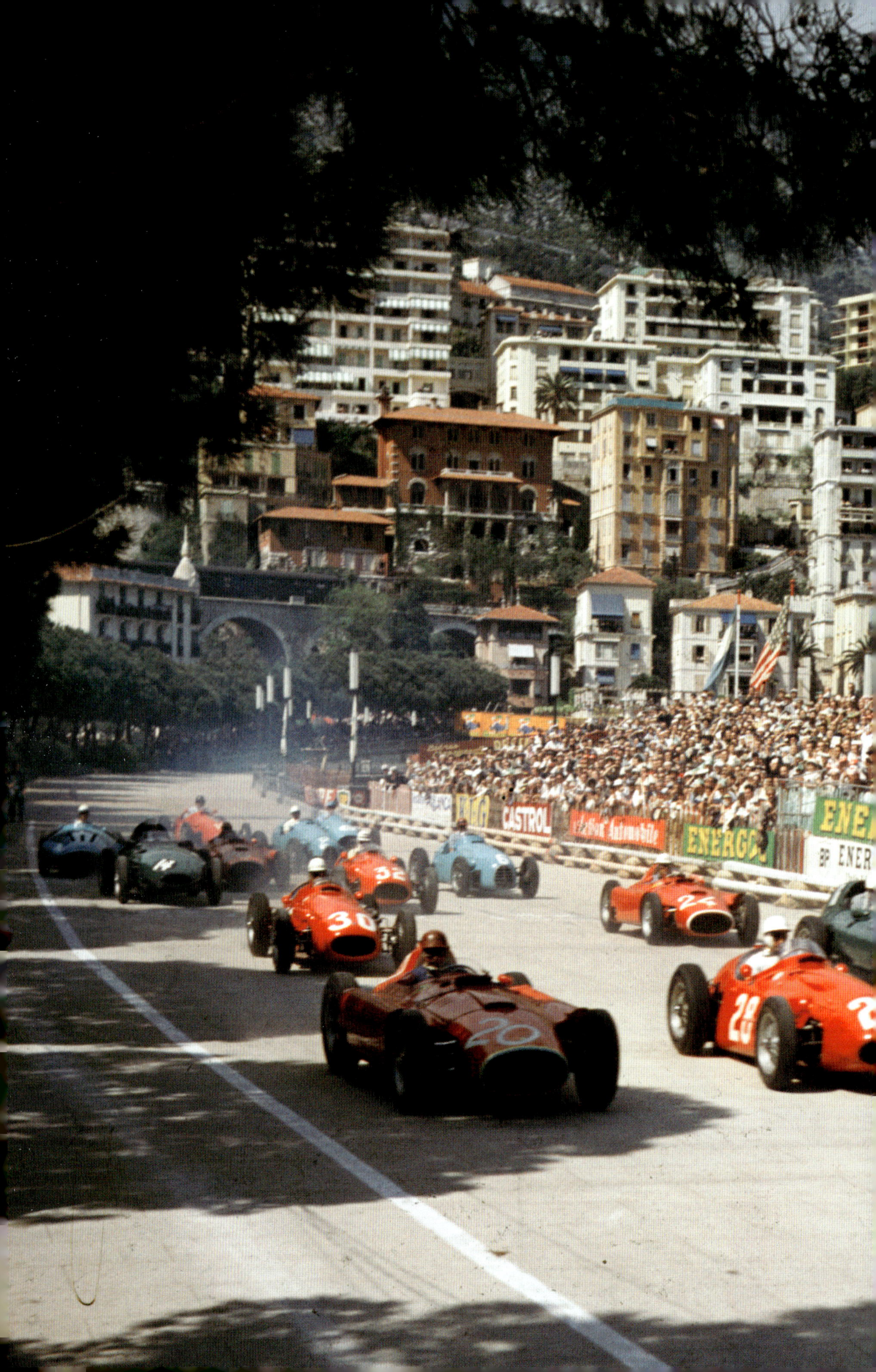
CASTROL
20
30
32
24
28

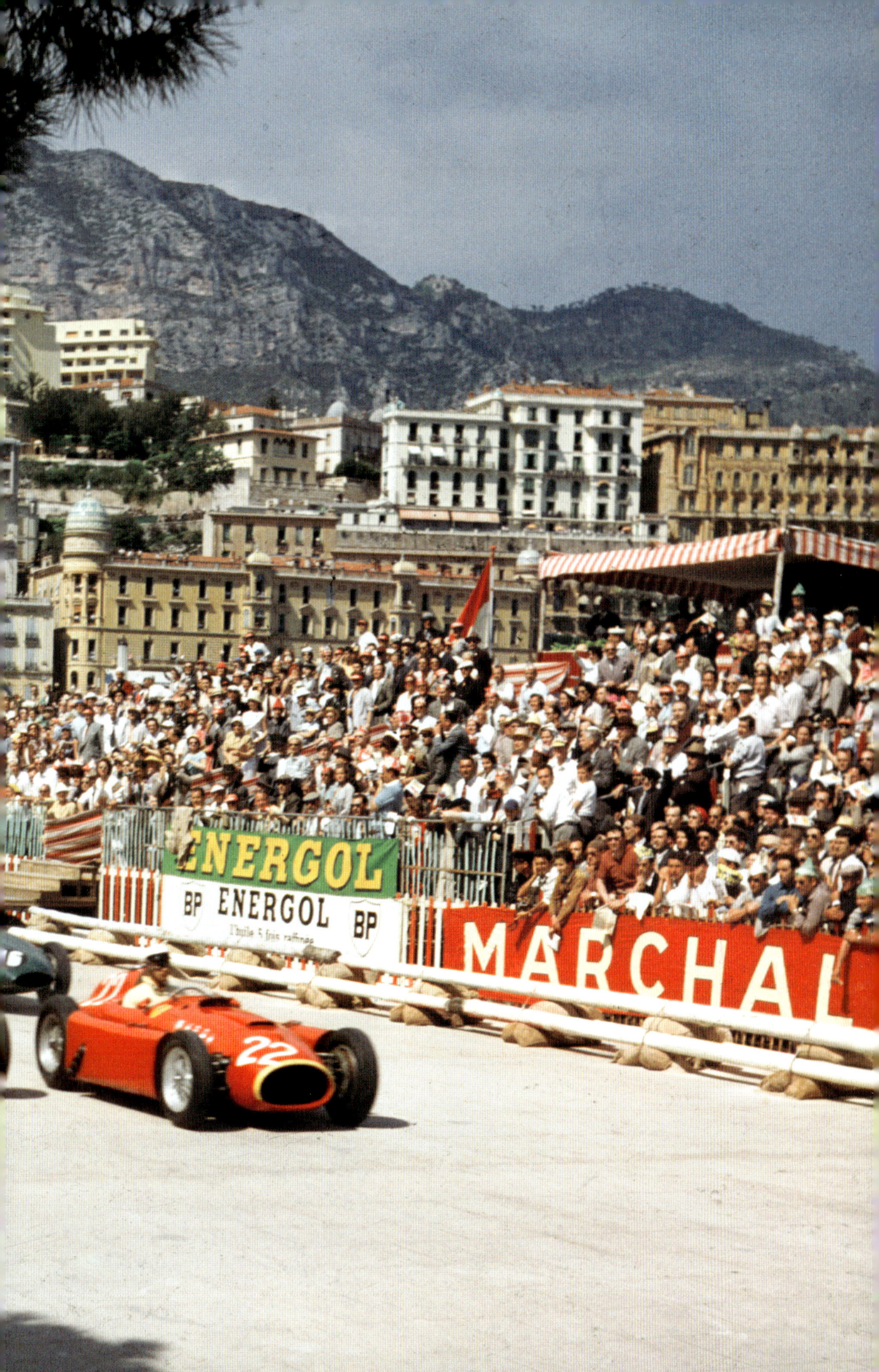
ENERGOL
BP ENERGOL BP
MARCHAL
22

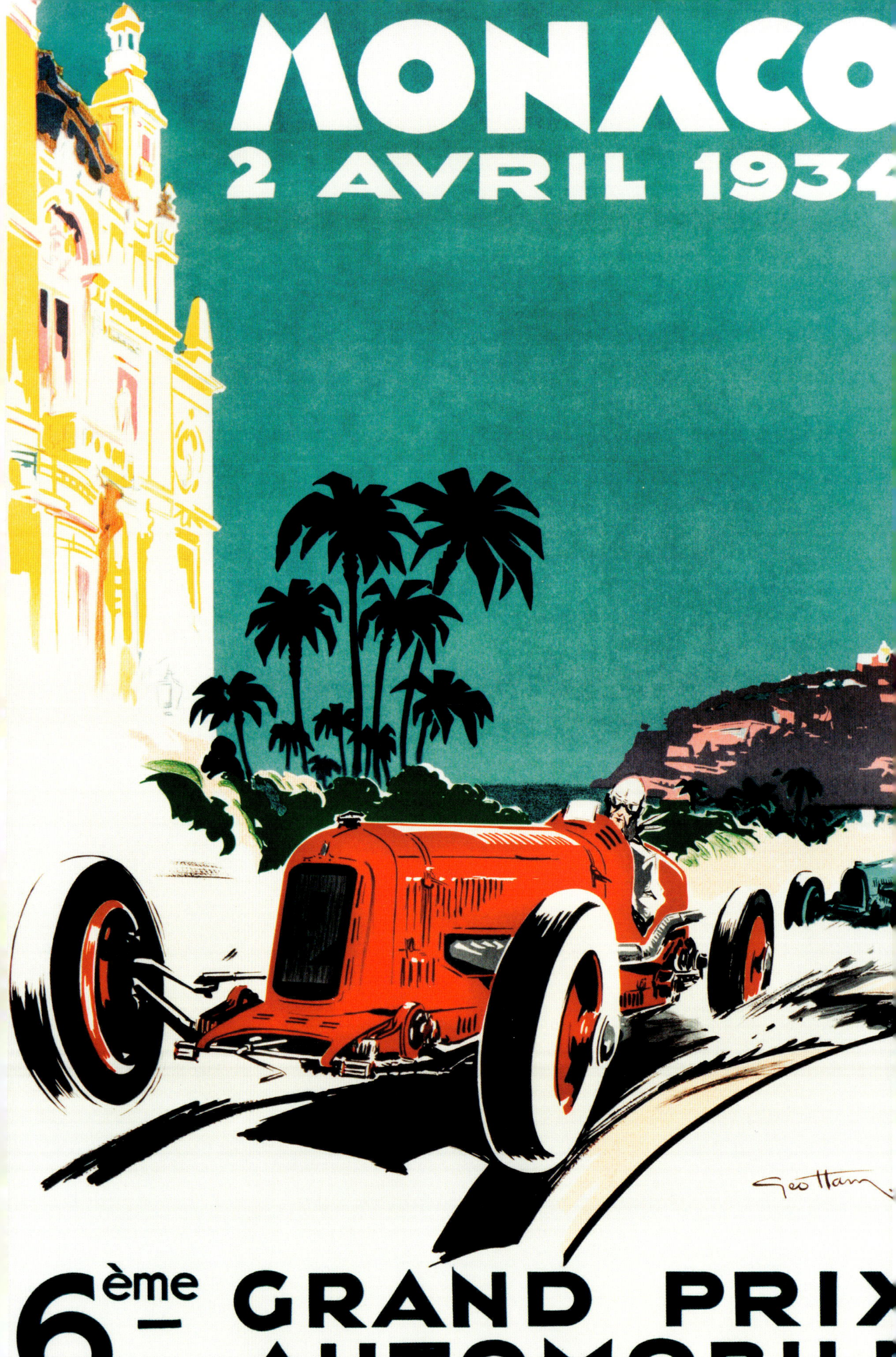
MONACO
2 AVRIL 1934
6ème GRAND PRIX
AUTOMOBIL
Geo Ham

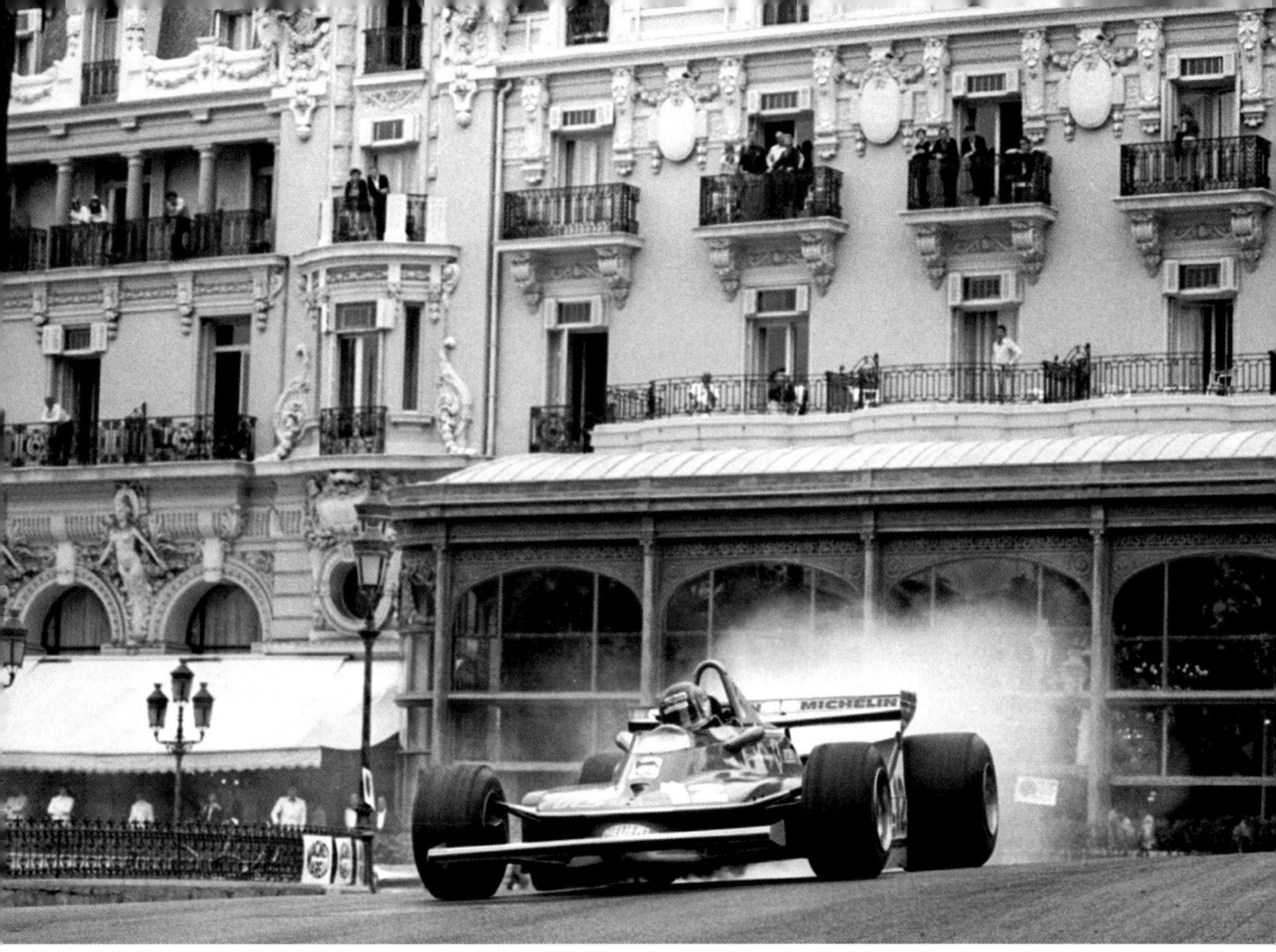

Gilles Villeneuve's engine blew at the end of Sunday morning warm-up for the 1975 race. He then retired from the Grand Prix on lap 55, in second position, with transmission problems. *Opposite:* Poster for the 1934 Grand Prix. *Previous pages:* The start of the 1956 Grand Prix. Stirling Moss (No. 28, center) went on to win the race.

compared to "a dance... a waltz" or, perhaps more accurately, "like being inside a bomb." In John Frankenheimer's 1966 movie *Grand Prix,* James Garner plays a driver who may have one more race left in him. The circuit has taken its toll. "You have to shift gears over 2,600 times during the race," he says ruefully. "That's an average of every three seconds."

The Indianapolis 500 and the 24 Hours of Le Mans are the other two competitions that make up the unofficial "triple crown" of motor sports, but neither has the glamorous cachet that distinguishes the Grand Prix—literally, "grand prize." The Grand Prix isn't auto racing's oldest competition but it is the one with the most breathtakingly scenic backdrop: namely, the Principality of Monaco. Ticket prices and hotel rooms are at a premium. Yachts with spectators fill the harbor. The grandstands are chock-a-block with fans. Hotel and apartment balconies are among the most coveted spectacle-viewing spaces. Just try getting into a restaurant, many of which are booked months ahead. The champagne flows and fireworks light up the sky. It's party time.

It doesn't last long—most genuine thrills don't—but the preparations start well in advance for what amounts to an afternoon event. Organized by the Automobile Club de Monaco, the circuit

Following pages: James Garner and Yves Montand on the set of the 1966 movie *Grand Prix.*

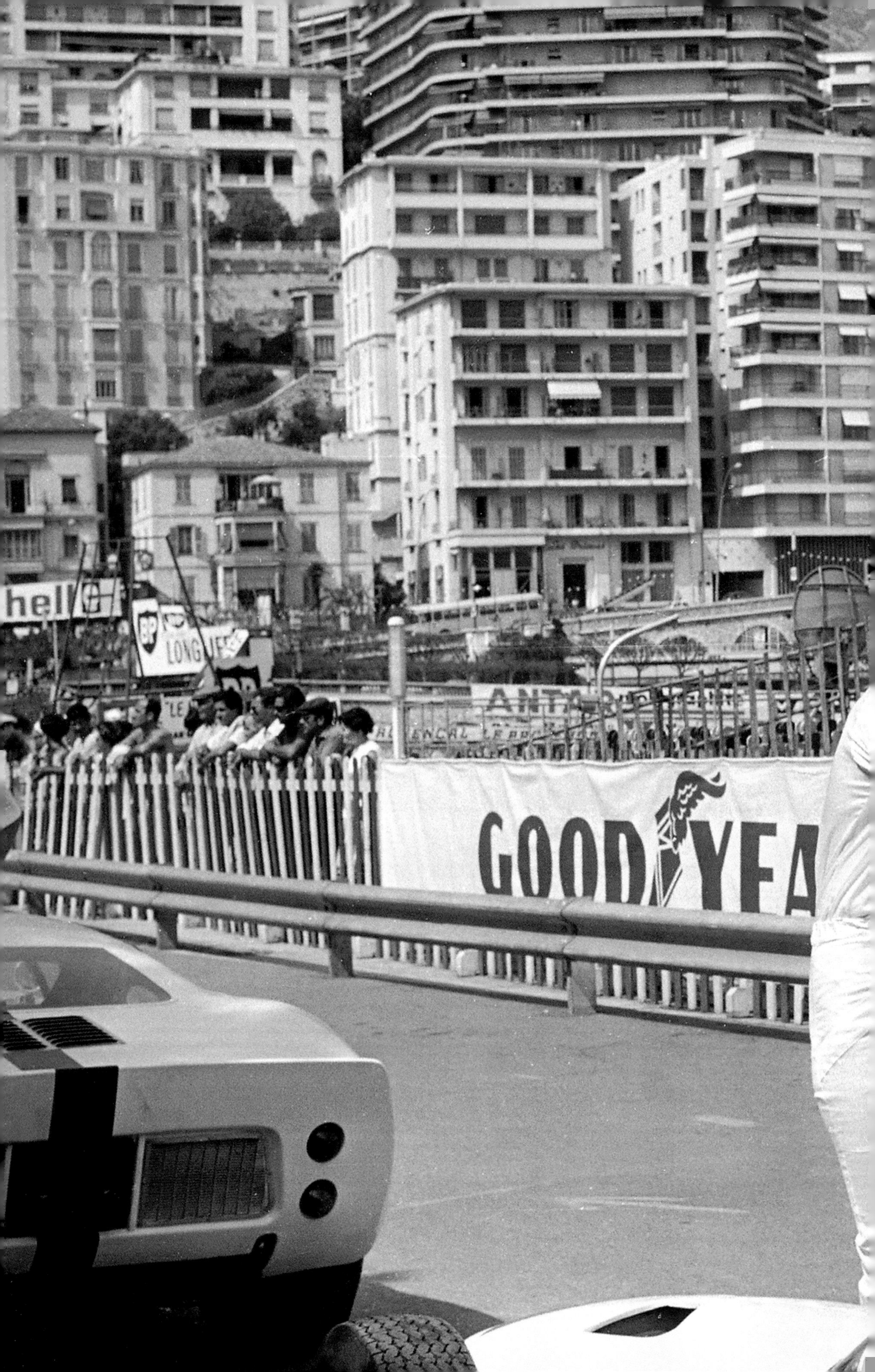
hell
BP
GOOD YEA

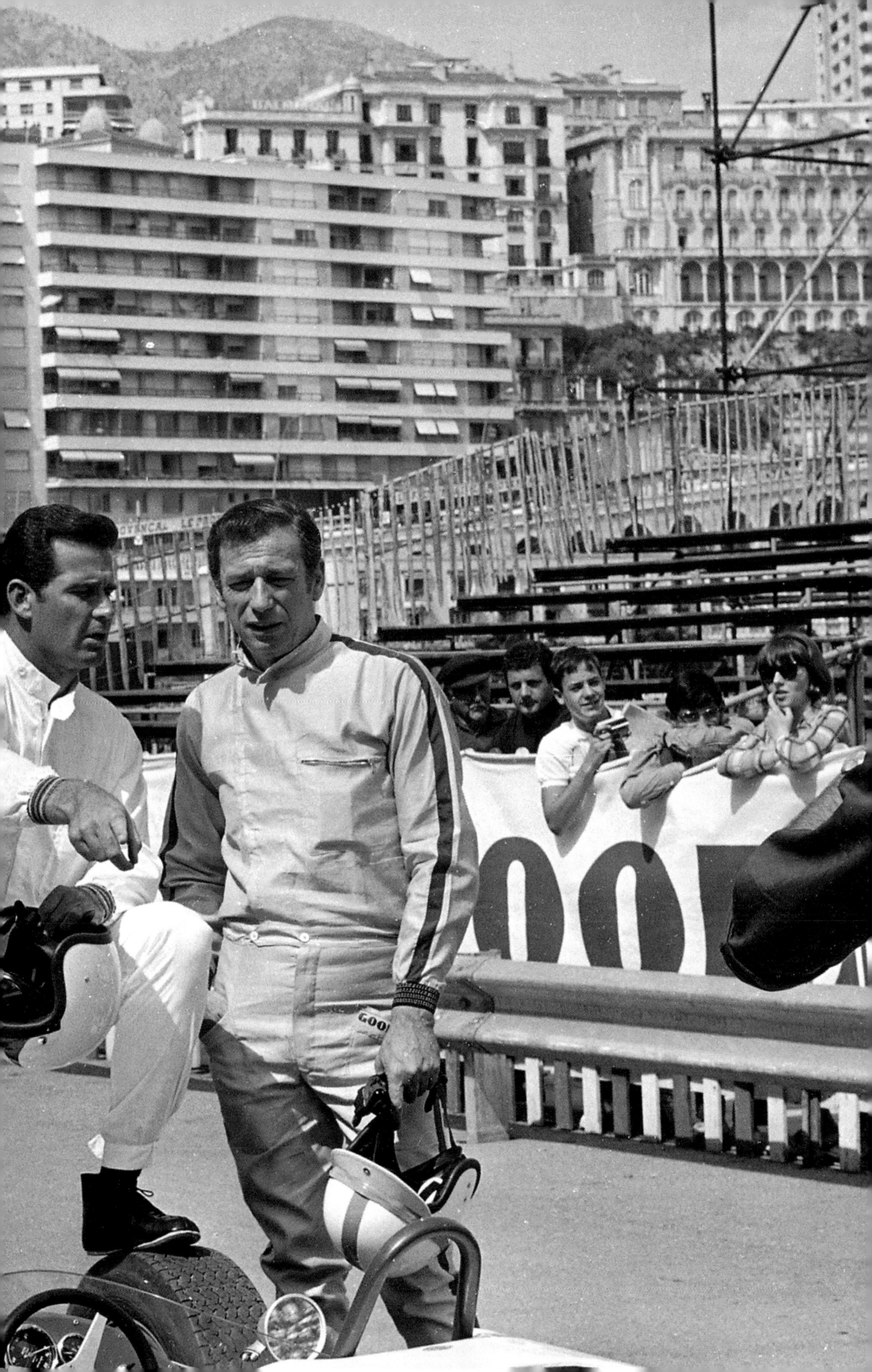

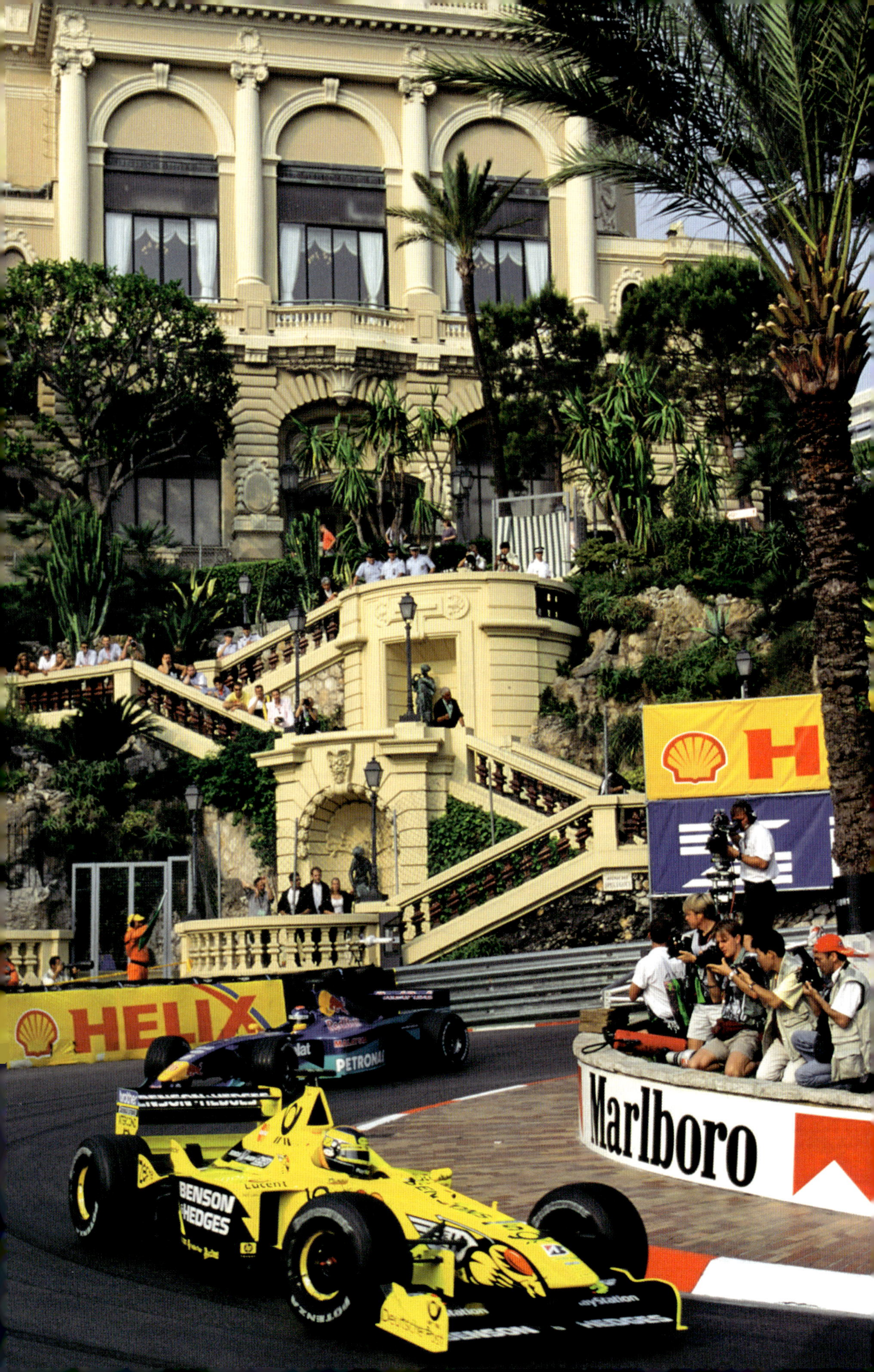
HELIX
Marlboro
PETRONAS
BENSON
HEDGES

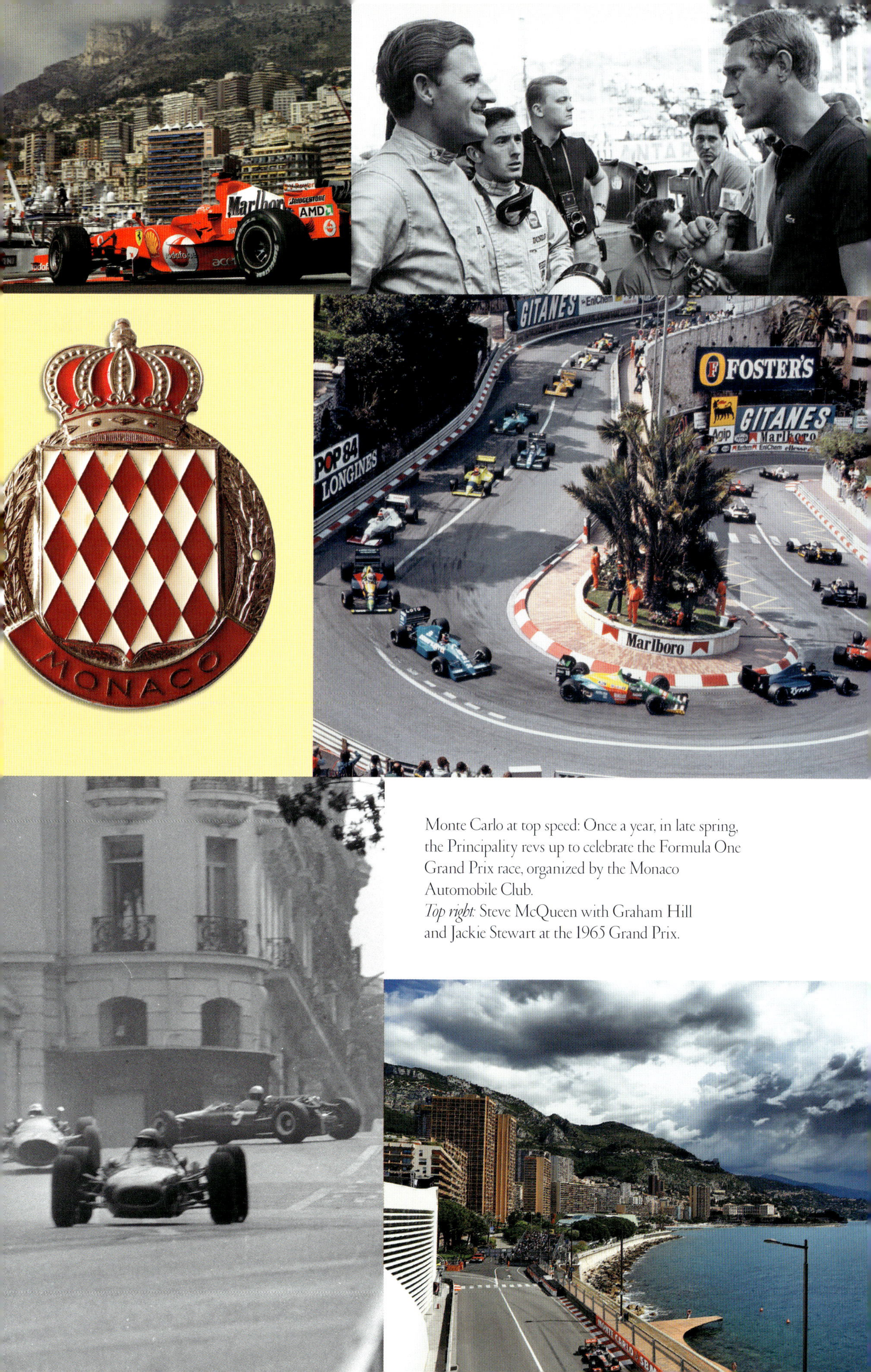

Monte Carlo at top speed: Once a year, in late spring, the Principality revs up to celebrate the Formula One Grand Prix race, organized by the Monaco Automobile Club.
Top right: Steve McQueen with Graham Hill and Jackie Stewart at the 1965 Grand Prix.

takes six weeks to construct and three weeks to remove after the race is over. More than 1,000 volunteers are involved: fly marshals, time marshals, technical marshals, and a host others, all of whom the ACM has to train. "We couldn't do it without the volunteers," says Michel Ferry, the ACM's general commissioner. "We also lose money on the Grand Prix," but, he continues, "fortunately, the government makes up the difference."

The first Grand Prix took place in 1929, during the rule of Prince Louis II. Organized by Antony Noghès, whose father was founding president of the ACM, it was won by a Bugatti driver, William Grover-Williams (who later worked for the Resistance in France, was captured by the Nazis and executed in a German concentration camp). As of 2014, seventy-two races have been held, elevating the careers of men like Niki Lauda, James Hunt, Graham Hill, Stirling Moss, Jackie Stewart, and Michael Schumacher. But it was Ayrton Senna of Brazil who had the most wins, with six victories—five consecutively between 1989 and 1993. (Senna died in the San Marino Grand Prix in 1994.) Of the manufacturers—"constructors," as they are known—McLaren has won fifteen Grand Prix, with Ferrari coming in second, at nine.

For those who are unfamiliar with Formula One, it is, according to its official Web site, the highest level of international

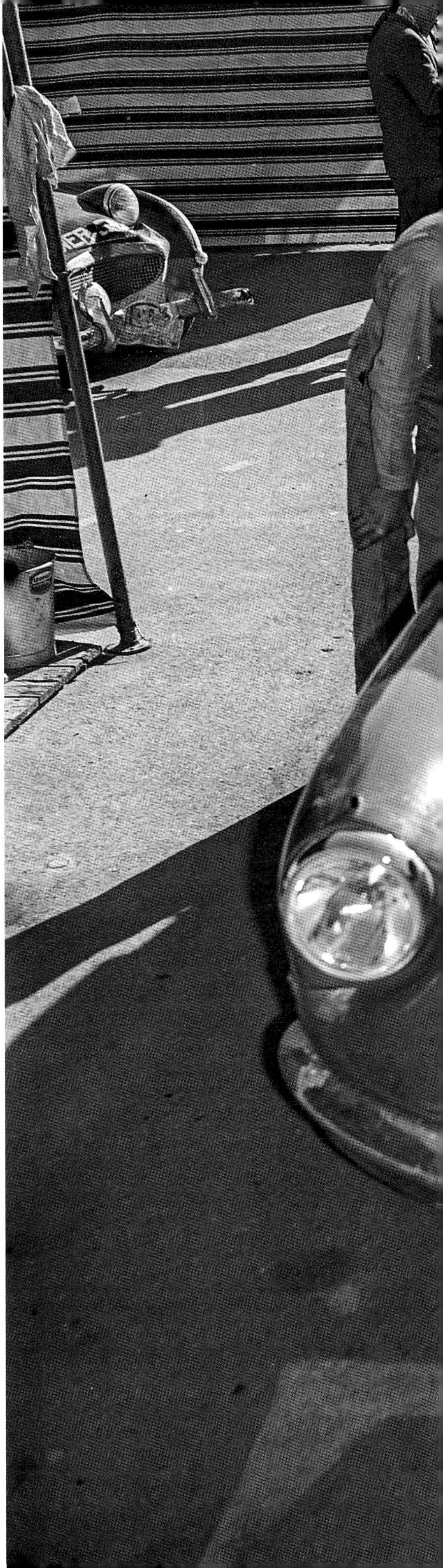

Former alpine skier Henri Oreiller was the driver of No. 132 at the Monte Carlo Rallye in 1962.

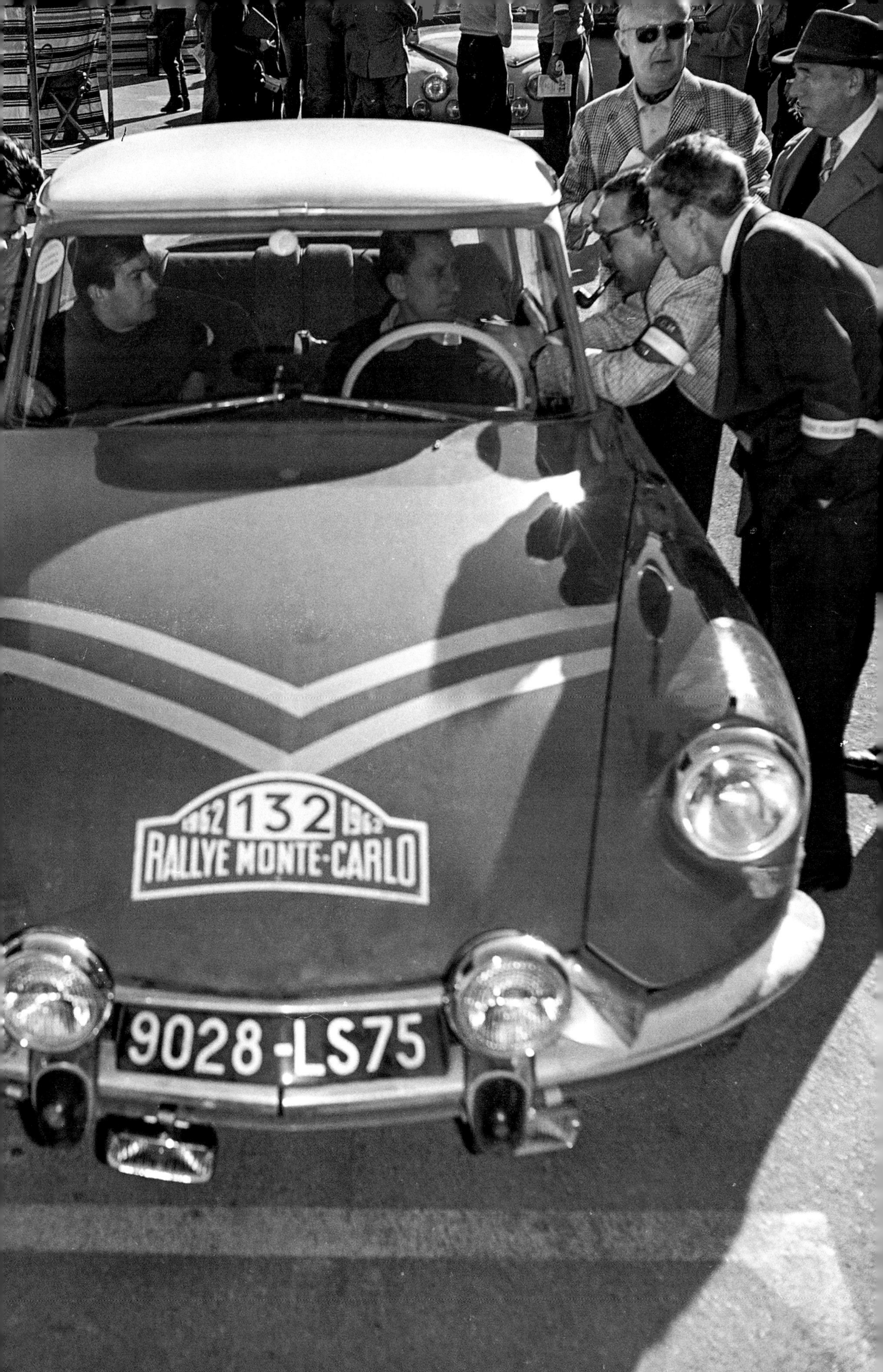
132
RALLYE MONTE-CARLO
9028-LS75

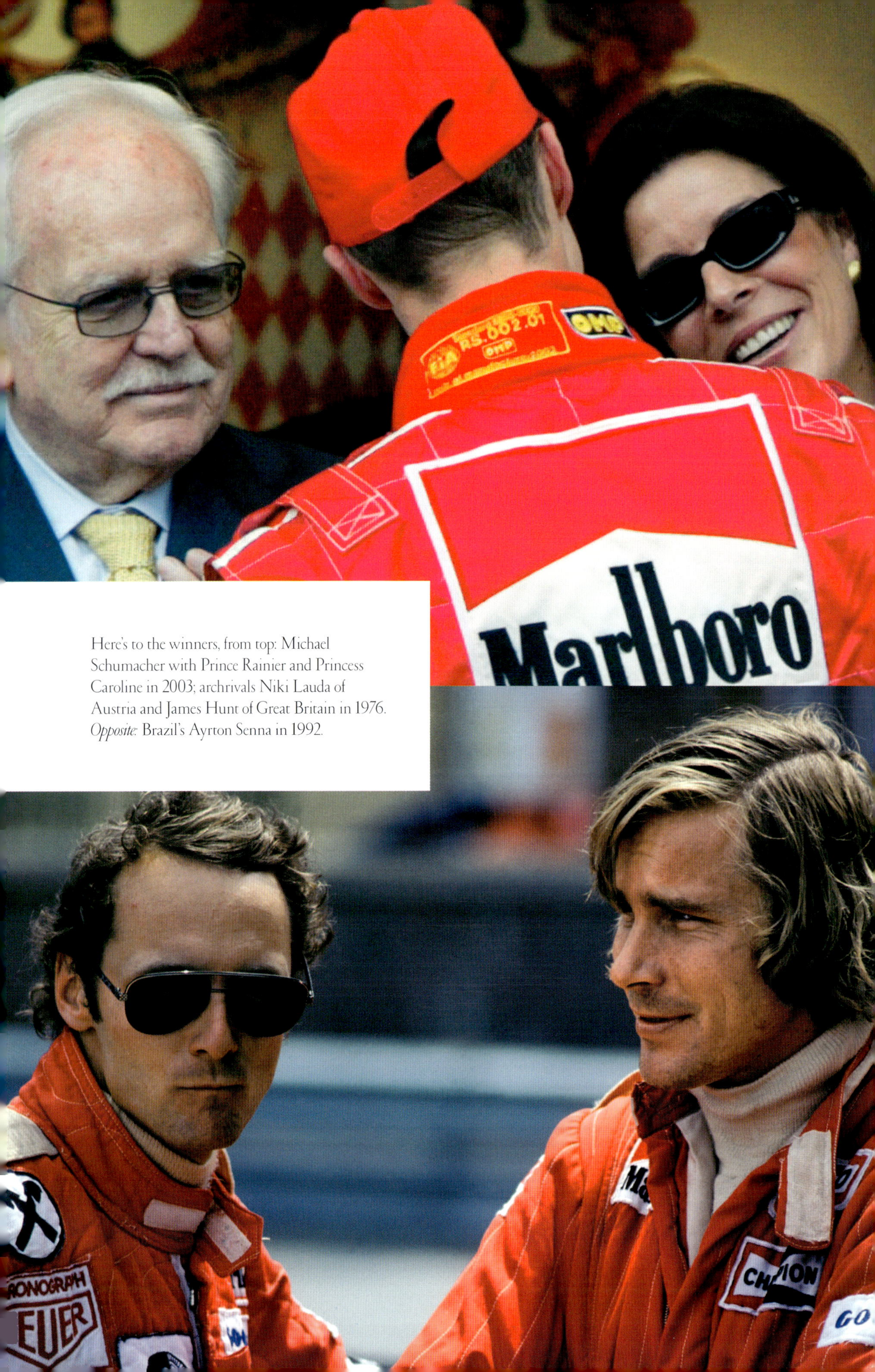

Here's to the winners, from top: Michael Schumacher with Prince Rainier and Princess Caroline in 2003; archrivals Niki Lauda of Austria and James Hunt of Great Britain in 1976. *Opposite:* Brazil's Ayrton Senna in 1992.

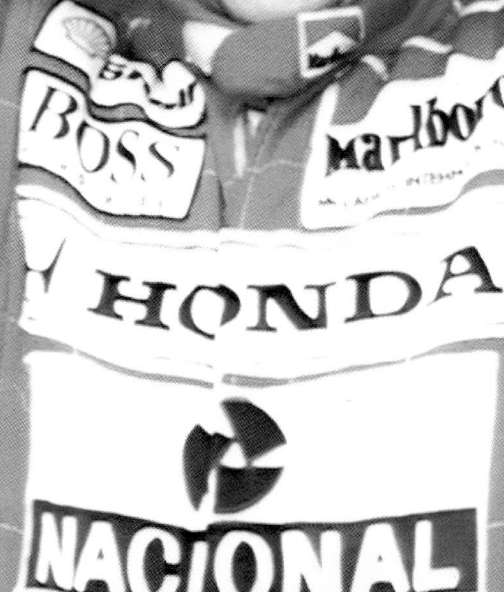
GOOD YEAR
BOSS
Marlboro
HONDA
NACIONAL

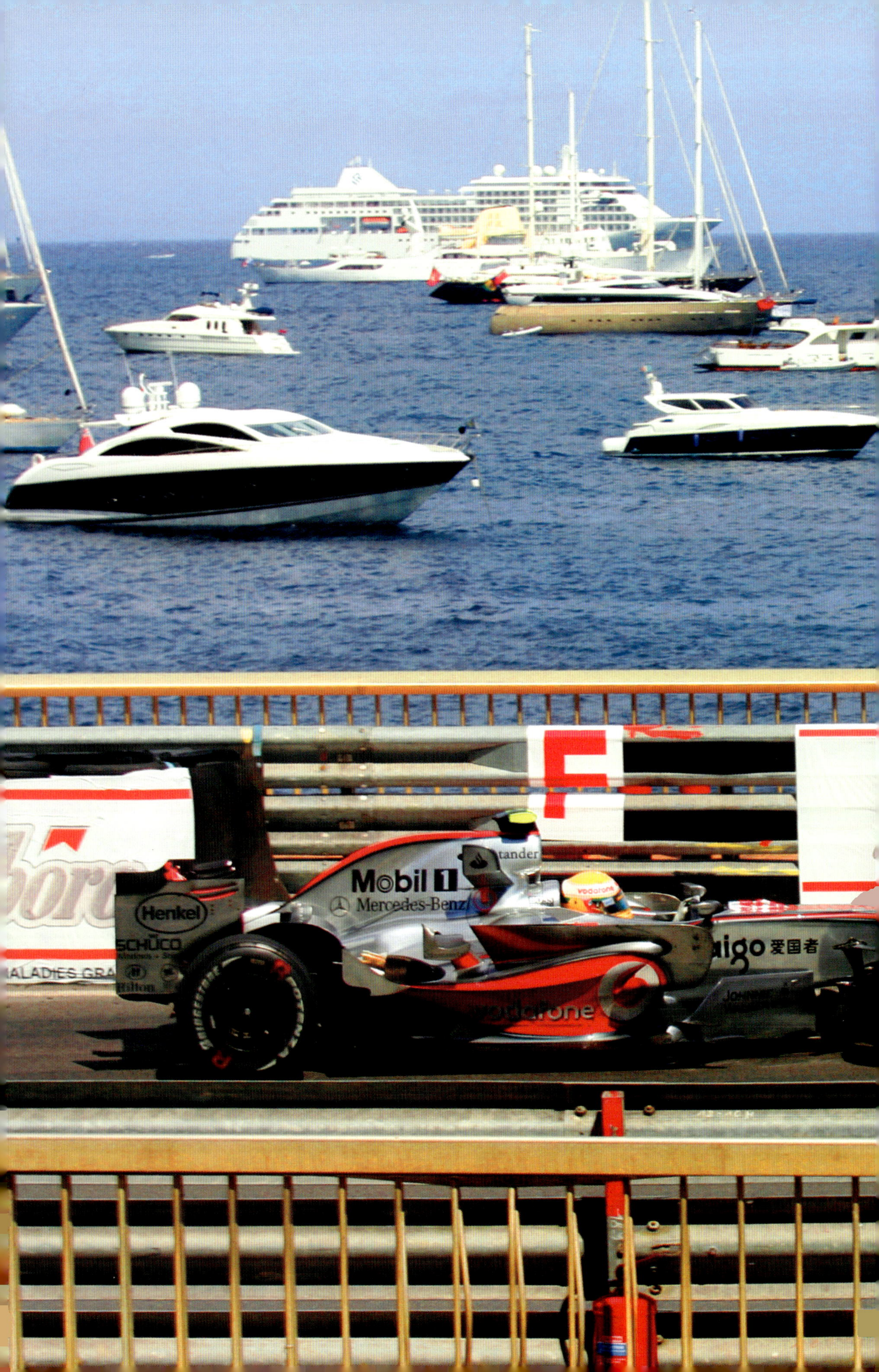
Mobil 1
Mercedes-Benz
Henkel
SCHÜCO
Hilton

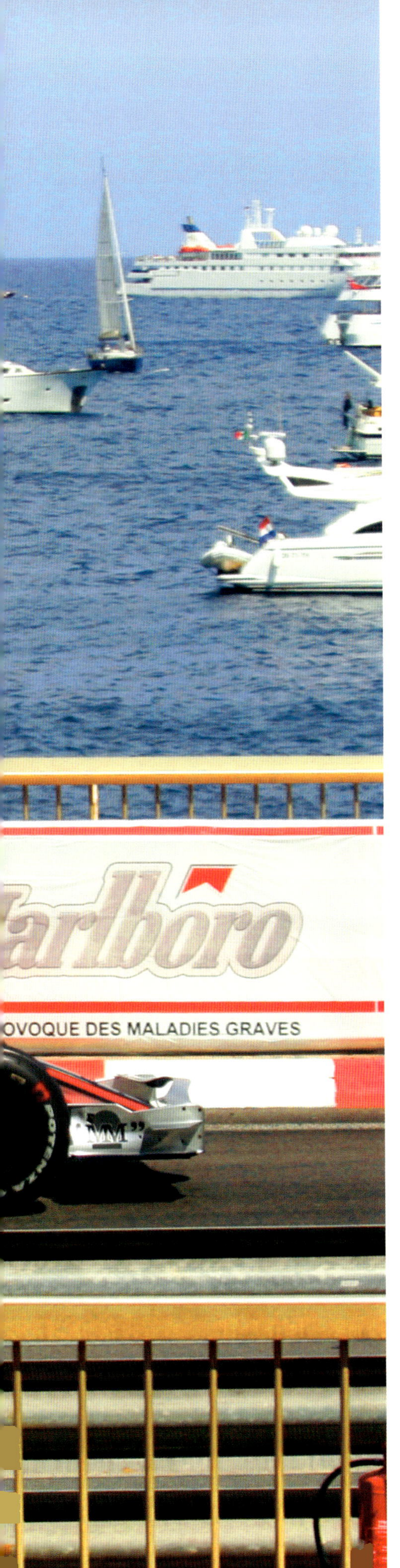

motorsport recognized by the governing body, the Fédération Internationale de l'Automobile. The "formula" refers to the code of rules that must be strictly followed in order to qualify. No racing car is faster (top speed: 220 mph) or more capable of making dangerous multi-turns.

The Grand Prix isn't Monaco's only automobile event: The Rallye de Monte-Carlo, a three-day spectacle that starts in Monte Carlo and finishes in the Alpes-Maritimes, is held every January. And every two years, two weeks before the Grand Prix, is the Historic Grand Prix, in which vintage Formula One cars are driven by their owners—typically, wealthy classic-car collectors.

The other major sporting event in Monaco, and one that rivals the Grand Prix, takes place not on the streets but on and by the sea: the Monaco Yacht Show. Each September architects, builders, sail-makers, outfitters, and brokers converge in Port Hercule in Monte Carlo to exhibit their magnificent and pricey wares. The show is the ultimate boys-and-their-toys event, unveiling mega-yachts and sailing vessels that are the stuff of some men's dreams. Like the Grand Prix, the best hotel rooms are hard to come by and rates soar—if you don't have your own yacht to stay on, you're out of luck.

When the yacht show is over and throughout the rest of the year, the port bulges with boats of all sizes—the bigger, the better (a riff on the old adage is even truer here: He who has the biggest toys wins). Cruise ships drop anchor at the breakwater that protects the harbor and the berths reserved for the ultra-wealthy.

A Formula One car whooshes past the yachts in the harbor, all of them anchored there to watch the spectacle.

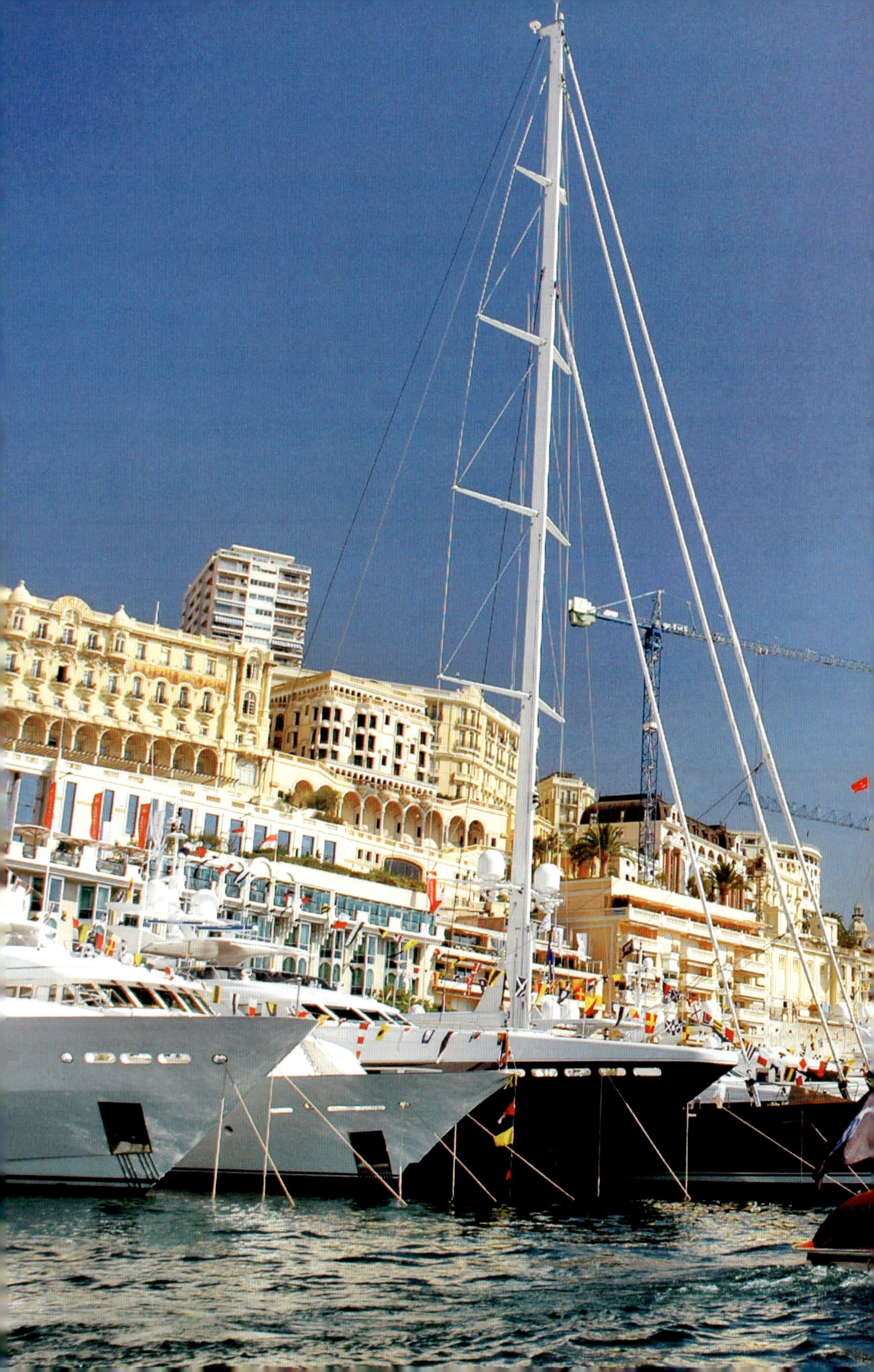

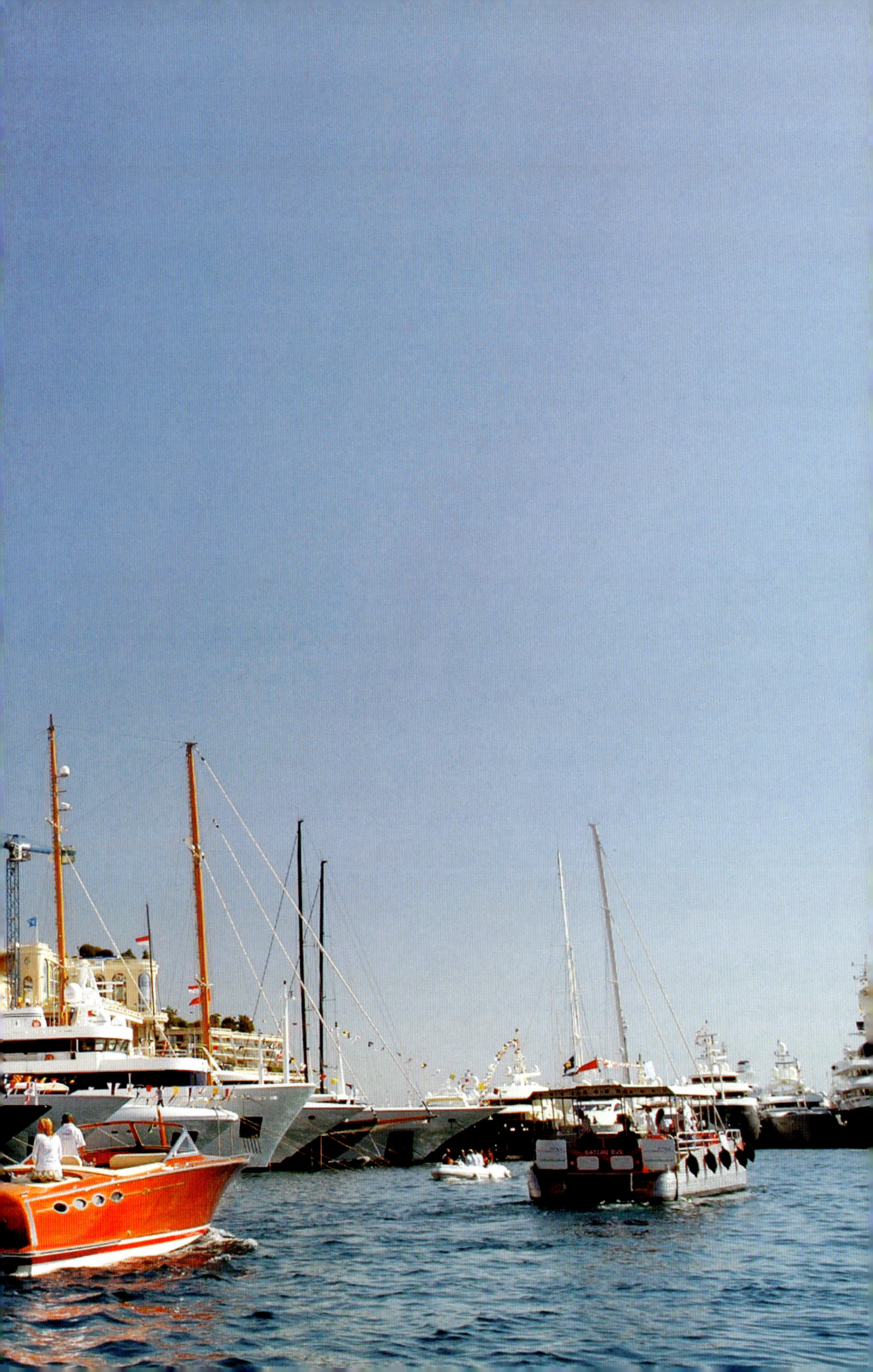

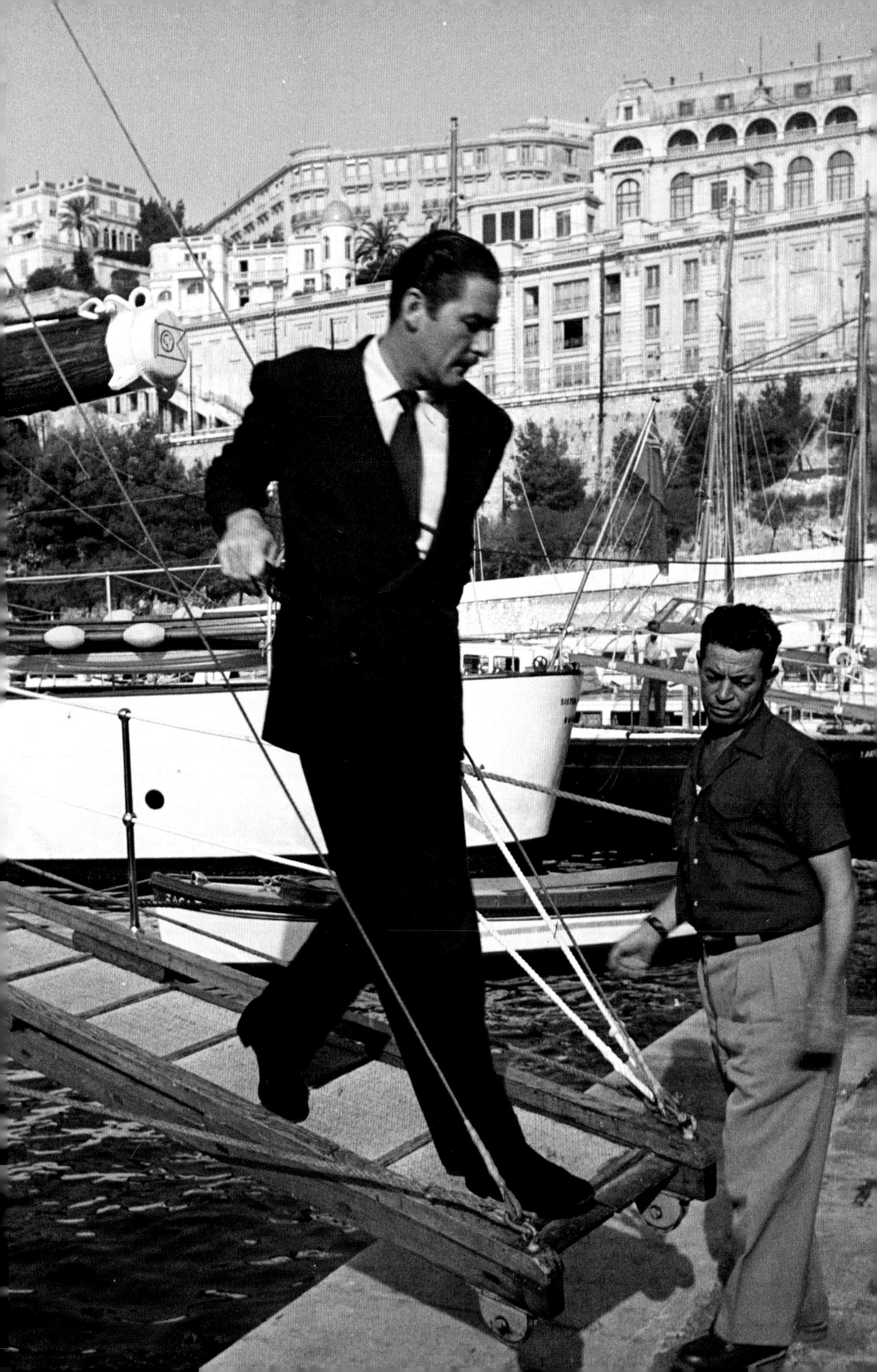

The Yacht Club de Monaco, the most exclusive of its kind, was founded in 1953 by Prince Rainier, an ardent sailor. He passed down his passion to his son Prince Albert II, now YCM president. If asked to name his favorite sailboat, Albert would surely say the *Tuiga*, a 15-meter gaff cutter dating back to 1909 and restored in 1993. Albert found it in Cannes and purchased it for the YCM in 1995. When it is not moored in the harbor for all to see, it participates in various regattas in the Mediterranean as well as during Monaco Classic Week in September. *Tuiga*, considered the Yacht Club's mascot, is, symbolically, a deep and reverent bow to the past. Demonstrating that the future is now, however, June 2014 brought a new headquarters for the YCM, designed by modernist architect Lord Norman Foster and as sleek and luxurious as any yacht in what is said to be the world's most glamorous harbor.

When Aristotle Onassis had control of the Société des Bains de Mer in the 1950s, he made sure the *Christina*, his 325-foot yacht, was front and center in Port Hercule. Originally built in 1943, the *Christina* was purportedly bought as scrap metal for $34,000 by Onassis, who then invested another $4 million to convert it into a luxury sea palace with eighteen staterooms—spacious enough for the likes of Elizabeth Taylor and Richard Burton, Winston Churchill, Rudolph Nureyev, John F. Kennedy, Onassis's mistress Maria Callas, and his trophy wife Jackie Kennedy Onassis (presumably not at the same time). His daughter Christina, the boat's namesake, inherited it and changed its name to *Argo*. In 1998, John Paul Papanicolaou, a family friend and fellow shipping tycoon, took it over, renovated, and renamed it the *Christina O*. For those who are legend-seekers, the *Christina O* is available for charter.

Another fabled yacht that made frequent stops in Monte Carlo was *La Belle Simone*, named after Simone Levitt, the second wife of Bill Levitt, who made his fortune in real estate—his claim to fame was developing Levittown, the postwar planned community on New York's Long Island, which made him forever known as the father of the American suburb. The yacht was Levitt's wedding gift to his wife as a way to have a perpetual honeymoon. "The rubies and diamonds came first," says Mrs. Levitt, now a widow in her eighties but with a sharp mind and a wry sense of humor. Built in Holland and launched in 1972, *La Belle Simone* was 275 feet long, had a crew of twenty-eight (thirty in high season), and spent many a summer plying the Mediterranean. "Summertime in Monte Carlo was always exciting," Mrs. Levitt remembers, as if in a reverie. "The Gypsy Kings came on board and played at our parties. Hubert de Givenchy not only dressed me for ten years, he also designed all the terrycloth robes and towels. I had four chefs on board and planned all the meals.

Dapper American movie star Errol Flynn in Monte Carlo for his wedding to Patricia Wymore, October 1950.
Previous pages: Port Hercule during the yacht show, which takes place every September.

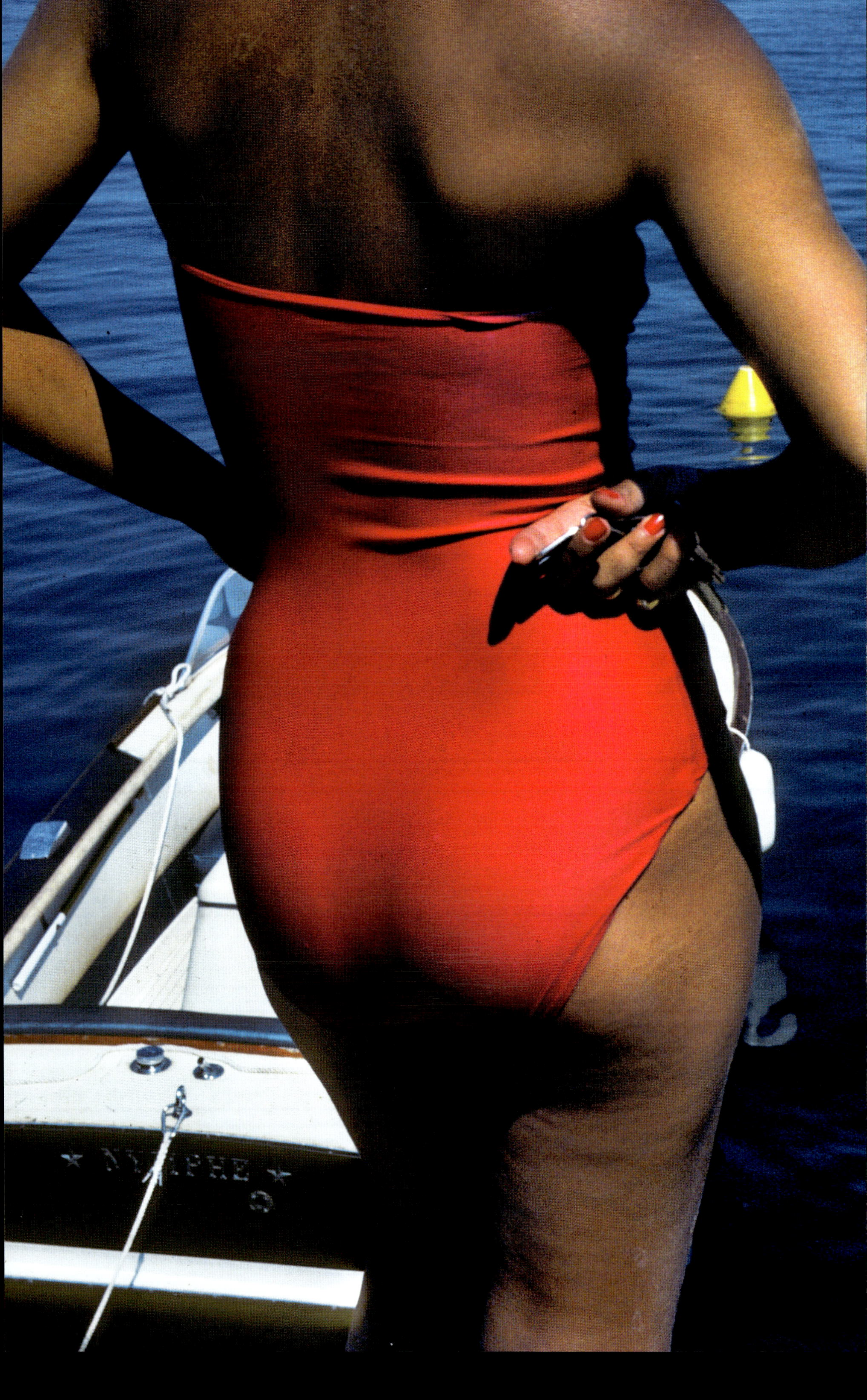

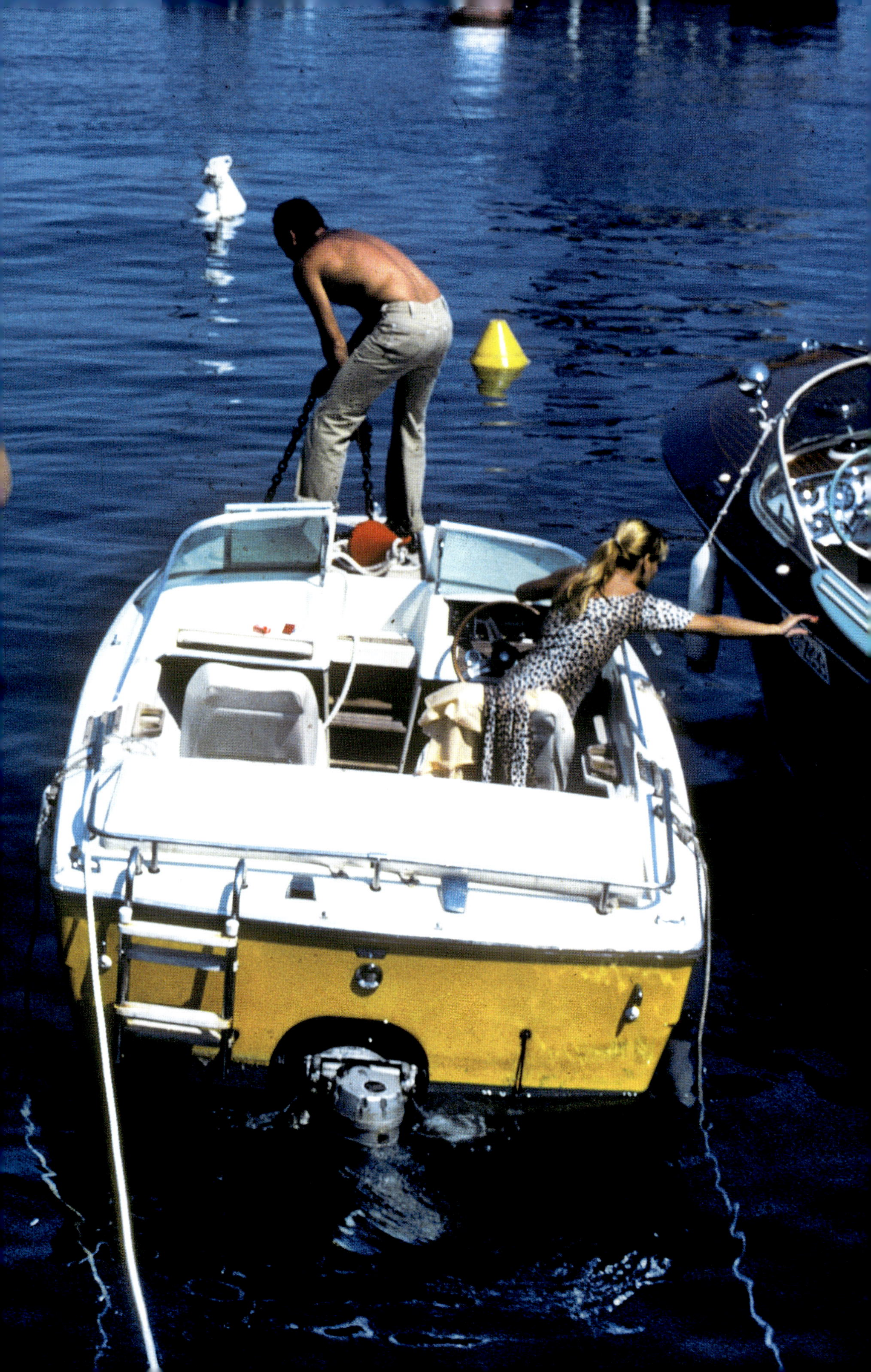

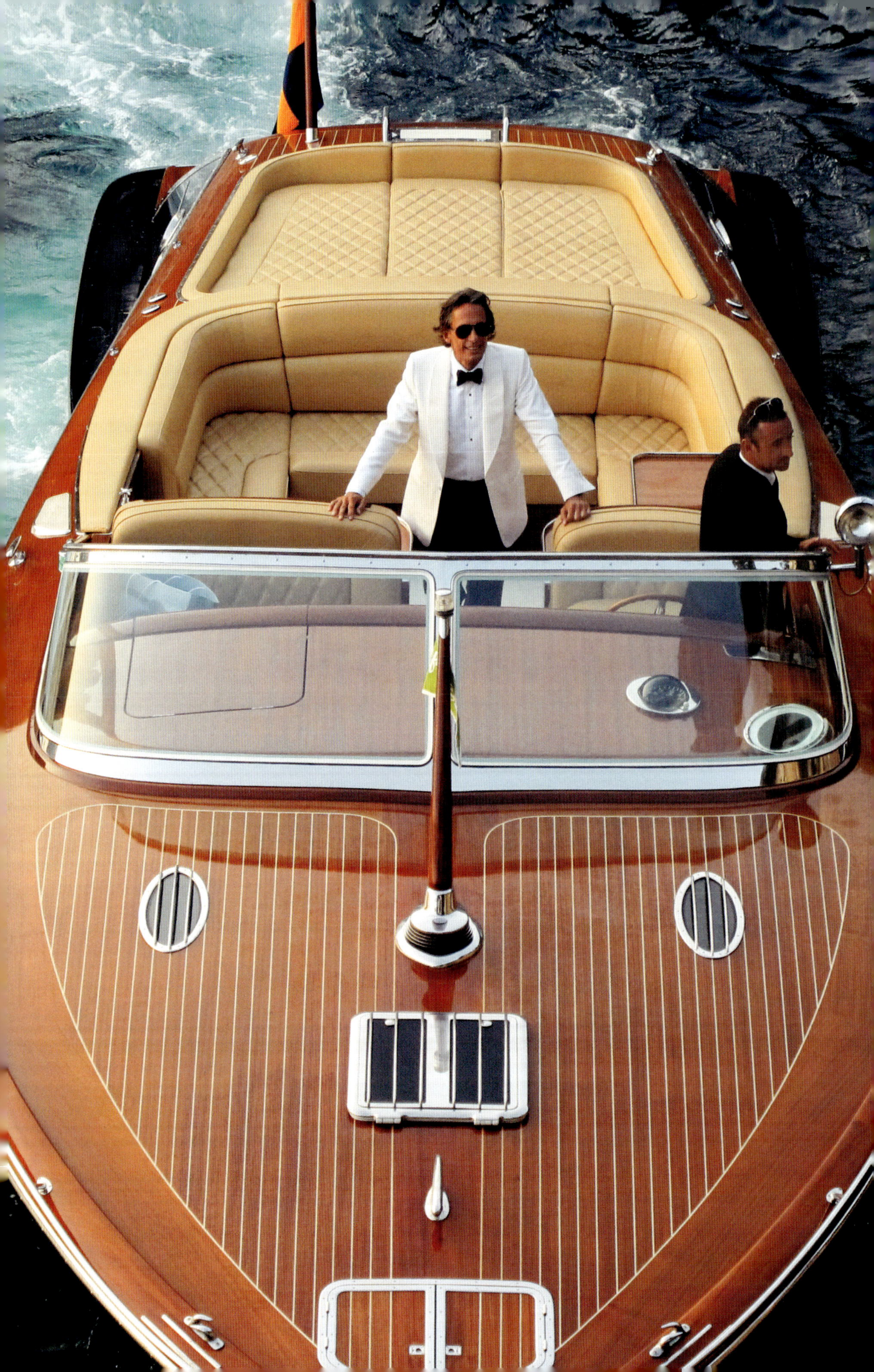

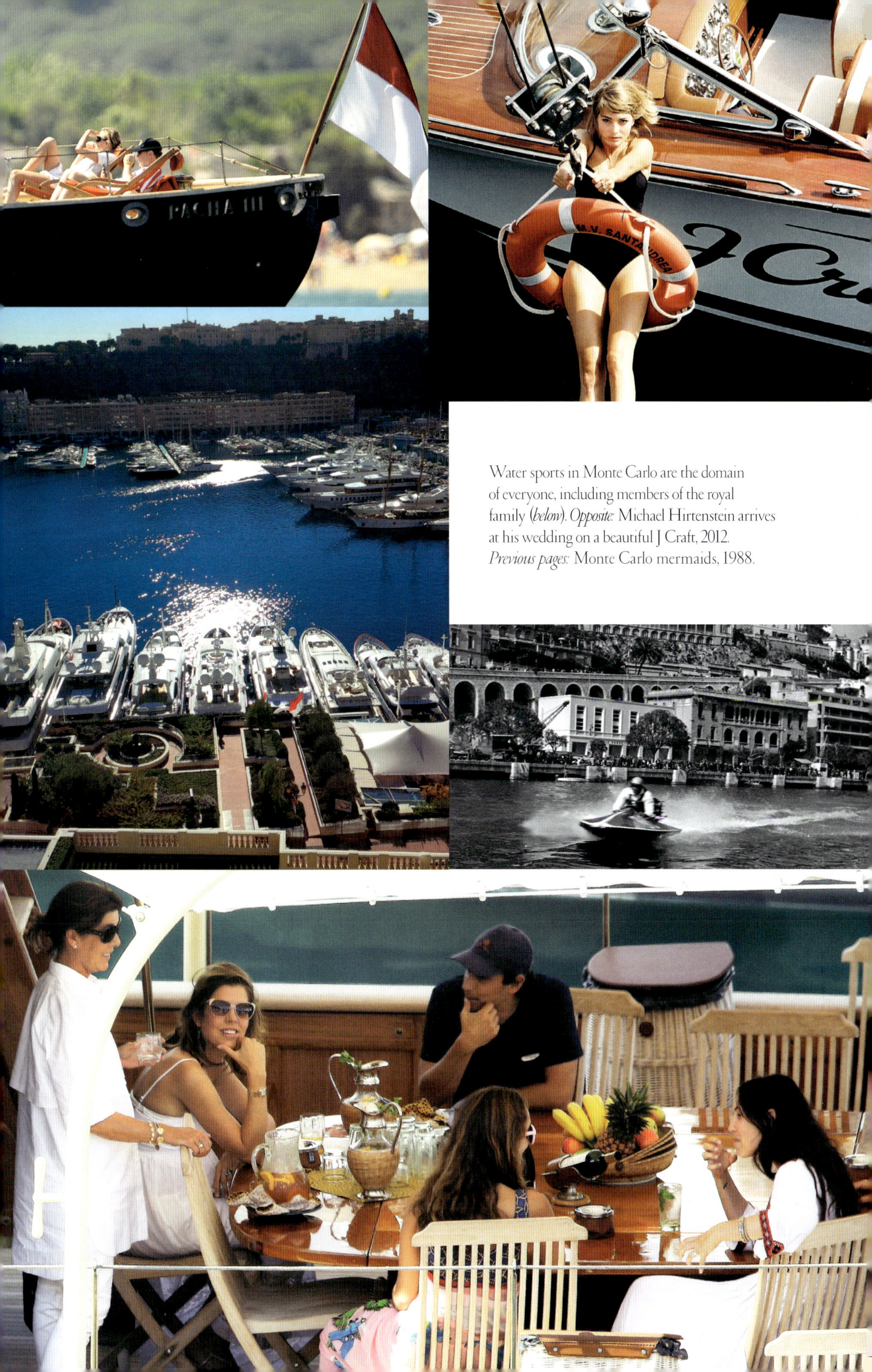

Water sports in Monte Carlo are the domain of everyone, including members of the royal family (*below*). *Opposite:* Michael Hirtenstein arrives at his wedding on a beautiful J Craft, 2012. *Previous pages:* Monte Carlo mermaids, 1988.

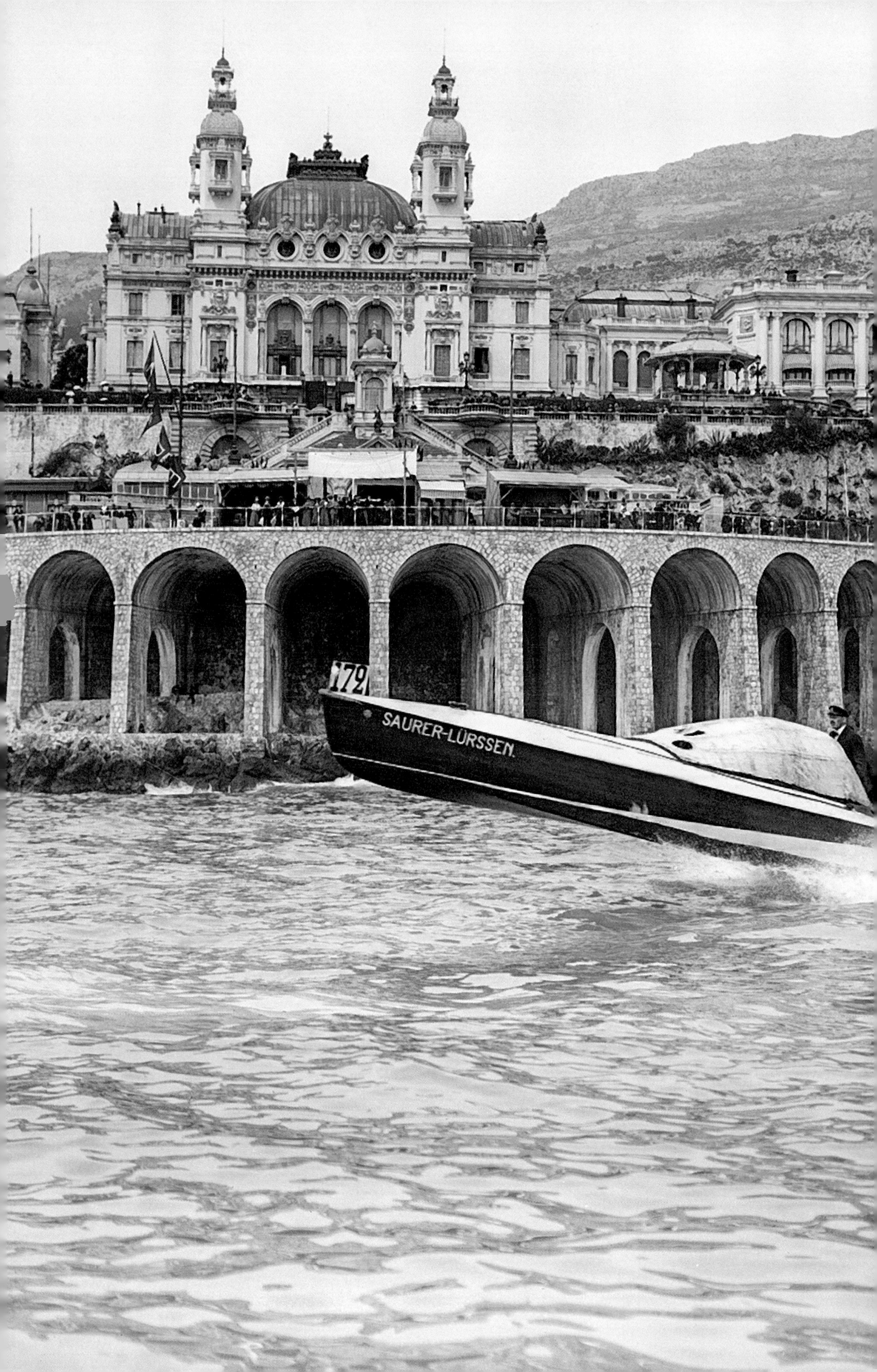
179
SAURER-LÜRSSEN.

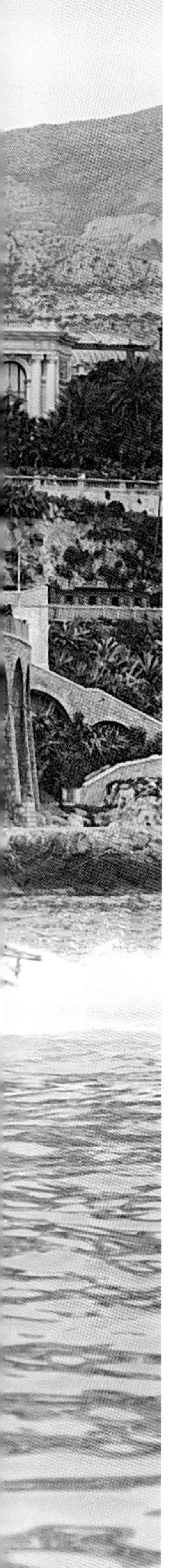

"When Princess Grace and Prince Rainier came to visit they didn't want any guests on board, so we had to send them to Monte Carlo on launches until the royal family left. But nobody minded. We had many famous guests—Anna Magnani, Michael Caine, Harry Belafonte. Even today I meet people who say, 'I was on your boat,' but I hardly remember them."

La Belle Simone was also the venue for two weddings: In 1979 Don Hewitt, the producer and creator of *60 Minutes*, married journalist Marilyn Berger. Five years earlier, British novelist and columnist Shirley Lord Rosenthal married architect David Anderson. Fashion scribe Earl Blackwell had introduced Rosenthal (then Lord) to the Levitts. "Bill suggested that David and I be married in Monte Carlo aboard *La Belle Simone*," recalls Rosenthal. "The Levitts' boat was next to *Ultima II*, owned by Revlon's Charles Revson, and was just a smidgen bigger, which caused some friction between the two men. Of course, the size of the boats then was nothing compared to the mega-yachts of today."

The ceremony was performed by *La Belle Simone*'s captain. To make it legal, the boat had to be twelve miles from land. Among the guests were the swells of that era: Estée Lauder, Rudi and Consuelo Crespi, the Brazilian cosmetic surgeon Ivo Pitanguy, Blackwell, and his fashion-writing pal Eugenia Sheppard.

"Those were enormously glamorous days in Monte Carlo," says Rosenthal. "Women wore jewels to the nines. Princess Grace was the shining light. There were movie stars galore."

"Yes," echoes Mrs. Levitt. "Ladies dressed for dinner; men were in black tie. It was a different time... a magical time."

That was then and this is now. Monte Carlo and Monaco are ramping up for a whole new generation. Rich Russians are the latest *arrivistes*. Several of the planet's most extravagant pleasure yachts call the harbor home. So densely populated is the Principality that the only way to build is up.

But even if you wanted to find an apartment, chances of securing one are slim, because this is one place on the Côte d'Azur where many wealthy families yearn to be, for all the important reasons: It's safe, it's sparkling clean, and the living is easy. What more could one ask for?

Skimming past the Casino, 1912.
Following pages: A rendering of Lord Norman Foster's design of the new headquarters of the Yacht Club of Monaco.

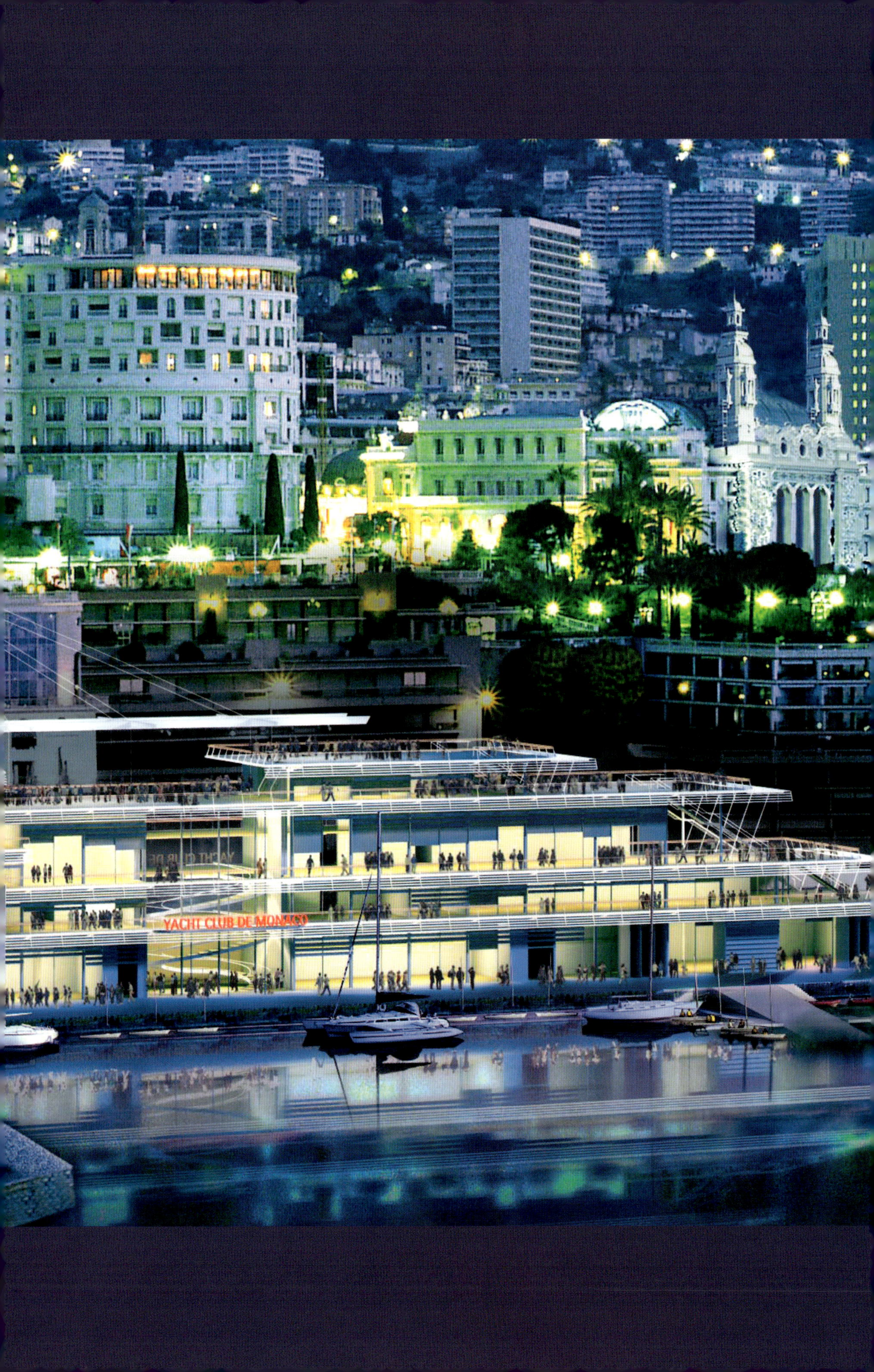
YACHT CLUB DE MONACO

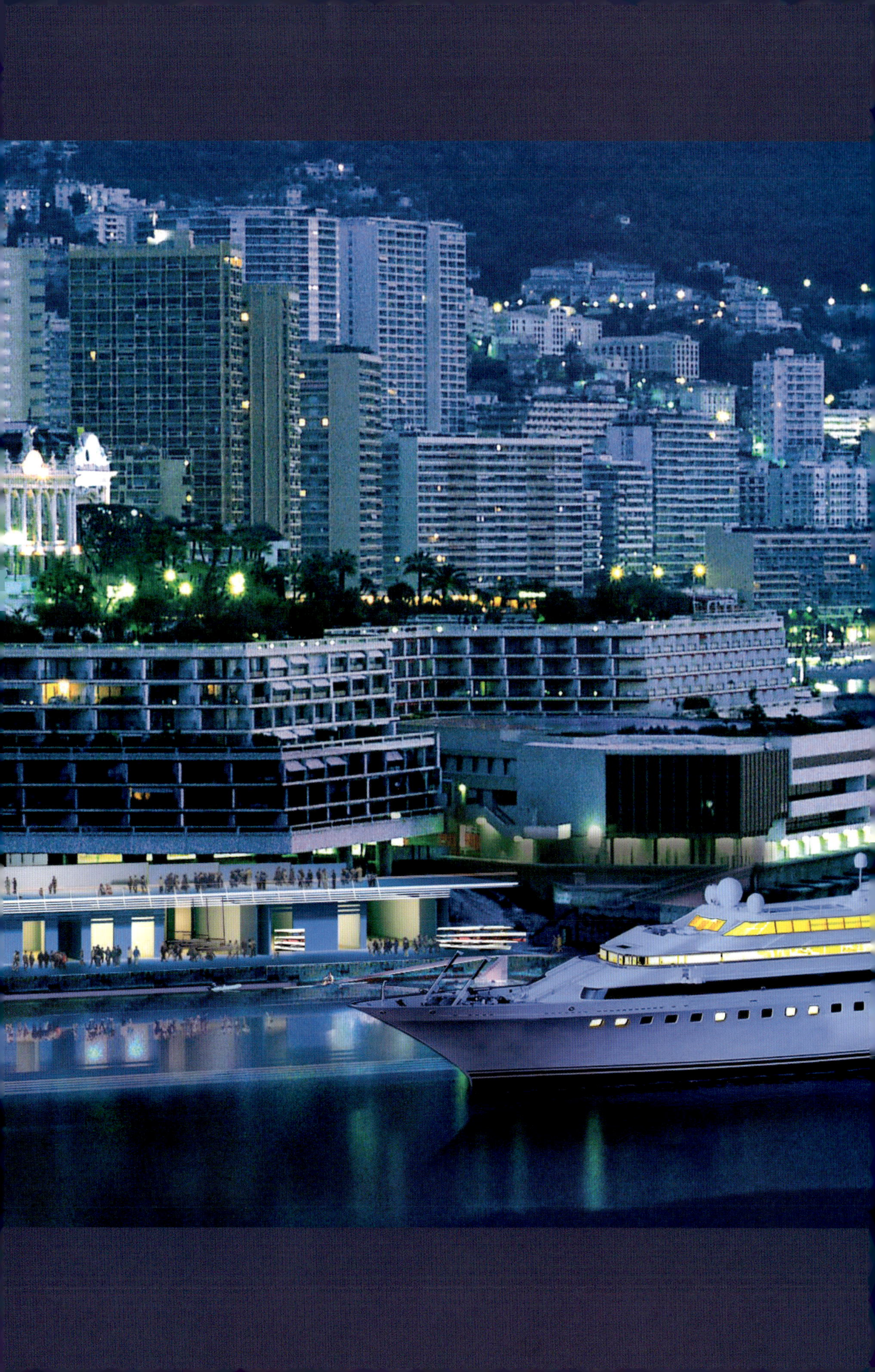

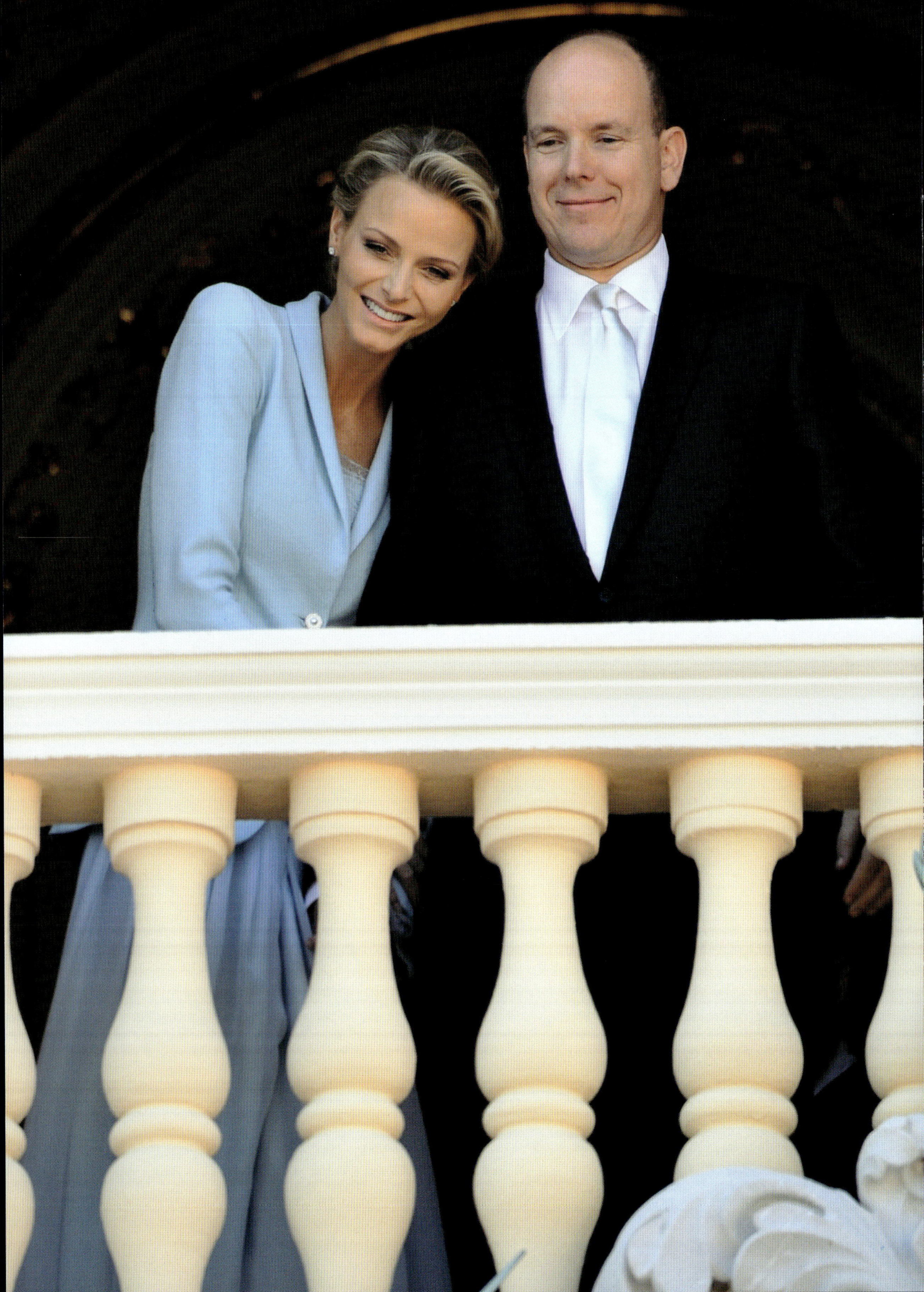

Changing Tides

"Monaco seems like the most benign of places, a slice of unreality on the French Riviera that is smaller than a square mile and has a population of about 36,000; a per-capita of more than $150,000; and an unemployment rate of zero."
—*The New York Times,* December 12, 2013

In the second decade of the twenty-first century, Monaco is on a roll. Even the 2008 global economic downturn didn't cause nearly as much damage as it did to other nations. In other words, the Principality is as solid as the rock it is built on. Prince Albert II has comfortably eased into his role as leader of his country. His wife, Princess Charlene, a former Olympic swimming champion for South Africa, has formed her own foundation focusing on sports as a powerful vehicle for positive change, particularly for young people.

Albert's sisters, Caroline (aka HRH Princess Caroline of Hanover) and Stéphanie, once rebellious in their youth, have matured as well, and each does her part with foundation work and furthering Monaco's involvement in the arts. Even *their* children are making their mark. In August 2013, Princess Caroline's son, Andrea Casiraghi, married Tatiana Santo Domingo, of the wealthy Colombian family, at a ceremony in Monaco. Andrea's sister, Charlotte Casiraghi, a great beauty, with her companion, Gad Elmaleh, gave birth to a baby boy, Raphael, in December of the same year. And the latest news is that Prince Albert and Princess Charlene are expecting their first child.

Despite their settling down, the royal family is still the target of gossip columns and celebrity magazines and a magnet for paparazzi whenever they emerge from the cocoon that is Monaco. Like the British royals—especially Kate and William—none of the Grimaldi heirs can make a move without a camera in their face or a reporter tailing them. A difficult way to live, but such less-than-royal treatment has always gone with the territory.

One doesn't have to be a Grimaldi to be a Monegasque, even though that family's heritage dates back further than any other native family. To be Monegasque comes with many privileges, not the least of which is living tax-free, thanks to Prince Charles' decree in 1869. Should a civil job become

Princess Charlene and Prince Albert II greet their subjects after their civil marriage ceremony on July 1, 2011.

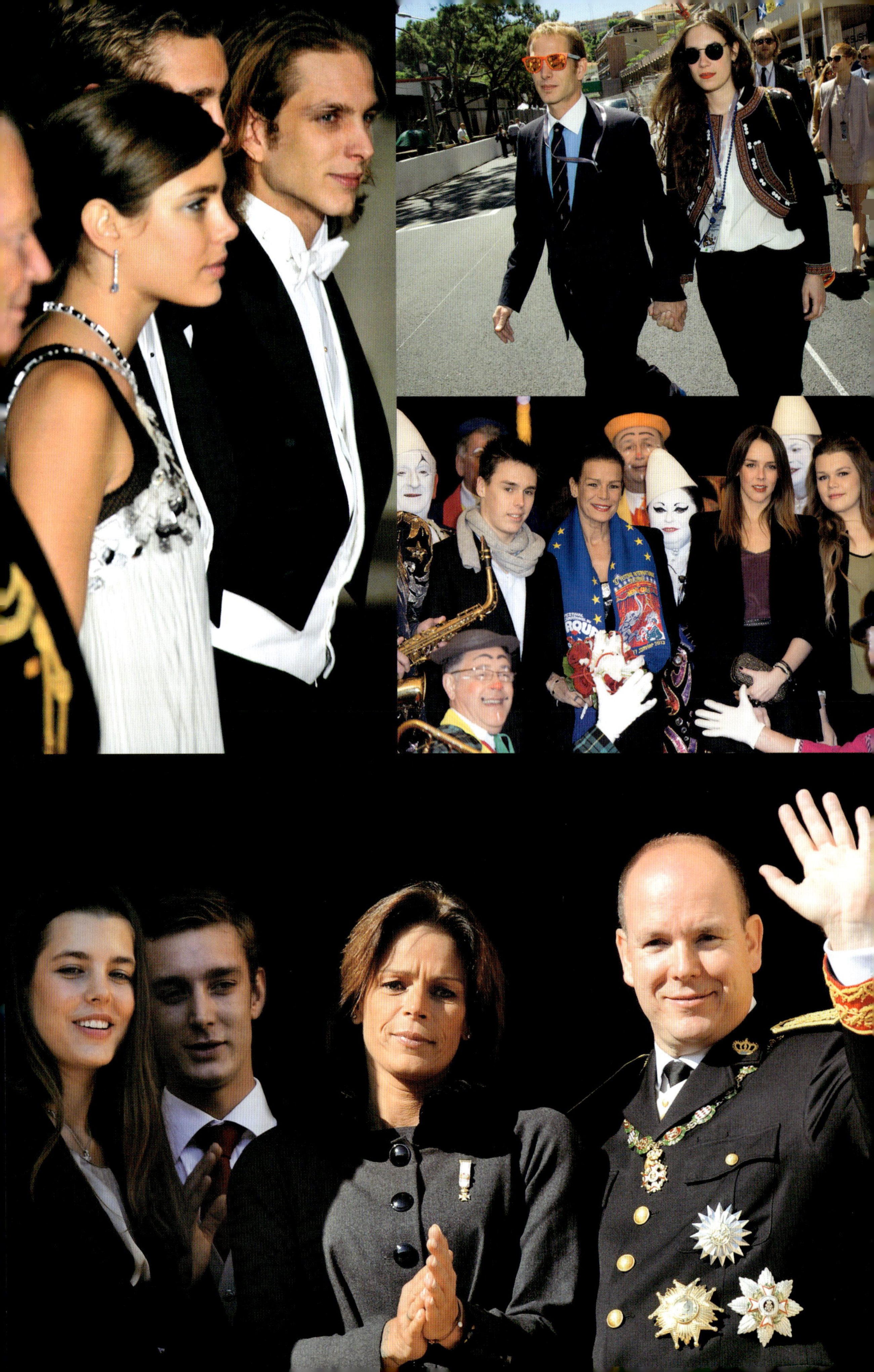

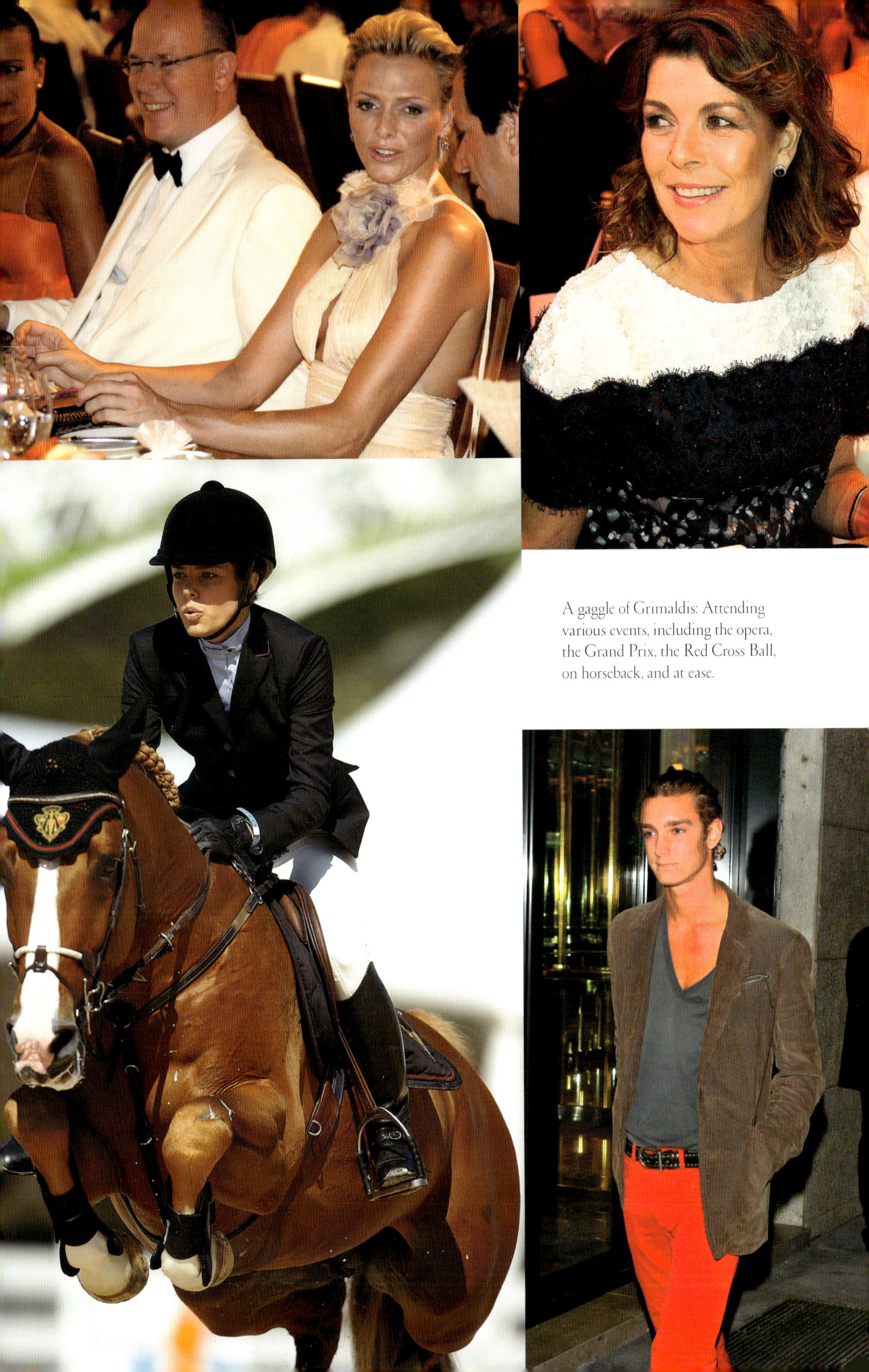

A gaggle of Grimaldis: Attending various events, including the opera, the Grand Prix, the Red Cross Ball, on horseback, and at ease.

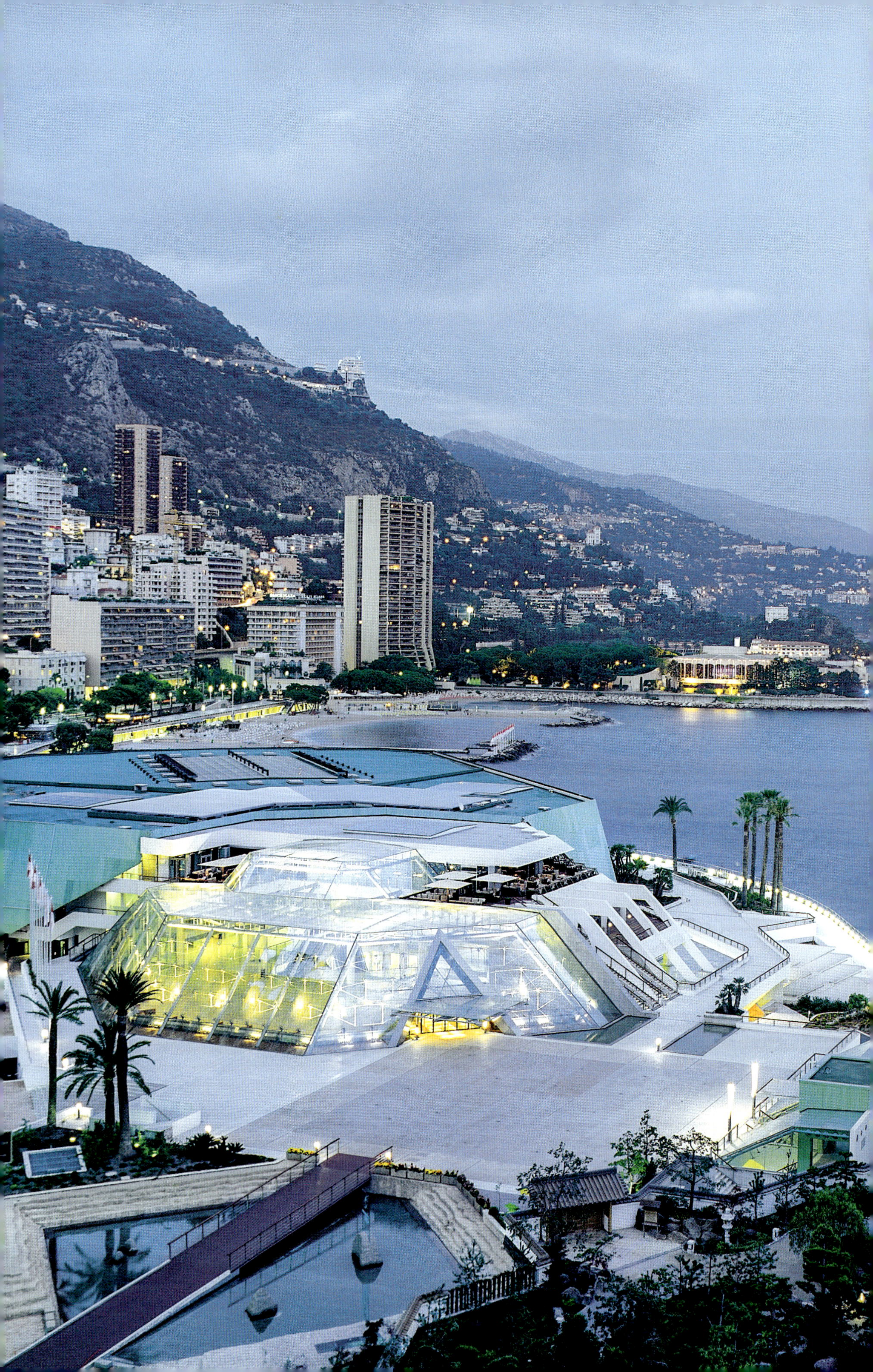

available, a Monegasque has the right of first refusal over an outsider. Schools are free and health care is generously subsidized.

Maguy Maccario Doyle, Monaco's newly appointed U.S. ambassador to Monaco, remembers growing up there as being simple and carefree. "Living in such a pretty place with a temperate climate was idyllic. While I knew there was a Prince and a Princess, they weren't a factor in my life. Sometimes I would see a photograph of Princess Grace in shop windows near my parents' art gallery and I thought she was pretty... that there was a lovely radiance about her." Doyle attended her first Red Cross ball at the age of eighteen. "It was Princess Caroline's first official appearance, at age sixteen, and I empathized with how nervous she was." In 1976 the young Doyle (then Maccario) went to work for the Monaco Government Tourist Office in New York City and there met Princess Grace. "I was asked to pick her up at the airport. I was only twenty-one." After some silence during the long drive into Manhattan, the two struck up a conversation and realized that they had made the same journey, but in reverse. "I went from an insular place to a big, complicated one. She had done the opposite. When I asked her how she made the difficult transition, she said, 'When I first arrived, everything was "no" or "impossible." I had to stay very

The Grimaldi Forum, situated between the sea and avenue Princesse Grace, is both a convention hall and a cultural arts center.

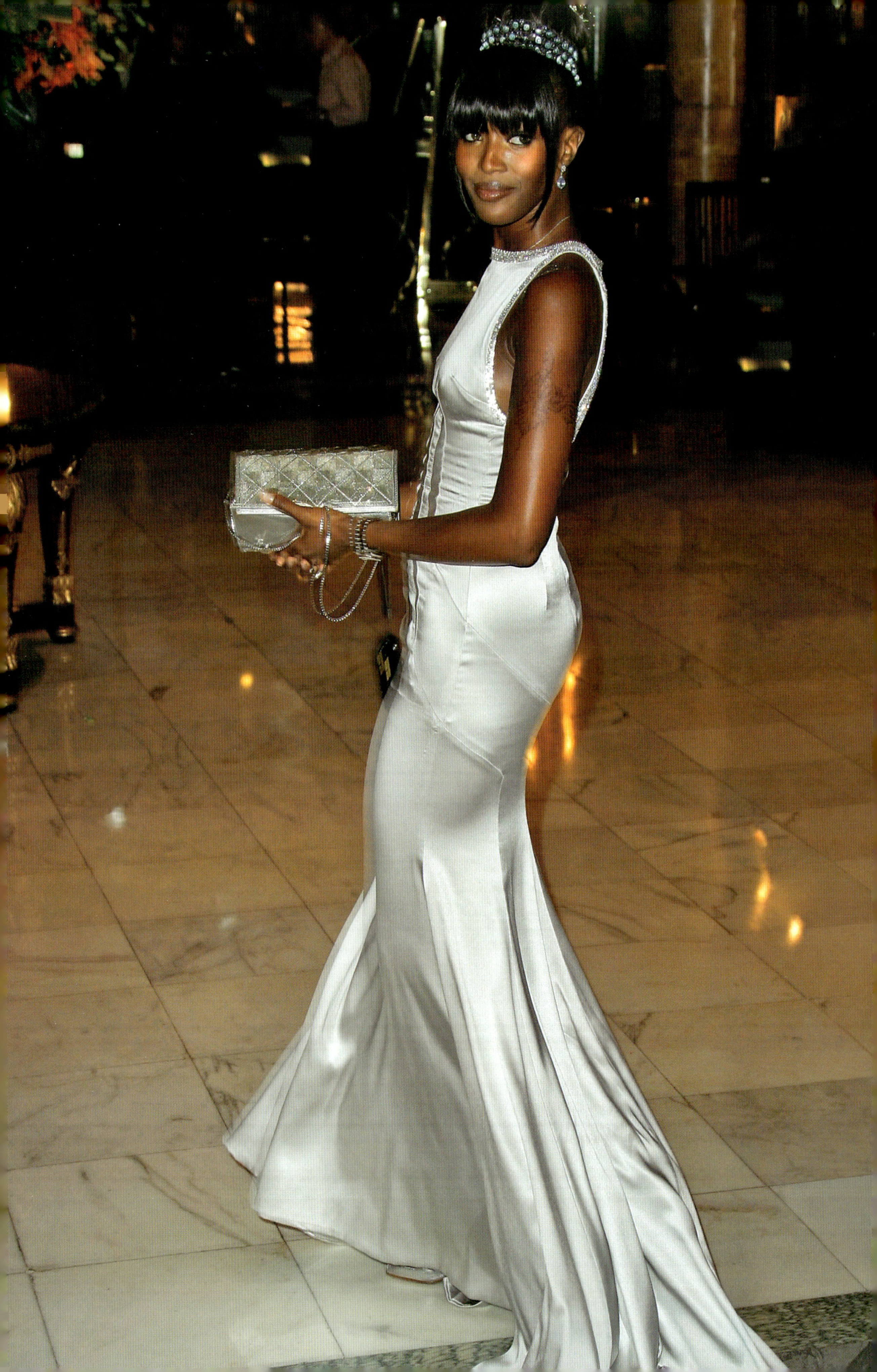

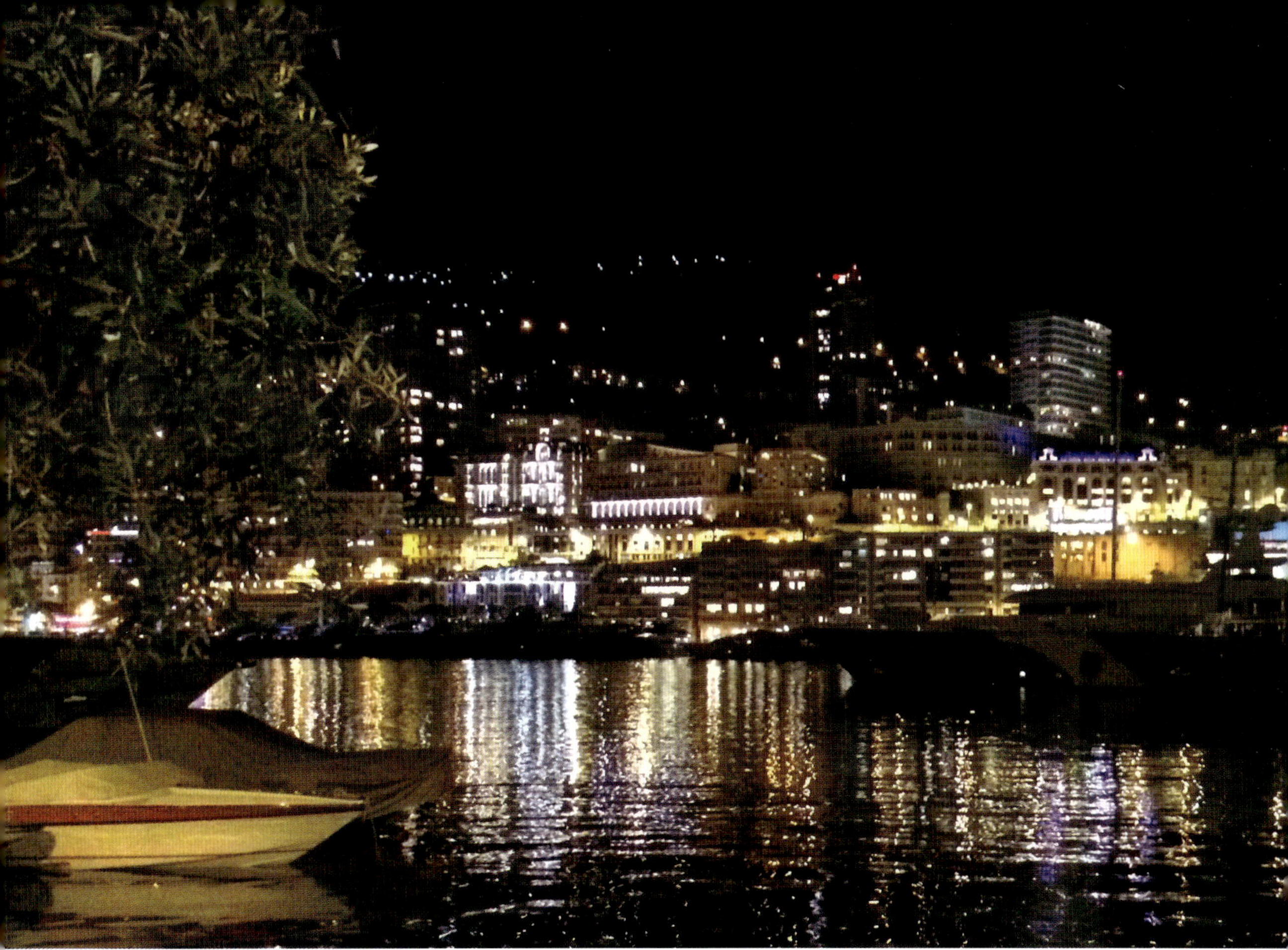

The harbor at night. *Opposite:* Supermodel Naomi Campbell at the Hôtel de Paris for the Better World gala, 2007. *Following pages.* The Red Cross Ball, established in 1948, commemorated its 60th anniversary with a spectacular fireworks display in 2008.

focused if I was to achieve what I wanted.'" Clearly, those words have served Doyle extremely well in her role as the Principality's first female ambassador.

Like Doyle, Kristina Orfali also grew up in Monaco and now lives in New York with her Monegasque husband, Pierre-André Chiappori. She describes her status as "a sense of privilege... like being among the happy few, given there are only around a few thousand people with a bright red passport bearing a beautiful coat of arms on the cover." Orfali returns regularly, and while recognizing "the absolute sense of security and coziness," she's not entirely comfortable with some of the changes that have taken place in the name of progress. "Gone forever are many of the charming Belle Époque buildings that graced Monte Carlo," she laments.

Orfali is not the only one. A *New York Times* article in 2012 entitled "Construction and Royalty Muffle Dissent in Monaco" reported on a small but peaceful demonstration that occurred protesting the proposed demolition of Monte Carlo's Sporting d'Hiver, a 1932 Art Deco building that was "once the site of the Principality's most glittering charity balls." It also houses upscale boutiques and art galleries that will have to relocate or maybe even close. Replacing the building will be a multiuse

Pages 142-143, from left: The 58th Red Cross Ball, 2006.; Beyoncé performs at the World Music Awards in 2008.
Pages 144-145: Glamour rules, *from left:* Baroness Stefanie von Korles at the Easter Gala, 1959; Princess Charlotte Casiraghi and brother Prince Pierre Casiraghi attend the Bal de la la Rose with Beatrice Borromeo, 2014.

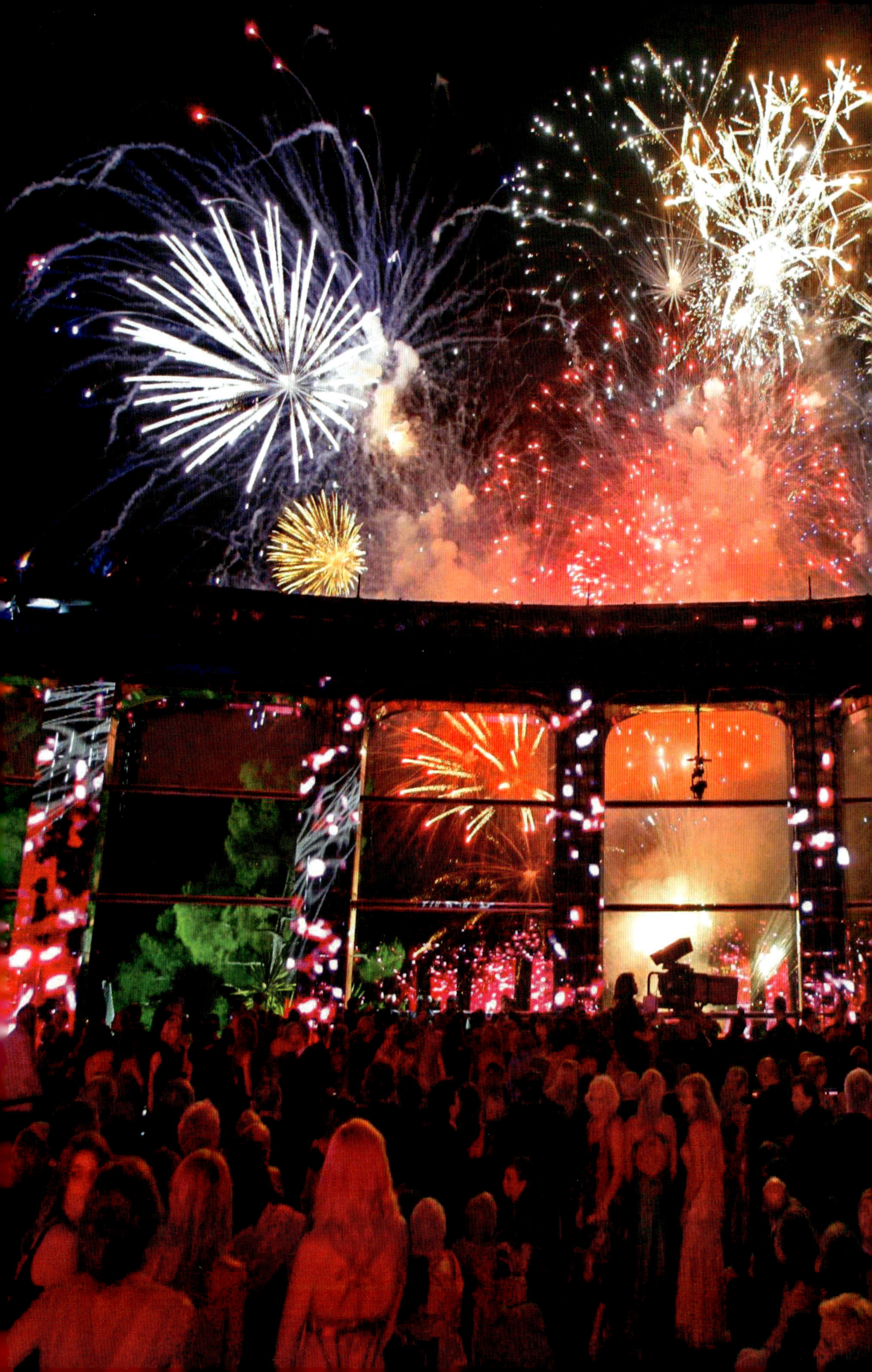

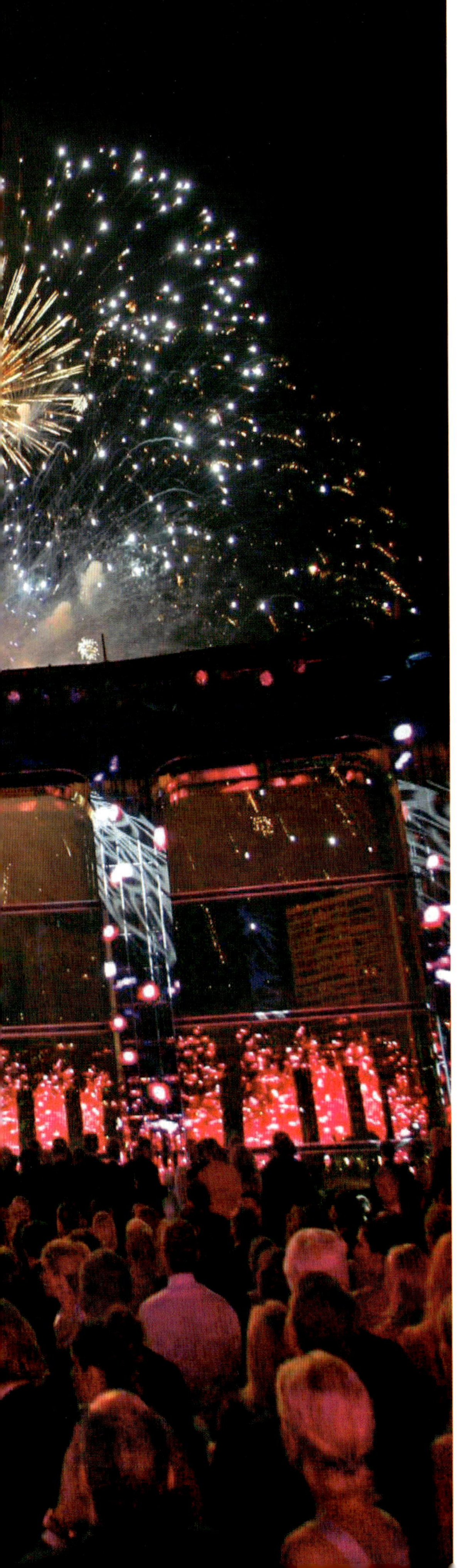

“I had my coming-out party at a debutante ball in Monaco. Can you imagine anything more glamorous? Those were the days.”

CATHY MOORE BARRETT

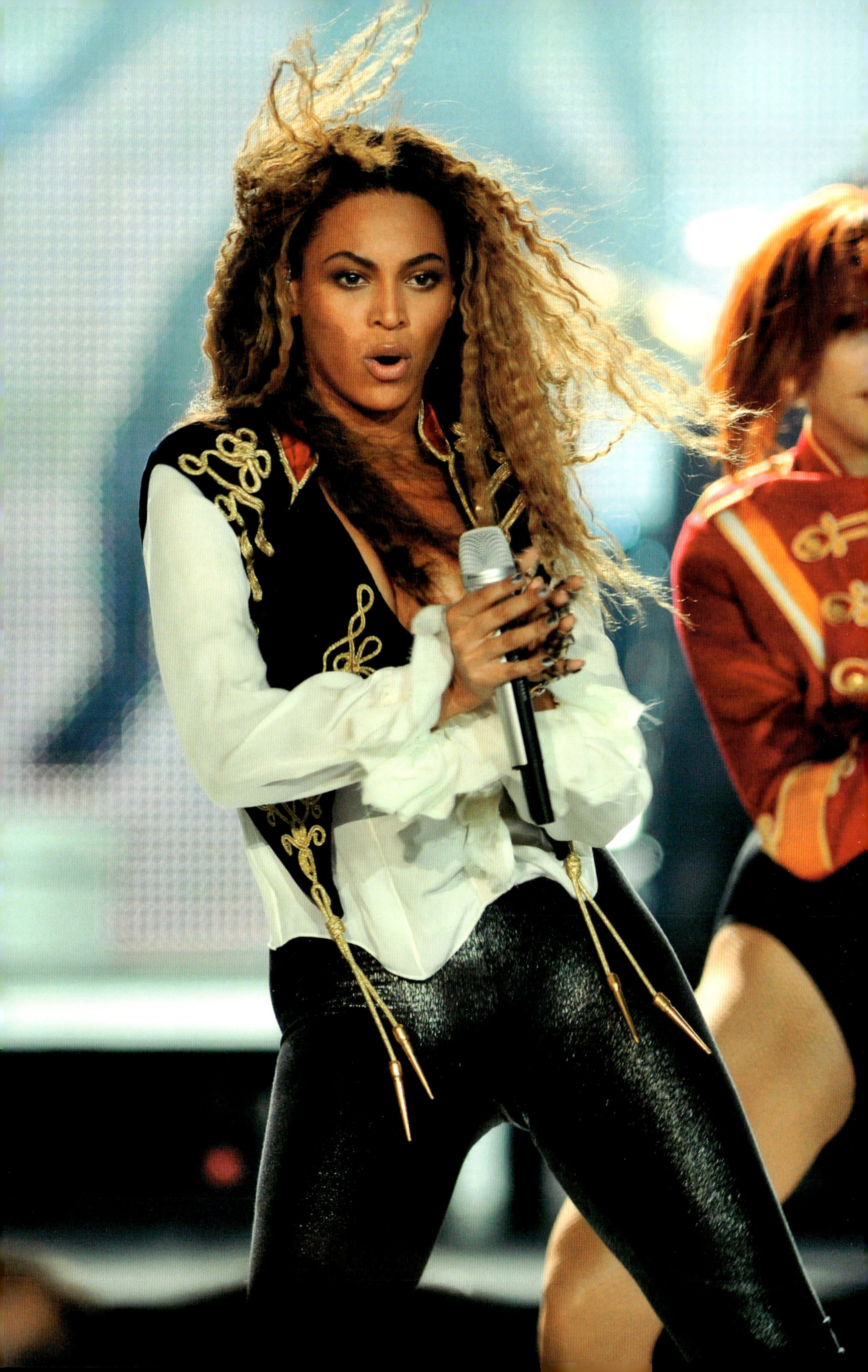

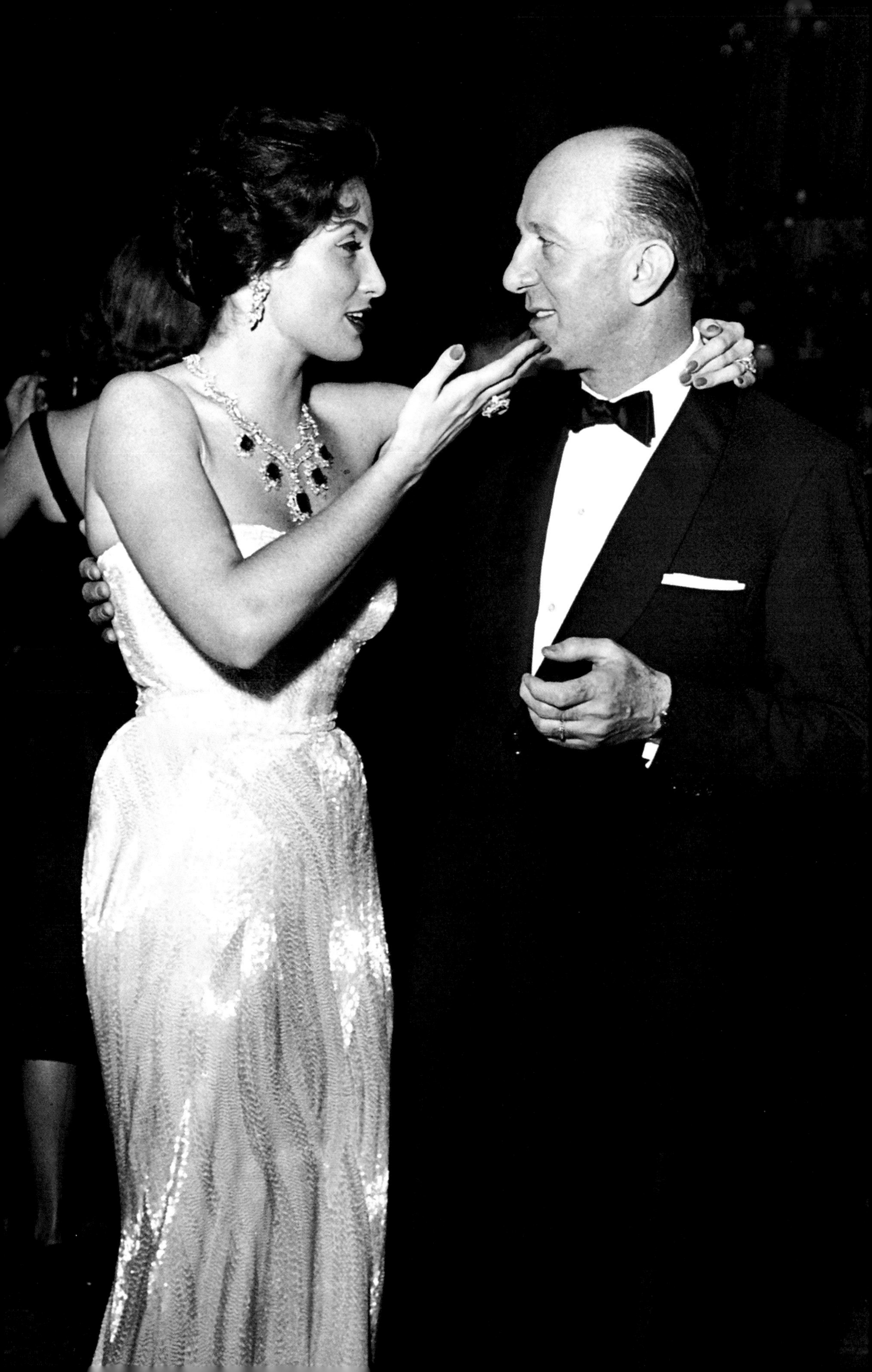

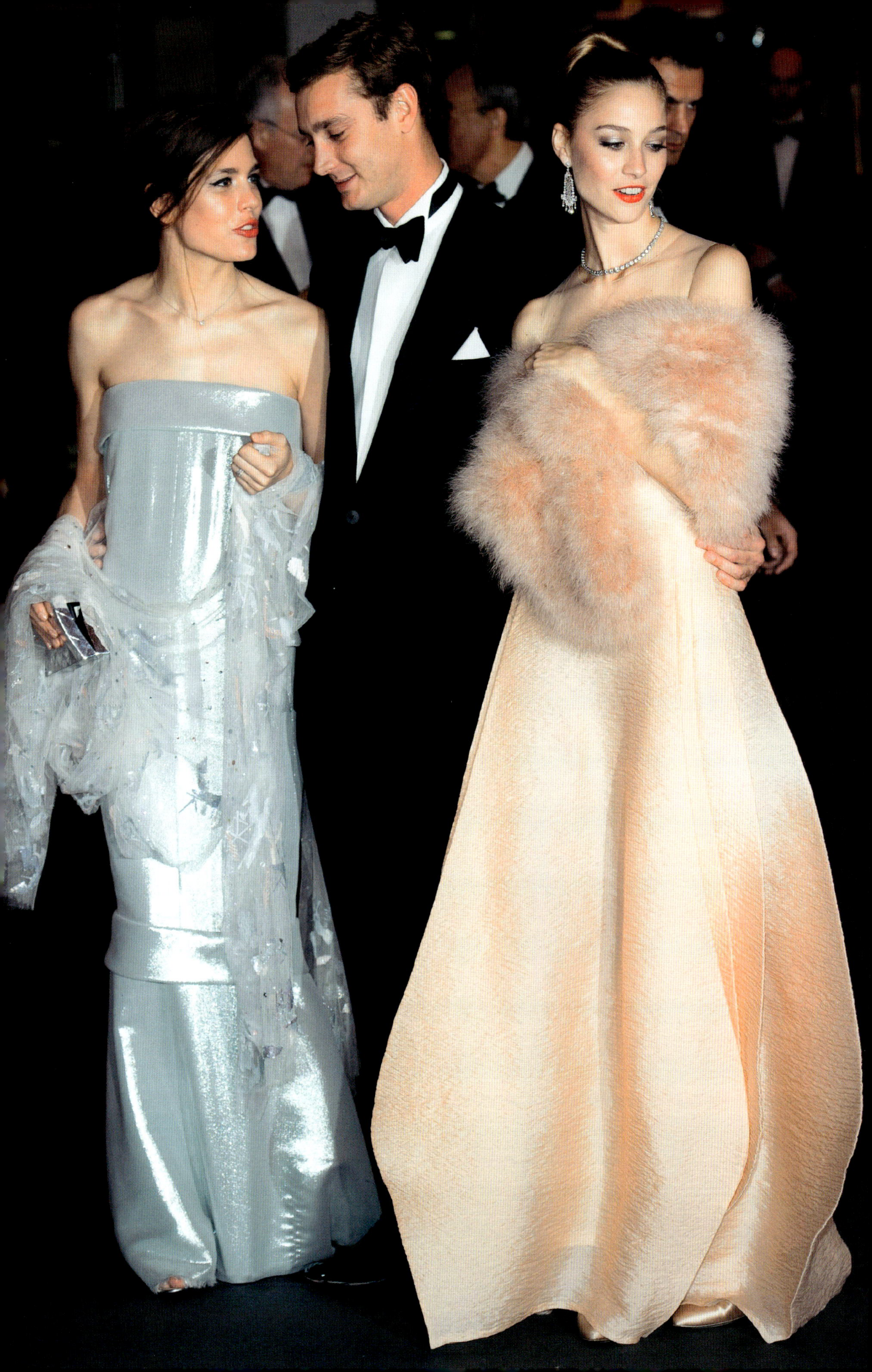

complex designed by British architect Richard Rogers. The Sporting d'Hiver is run by the Société des Bains de Mer, 69 percent of which is owned by Prince Albert and his family. Also planned is a major renovation of the Hôtel de Paris.

The *Times* article acknowledges that construction has been moving apace in Monaco for the last two decades—nothing new on the Côte d'Azur, which is constantly assailed for its predilection for overbuilding. In Monaco, many of the new occupants of the high-rises are Russian oligarchs. The Russians have a long history in Monaco, dating back to the nineteenth century, when Tsar Nicolas was one of the first visitors to the Casino and the Hôtel de Paris. Today, Russians are everywhere in evidence as well as in residence, as they are in many of the most sought-after resorts communities in Europe, including the Costa Smeralda in Sardinia.

Among those who have lived in Monaco for years under the "soft-tax" provisions are several top athletes and race car drivers, singer Dame Shirley Bassey, and actor Sir Roger Moore, who played James Bond in two movies that were filmed in Monte Carlo. Moore recounts all of the qualities that attracted him: "It is about eighteen years that I have had the pleasure of living in Monaco. I came because Kristina [Moore's wife] was already living here and I had put my house

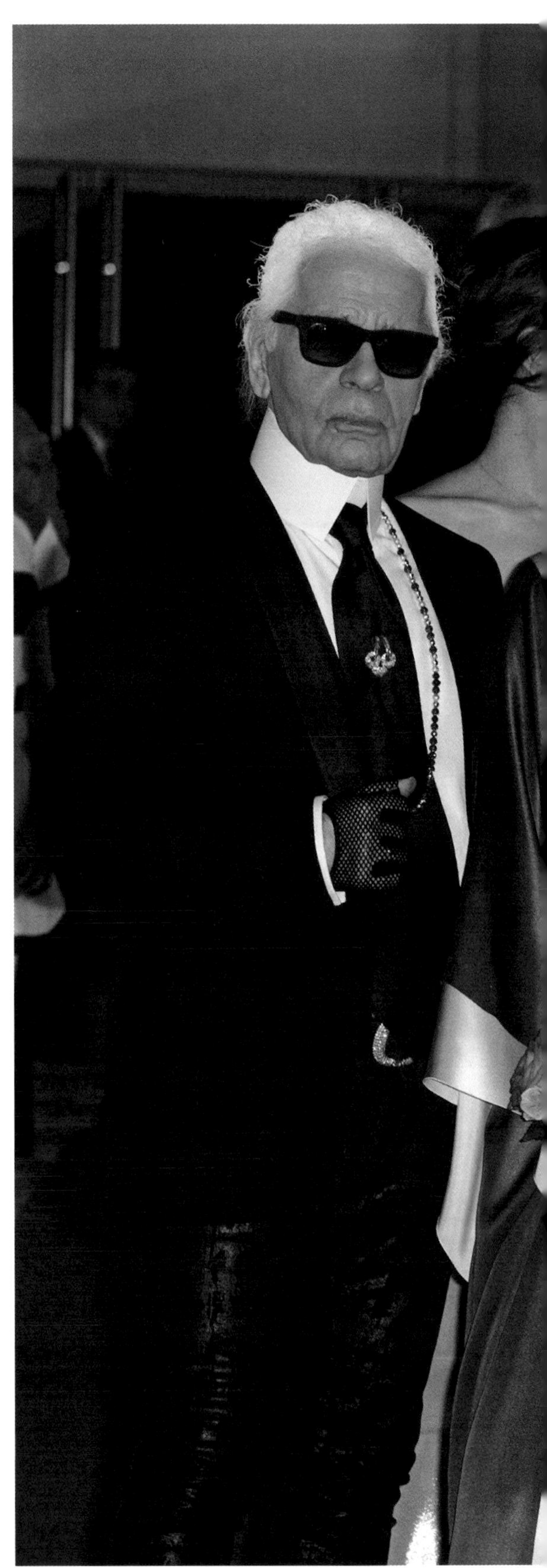

Couturier and family friend Karl Lagerfeld at the 60th Bal de la Rose with Caroline Princess of Hanover, Princess Charlene, and Prince Albert in March 2014.

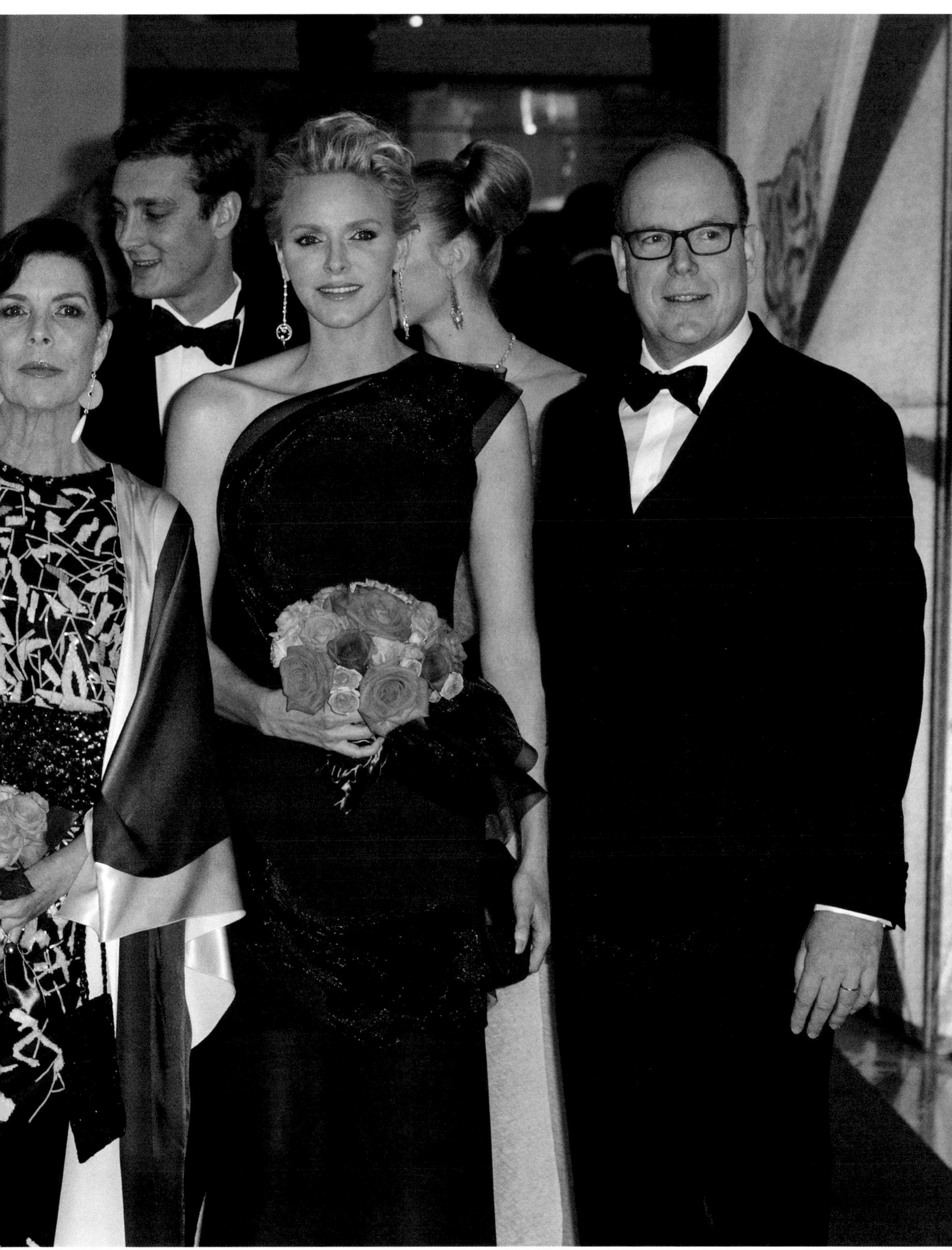

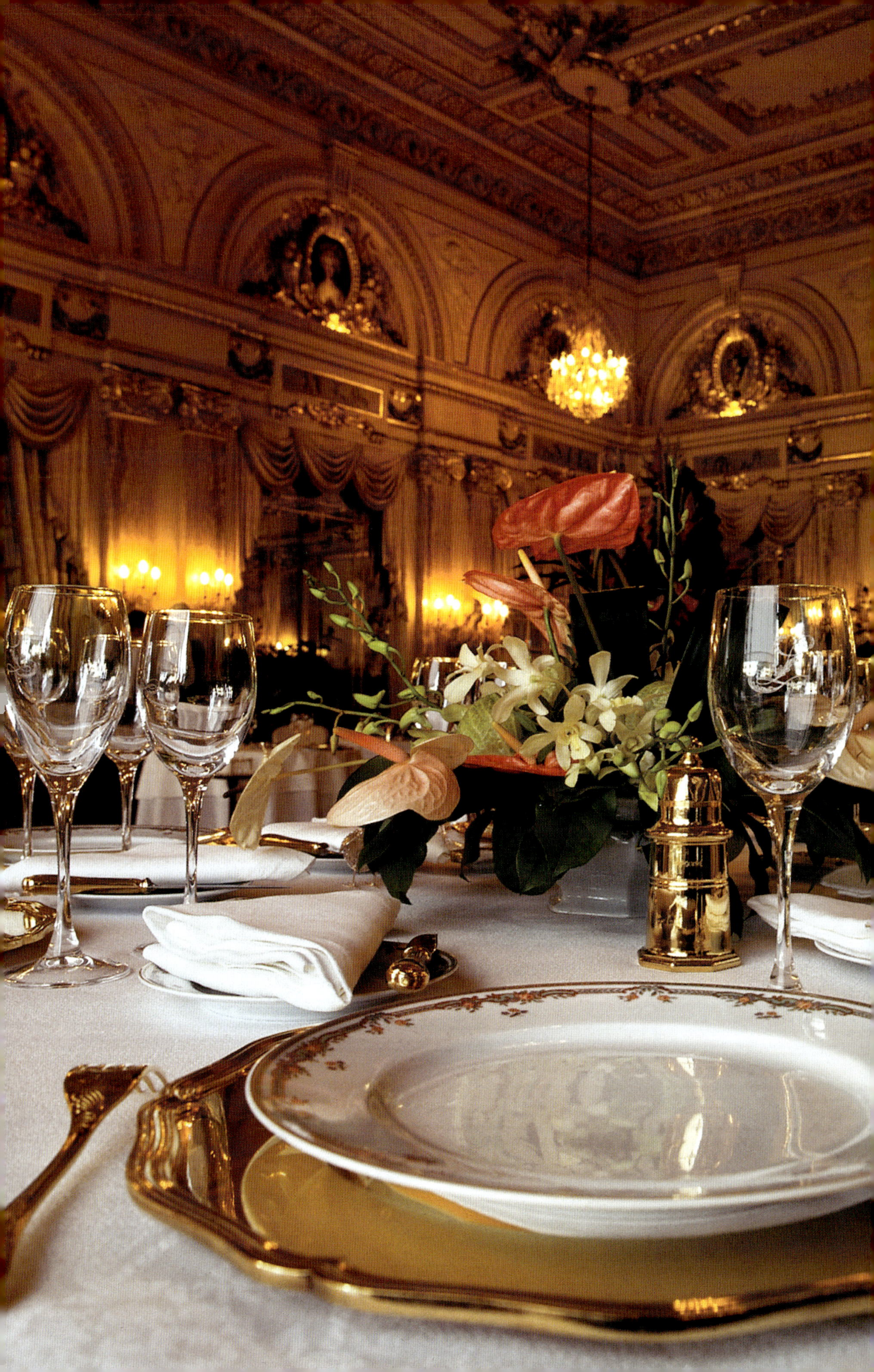

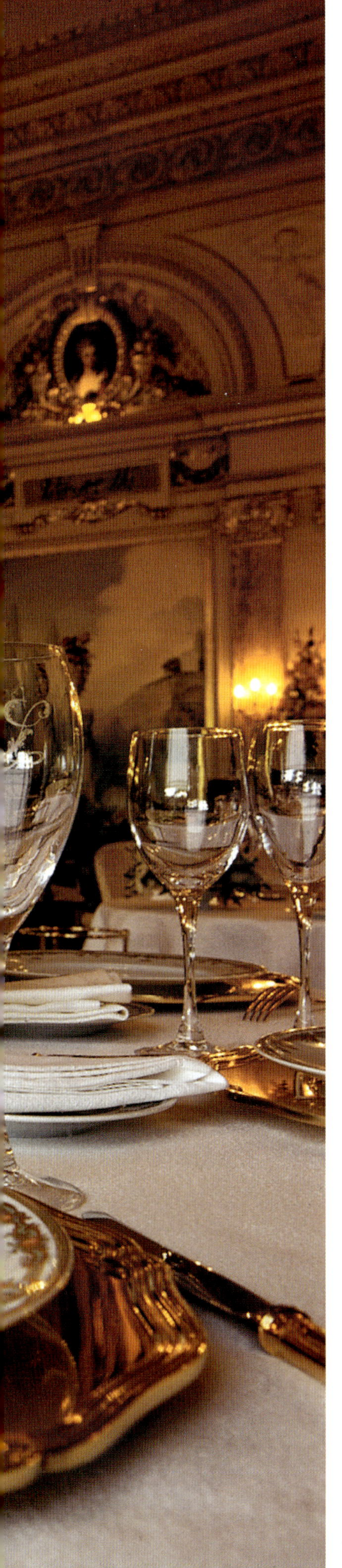

in St.-Paul-de-Vence up for sale. The security of Monaco appealed to me then, and it still does. It is one of the few places in the world where a lady can walk safely on the streets at any time of the day or night. There's a smart police force, polite and efficient. Medical care is readily available—the Princess Grace Hospital, the Centre Cardio-Thoracique, immediate response to emergency calls. Every type of restaurant is within walking distance: Bouchon, the Café de Paris, there are many first-rate Italian places—La Piazza and Michelangelo—as well as those two top chefs, Joël Robuchon and Alain Ducasse."

Ducasse arrived first. In 1987 he promised Prince Rainier that, if hired, he would deliver three Michelin stars to the Louis XV restaurant in the Hôtel de Paris in no fewer than four years. It only took thirty-three months: In 1990 the Louis XV received its triple-star rating and has held on to it ever since. "My encounter with Monaco was a milestone, an important and magical moment in my life," says Ducasse. "It is on this small rock between France and Italy that I focused my 'Rivieras.' I know today that this land is part of my destiny"—as it has been for countless others.

In fact, if it weren't for Monaco, there would be a lot of unemployed French. Almost every day the population more than doubles, with 45,000 workers entering the Principality, most of them from France and some from Italy. No wonder Monaco is called "the lung of France."

But to *live* in Monaco is something else. Unless you are Monegasque, only the superrich (these days, primarily those Russians) can afford it, and even then the question is, where? Available apartments are rare and there is hardly any space to build, unless, that is, something is razed to make room for it. For something new to go up, something old must come down—and therein lies the dilemma.

The splendor of it all: A place setting at Alain Ducasse's three-star Louis XV restaurant at the Hôtel de Paris.

Essential Monte Carlo

LAY OF THE LAND

Monte Carlo is one of five towns in the Principality of Monaco. The others are Monaco-Ville, La Condamine, Fontvieille, and Jardin Exotique. Monaco-Ville, the oldest, is where the palace, Oceanographic Museum, and several other historic sites are located.

HOW TO GET THERE

Fly into Nice Airport and either rent a car, hire a taxi, or have your hotel arrange for a pickup (a 30- to 40-minute ride). To get there in practically no time, take the seven-minute ride on **Heli Air Monaco**'s helicopter (www.heliairmonaco.com).

WHERE TO STAY

The elegant, old-world **Hôtel de Paris** and its posh sister property, the **Hermitage**, are both run by SBM and situated in the center of Monte Carlo. (Note: The Hôtel de Paris is about to undergo a major renovation in fall 2014 and may be closed for a few months.) The **Métropole**, equally top notch, draws the young and the hip. You can't miss with any of these if you want to be in the heart of Monte Carlo. If you'd rather be right on the water, there is the SBM's swank 1930s-vintage **Monte Carlo Beach** hotel with the **Elsa** restaurant (named for Monte Carlo habitué and social butterfly Elsa Maxwell), and its **Monte Carlo Bay Hotel and Resort**.

All roads lead to Monte Carlo.

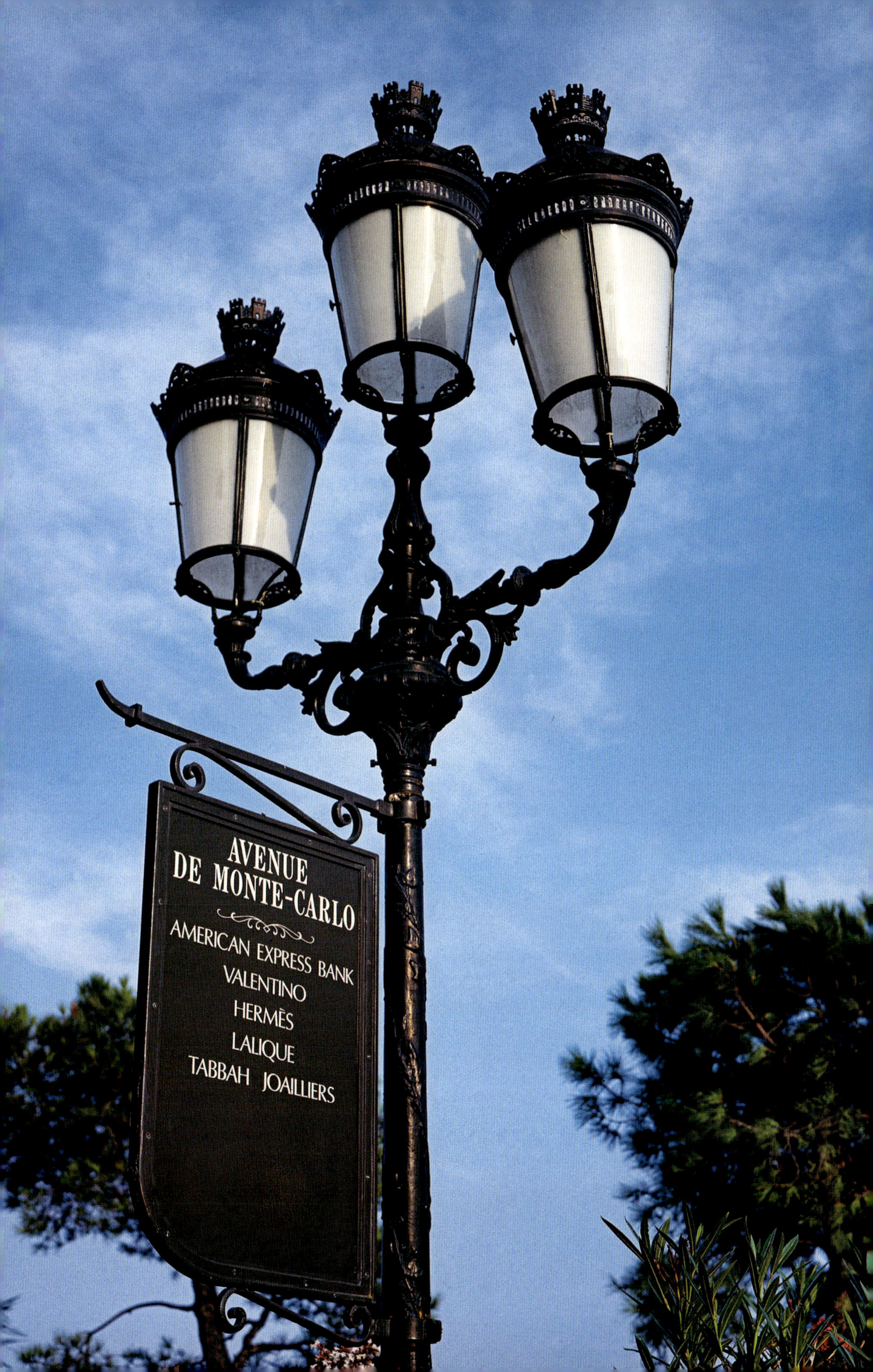
AVENUE
DE MONTE-CARLO
AMERICAN EXPRESS BANK
VALENTINO
HERMÈS
LALIQUE
TABBAH JOAILLIERS

WHERE TO EAT AND DRINK

There's no dearth of choices here, starting with **Alain Ducasse**'s three-star **Louis XV** in the Hôtel de Paris for a truly sublime and unforgettable haute cuisine experience. The hotel's legendary wine cellar, dating back to Monte Carlo's beginning, stores 300,000 bottles under the care of sommelier Patrice Franck, and you can dine in the *cave*. The rooftop Grill is lovely and offers superb views—and its roof opens up in good weather, affording dinner under the stars. At the Hermitage, the intimate **Le Vistamar** is *the* place for fine dining. The two excellent restaurants at the Métropole are under the tutelage of **Joël Robuchon**. The two-star **Le Jardin** serves classic French food. If you do nothing else, order the justly famous mashed potatoes, which are seemingly made with a few potatoes, a pound of butter, and a quart of cream. **Yoshi**, the hotel's Japanese restaurant, serves some of the freshest, most delectable sushi west of Tokyo. Ditto **Maya Bay** and the new **Nobu**. Go to the enormous and lively, sometimes loud (there's a DJ) **Buddha Bar** for pan-Asian cuisine. Rampoldi, a longtime favorite, is unfortunately now closed, but the Italian restaurant **Polpetta** still offers good food and celebrity sightings. In Monaco-Ville are **Castelroc** for local cuisine (best for lunch; try the *barbajuan*) and the cozy (18 seats) and tasty **La Montgolfière**. Open in summer is the outdoors **La Vigie** at the Monte Carlo Beach hotel. **La Chaumière** high up in the Jardin Exotique is a one-star wonder. Other great choices include **Cipriani**, **Bouchon**, and **Beef Bar**. The **Café de Paris** in Casino Square is a must for an early morning café or late afternoon cocktail. Three other favorite spots for drinks, tea, or a light meal are the **Bar Américain** off the lobby of the Hôtel de Paris, the **Crystal Bar** at the Hermitage, and the **Métropole**'s lobby bar. Beneath the Métropole is a shopping mall with all sorts of good fast-food choices. If you get hungry in the heat of gambling, there is always the Belle Époque-style **Le Train Bleu** to sustain you Purists may prefer **L'Hirondelle** at the Thermes Marin Monte-Carlo for salubrious spa cuisine. If you want to dance, go (late, of course) where many of the rich and famous have gone before you: to **Jimmy'z** at **Le Sporting Monte-Carlo**.

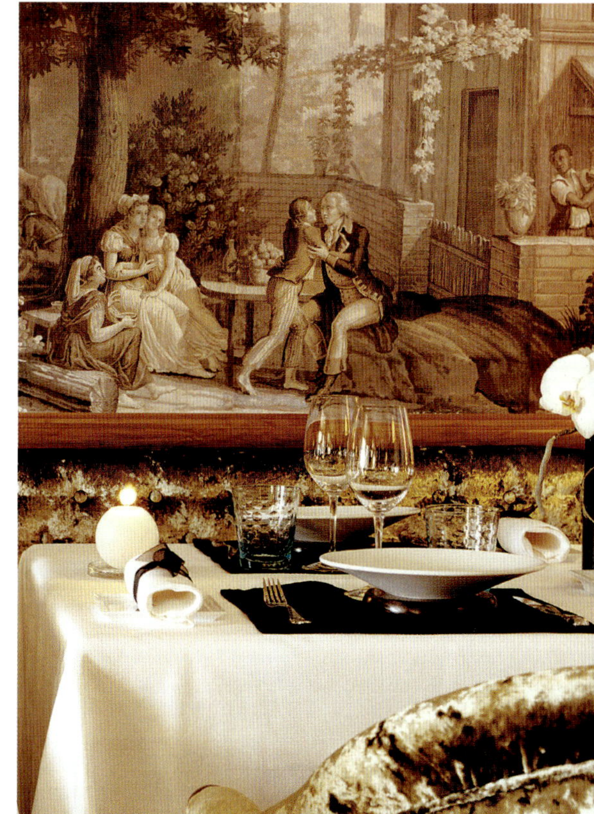

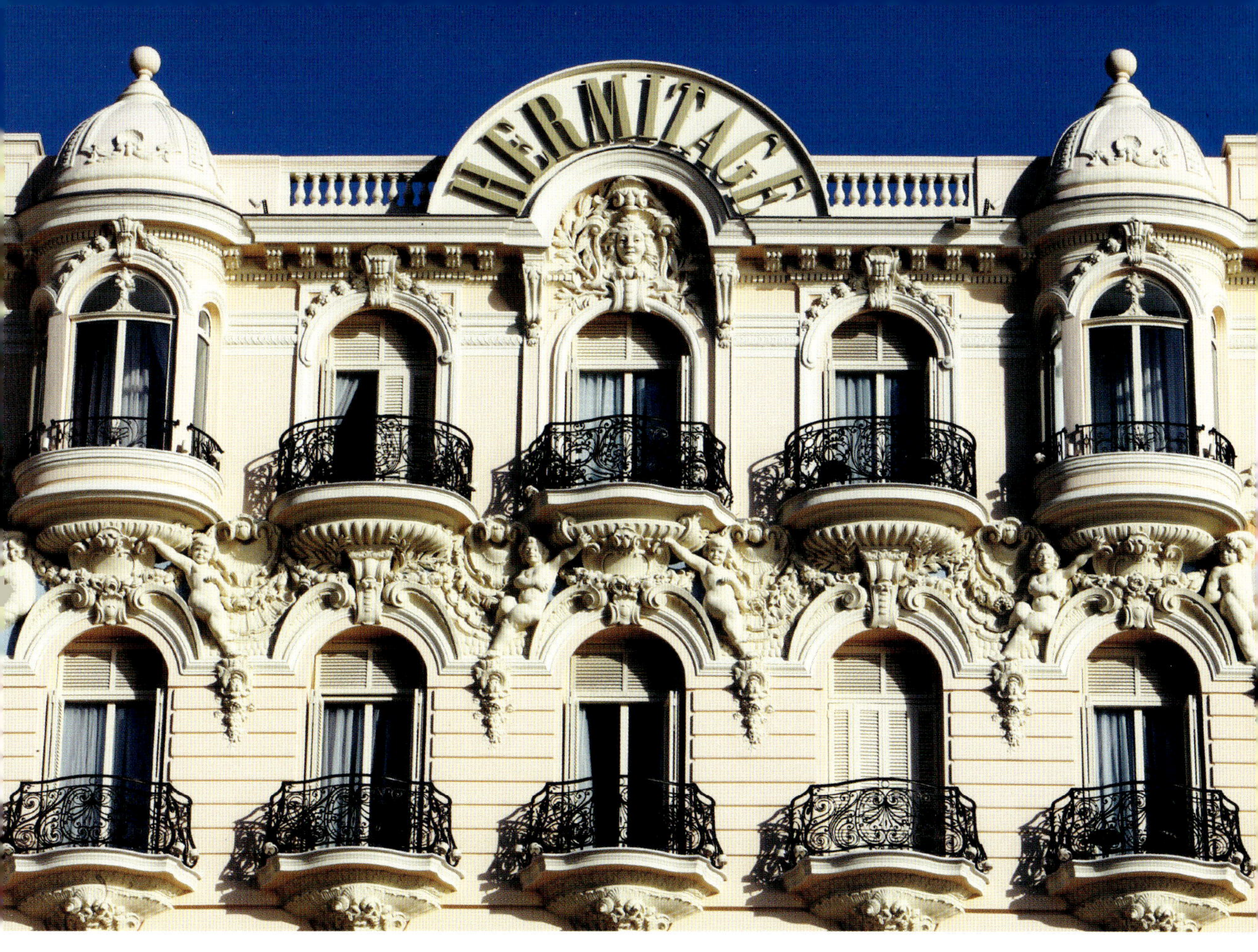

A Monte Carlo confection: Exterior of the Hotel Hermitage. *Opposite:* Joel Robuchon's restaurant at the Hotel Métropole.

GETTING AROUND

Most people walk or take one of the five bus routes for 1 euro or get a 10-trip card for 6 euro. It may be the best bargain in the Principality.

SIGHTSEEING

In Monte Carlo: Casino Square (including the **Casino** itself and the **Salle Garnier**), the **Villa Sauber** museum, the **Japanese Gardens**, and **Larvotto Beach**. In Monaco-Ville: the **Palace** (the changing of the guard occurs at 11:55 a.m. every day in Palace Square), the **Oceanographic Museum and Aquarium** (you can have lunch there), the **1875 Cathedral**, and the **Princess Grace Irish Library**. In Condamine: Walk along the **Port Hercule**, the main harbor; check out the **Condamine Market**; pay your respects at the church of **Sainte-Dévote**. In Fontvieille, visit the **Princess Grace Rose Garden**, Prince Rainier III's **Private Collection of Antique Cars**, the **Stamp and Coin Museum**. In the Jardin Exotique: Amble through the garden and the **Museum of Prehistoric Anthropology**, then visit La Paloma, which houses the **Nouveau Musée National**, focused on contemporary art installations.

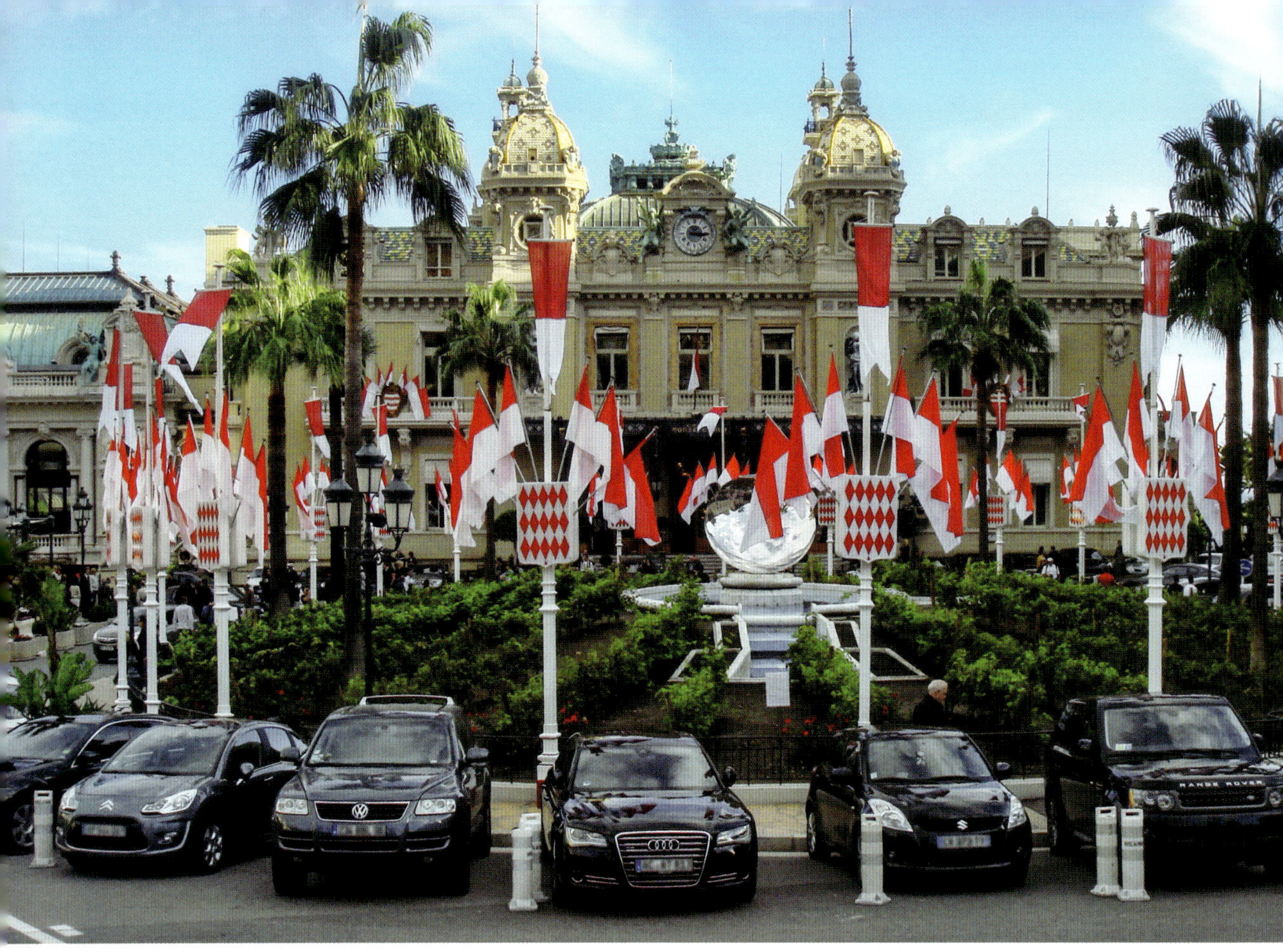

The Place du Casino, also known as Casino Square. In the background is the Casino itself.

CASINO-GOING

There are several casinos in Monte Carlo but the queen bee is the one in Casino Square (entry fee, 10 euro; minimum age of 18, proof of identity required). There are slot machines for novices; English, French, and European roulette; blackjack; craps; and ultimate poker for old hands.

NEW AND WORTH YOUR WHILE

Part of the development of the port of Monaco, Lord Norman Foster's modernist **Yacht Club**, which opened in June 2014, looks itself like the sleekest yacht in the harbor, looming over 9,000 square meters, located on Quai Louis II, an extension of the Quai des États-Unis. Established by Monaco-based real estate magnate and ardent collector Majid Boustany, the **Francis Bacon Art Foundation**, opened in October 2014, is a private, nonprofit institute for scholars, researchers, and the general public, by appointment only. Its particular emphasis is on the time that the artist lived and worked in Monaco and southern France, from 1946 to the early '50s. The Foundation is on the first floor of Villa Elise, 21 Boulevard d'Italie, in the heart of Monte Carlo.

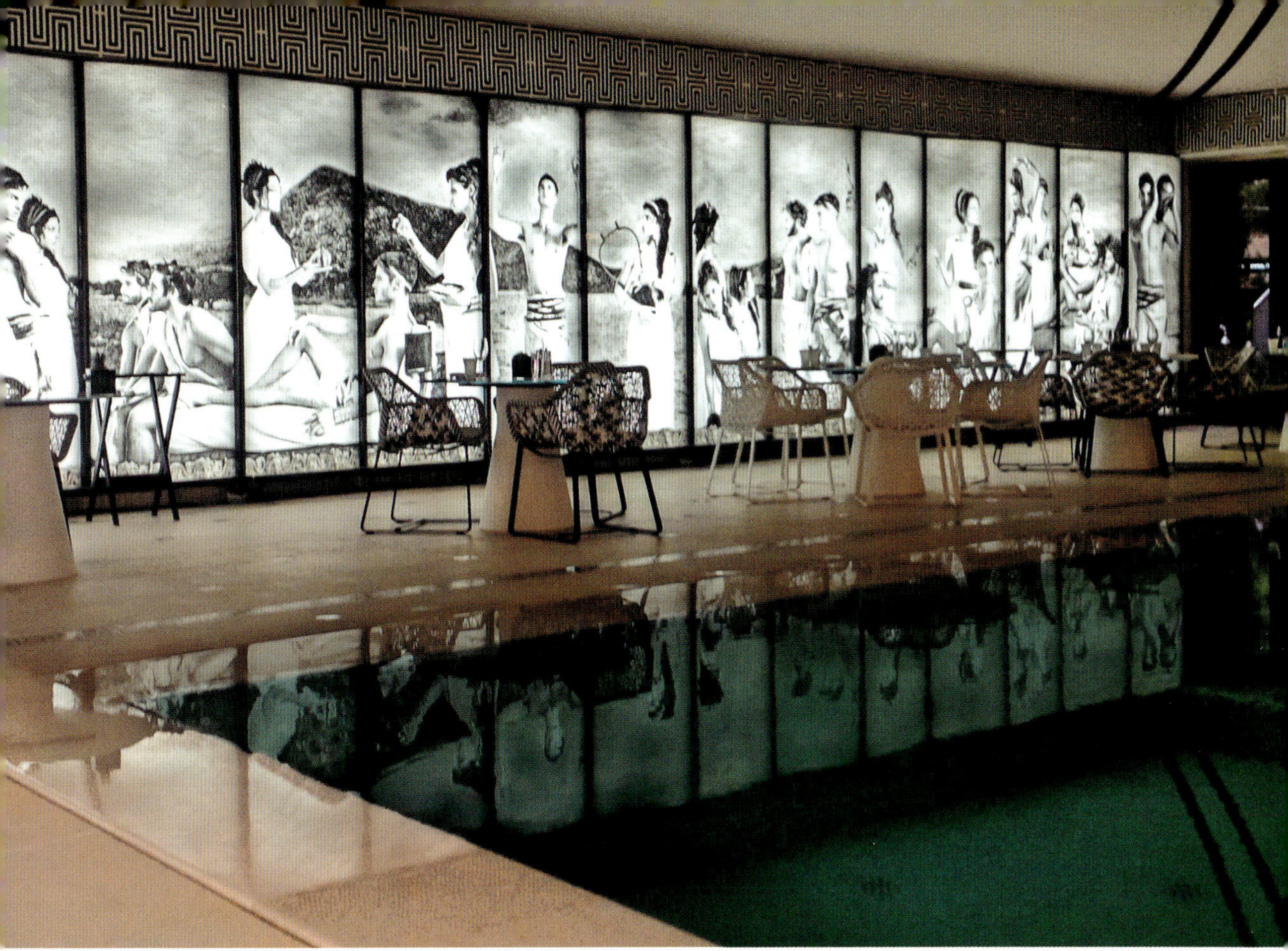

The sleek Odyssey Pool, designed by Karl Lagerfeld, at the Hotel Métropole.

SHOPPING

Almost all of the big names—Chanel, Dior, Louis Vuitton, Hermès, and more—are here, plus there's a Zara across from the Hermitage. There are also many galleries (Marlborough and Monaco Fine Arts are two of the best-known), gift shops, and antique stores—a standout is **Czarina**, owned by Adriana Ella, whose eclectic taste has made it one of Monte Carlo's go-to boutiques. Top galleries include the **Marlborough, Monaco Fine Arts, Maison d'Art, Robert Zehil**, and **Adriano Ribolzi**. Some of these may be closed during the redevelopment of Casino Square or may have moved to another spot, whether temporary or permanent. Let your concierge point the way.

SPAS

Just about every major hotel has some sort of spa facility. The Métropole has its own **ESPA** as well as **Odyssey**, a sexy new swimming pool designed by Karl Lagerfeld as an homage to ancient Greece. The pool is open-air in summer and covered in winter. The **Therme Marins** used to be shared by the Hôtel de Paris and the Métropole, but the Hôtel de Paris will soon have its own.

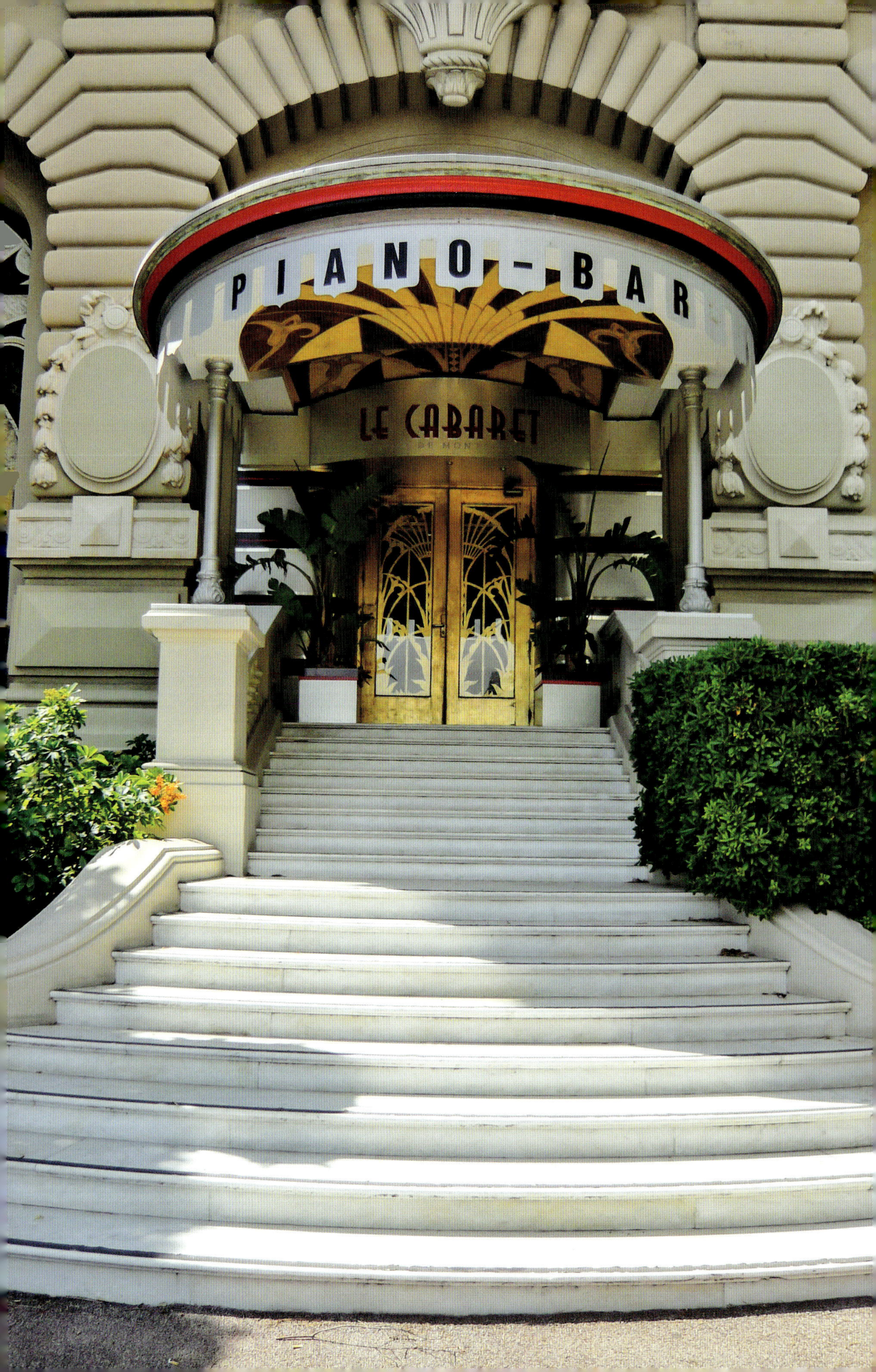
PIANO-BAR
LE CABARET

DRESS CODES

Monaco is a rather proper place, so you won't see topless bathers (à la St. Tropez) at Larvotto Beach or shirtless men on the streets. Rise to the occasion and look like you belong.

EVENTS

January: Monte Carlo Rallye and International Circus Festival. **March:** Bal de la Rose (Rose Ball). **April:** Monte-Carlo Rolex Masters and Monte-Carlo Ballet. **May:** Formula One Grand Prix, International Swimming Meet, International Jumping. **July:** International Fireworks Festival and Monte-Carlo Philharmonic concerts. **August:** Red Cross Ball. **September:** Yacht Show and Monaco Classic Week. **November:** Monegasque National Day celebrations. The opera season begins in the fall.

SIDE TRIPS

No matter in which direction you drive, you'll find yourself in Riviera-land. Close by are Cap d'Ail, Villefranche, Èze, St.-Jean-Cap-Ferrat, and Nice. Farther west are Beaulieu, Juan-les-Pins, Antibes, Cap d'Antibes, Cannes, St. Tropez. High up in the hills you'll reach Vallauris, Vence, St.-Paul-de-Vence, and Mougins. And if you head east you will cross the border into Italy.

MONTE CARLO IN THE MOVIES

Begin your cinematic journey with *The Red Shoes,* then seek out the following: Ernst Lubitsch's 1930 confection *Monte Carlo*; *Affair in Monte Carlo*; *Monte Carlo Baby*; Alfred Hitchcock's *To Catch a Thief,* for Grace Kelly and Cary Grant's swervy drive along the Grand Corniche; *Madagascar 3* opening sequence; *Grand Prix*; *Never Say Never Again*; *GoldenEye*; *A Man and a Woman*; *Ocean's Twelve*; *Iron Man 2.*

BACKGROUND READING

Monaco and Its Princes by Alain Decaux (Perrin); *Riviera: The Rise and Rise of the Côte d'Azur* by Jim Ring (John Murray); *Monaco: Enchantment of the World* by Martin Hintz (Children's Press); *Jeux de Dames à Monte-Carlo* by Bernard Spindler (Rocher); *Albert II de Monaco: L'Autre Prince* by Christiane Stahl (Rocher); *The Red Shoes* by Michael Powell and Emeric Pressburger (A Wyatt Book for St. Martin's Press); *Nemesis* by Peter Evans (HarperCollins); *Inside Monaco* by Siri Campbell (Post Oak Press).

The Piano Bar is part of the Casino complex.
Following pages: Still from *The Persuaders!* TV movie *Mission: Monte Carlo,* starring Sir Roger Moore and Tony Curtis, 1972.

Acknowledgments

First and foremost, my gratitude goes to my longtime friend, Ambassador Maguy Maccario Doyle, at the Monaco embassy in Washington, D.C., and to her trusty team, most of all Elle Berdy and Karla Modolo at the Monaco Consulate in New York.

In Monaco, I wish to thank Lætitia Pierrat of the Princely Palace Press office; Thomas Fouilleron of the Princely Palace Archives; Robert Calcagno of the Oceanographic Museum; Caroline O'Conor of the Princess Grace Foundation; Judith Gantley of the Princess Grace Irish Library; Michel Dotta of the Chambre de Développement Économique (Chamber for Economic Development); Michel Ferry of the Automobile Club of Monaco; Bernard d'Alessandri and Isabelle Andrieux of the Monaco Yacht Club; Jean-François Gourdon of the Monaco Tourist Bureau; Jean-Claude Messant and the late Odile Firmin-Guion of the Hôtel Métropole Monte-Carlo; Jean-Marie Véran and Christiane Cane of the Fondation Princesse Charlène de Monaco; Marie-Claude Beaud, Nathalie Rosticher, and Elodie Biancheri of the Nouveau Musée National de Monaco; chef Alain Ducasse and his associates Emmanuelle Perrier and Kimberley-Marie Blanchot. At Monte-Carlo SBM my thanks go to Charlotte Lubert-Notari; Véronique Burki-Despont; Hélène Bustos; Eric Bessone; Guillaume Jahan de Lestang; Floreana Rubega and Patrice Franck at the Hôtel de Paris, and Pascal Camia at the Hôtel Hermitage. My sincere appreciation to Sir Roger Moore, Bernard Spindler, Wendy Lauwers, Majid Boustany, and Adriana Elia for their impressions and insights. In London: a tip of the hat to Bettina von Hase and Jean Rafferty.

In the States, a deep bow to Jamie Niven, Robert Wolders, Shirley Lord Rosenthal, Simone Levitt, Cathy Moore Barrett, Mark McGowan, Harry Slatkin, Steven Stolman, Kristina Orfali, Anne Busquet, Martin Hintz, Shamin Abas, Matthew Lefkowitz, Angela Vecellio, Linda Nardi, and Anne Schinnerer.

Last and most certainly not least, I am indebted to my associates at Assouline: to Amy Slingerland or her deft editing; to Esther Kremer for her ongoing guidance; to Stéphanie Labeille-Sczyba and Eduard de Lange for keeping the "spirit" of these books alive; and above all to Martine and Prosper Assouline for entrusting me with a fourth book in this series. *Merci mille fois!*

Pamela Fiori

This book would not have been possible without the gracious participation of Ambassador Maguy Maccario Doyle, the Embassy of the Principality of Monaco, the Consulate General of Monaco in New York, and the Société des Bains de Mer, Monaco. Assouline would also like to thank the following individuals for their invaluable assistance: Bob Adelman; Anna Gibson, The Advertising Archives; Stephanie Marsh and Angelika Pirkl, akg-images Ltd.; Louise Dear, Jasmine Gould, Starr Hackwelder, Oren B. Silverstein, Lisa Vazquez Roper and Darlene Wilkins, Alamy Inc.; Matthew Lutts, AP Images; Christian Roti and Vincent Vatrican, Archives Audiovisuelles de Monaco; Gerard Dubois, Automobile Club de Monaco; Jessica Pinal, Ballets de Monte-Carlo; Randy Bauer, Aaron Perez, and Aide Wimber, Bauer-Griffin LLC; Elle Berdy and Karla Modolo, Consulate General of Monaco; Oscar Espaillat, Corbis; Wolfgang and Ursula Frei, Edward Quinn Archive Ltd.; Doug Fallone, Everett Collection, Inc.; Jay Lopez and Gayle Mault, Foster + Partners; Sarah Zimmer and Courtney Hopkins, Getty Images; Nelly Dhoutaut, Hachette Filipacchi Médias, SA; Myriam Rachid, Hôtel Métropole Monte-Carlo; Johan Attvik, J Craft Boats; Robert Littleford; Michael Shulman, Magnum Photos; Geneviève Berti, Monaco Media Bureau; Johan Pizzardini, Monaco Yacht Show S.A.M.; Michel Dagnino, Pauline Herouan and Patrick Piguet, Musée Océanographique de Monaco; Thomas Fouilleron and Laetitia Pierrat, Palais Princier de Monaco; Irene Halsman and Steve Bello, Philippe Halsman Archives; Toby E. Boshak, Princess Grace Foundation–USA; Alla Diment, Holly Taylor and Laura Watts, Rex USA; Charlotte Lubert-Notari and Hélène Bustos, Société des Bains de Mer (SBM); Gul Duzyol and Fabienne Toublanc, SIPA; Dr. Astrid Krüger, Beate Datzkow and Uta Koch, Stadtarchiv Bad Homburg; Keiichi Tahara; Amy Wong, Time Inc.; Justine Pippitt-Zagolin and Billy Vong, Trunk Archive; Chris Delmas and Richard Michel, Visual Press Agency; Isabelle Andrieux, Bernard d'Alessandri and Sonia Thévenet, Yacht Club de Monaco.

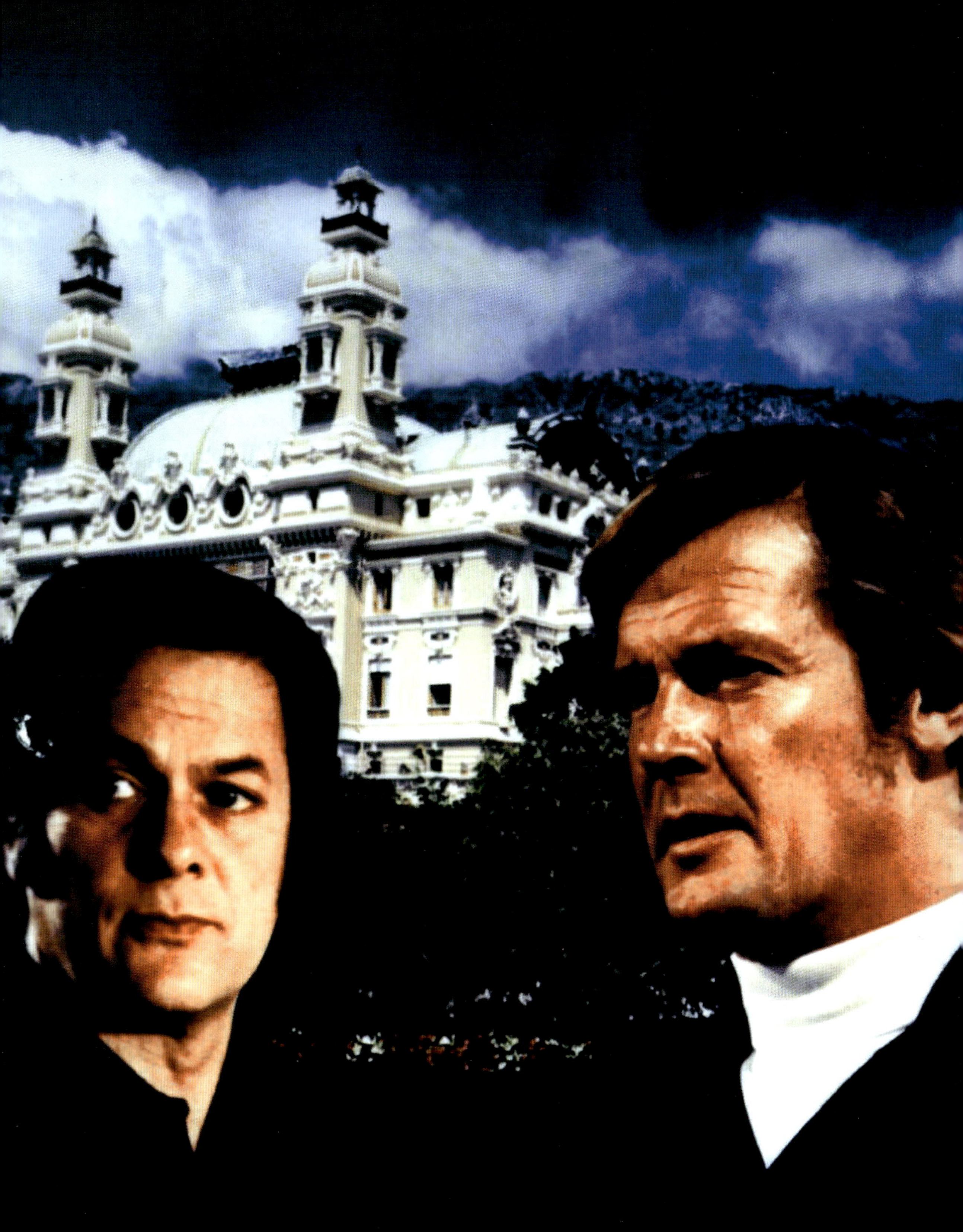

Credits

A portion of "Grace Personified" first appeared in *Town & Country* November 2007.

Pages 4-5: Photo Edward Quinn, © edwardquinn.com; pages 10-11: © Archives Monte-Carlo S.B.M; pages 12-13: Jacques Enrietti © Archives Monte-Carlo S.B.M; page 15: © Pictorial Press Ltd/Alamy; page 16: Ploton © Archives Monte-Carlo S.B.M; pages 18-19: © Mary Evans Picture Library/Alamy; page 20: © Keiichi Tahara; page 21, clockwise from top left: © Pamela Fiori, Jacques Enrietti © Archives Monte-Carlo S.B.M, © Keiichi Tahara, © Patrick Swan/*/Design Pics/Corbis, © Archives Monte-Carlo S.B.M, © Archives Monte-Carlo S.B.M; page 22: © Condé Nast Ltd–Eugene Vernier/Trunk Archive; page 23: © Keiichi Tahara; pages 24-25: Jean-Jacques L'Heritier © Archives Monte-Carlo S.B.M; pages 26-27: © Bertrand Gardel/Hemis/Corbis; pages 28-29: © Archives Monte-Carlo S.B.M; page 31: © Geoffroy Moufflet/Archives du Palais de Monaco; page 33: © Gaëtan Luci/Palais de Monaco; pages 34-35: © Keiichi Tahara; page 36: © Archives Monte-Carlo S.B.M; page 36: © Stadtarchiv Bad Homburg; page 37: © Gaëtan Luci/Palais de Monaco; page 37: © Archives du Palais de Monaco; page 39: © Fernand Detaille/Archives du Palais de Monaco; page 40: © Gaëtan Luci/Palais Princier de Monaco; pages 42-43: © Stevens Frémont/Corbis; pages 44-45: Jacques Enrietti © Archives Monte-Carlo S.B.M; page 46: Jacques Enrietti © Archives Monte-Carlo S.B.M; page 47: © Archives Monte-Carlo S.B.M; page 49: © Pictorial Press Ltd/Alamy; pages 50-51: (1, 2, 6, 10, 12, 15) Robert Oggero © Archives Monte-Carlo S.B.M, (3, 8) Photo Edward Quinn, © edwardquinn.com, (4) Thevenin/SIPA, (5) © Keiichi Tahara, (7) © akg-images/picture-alliance, (9, 14) Jacques Enrietti © Archives Monte-Carlo S.B.M, (11) Ploton © Archives Monte-Carlo S.B.M, (13) Detaille © Archives Monte-Carlo S.B.M; pages 52-53: Ploton © Archives Monte-Carlo S.B.M; pages 54-55: © Monaco Yacht Show; pages 56-57: © Philippe Halsman/Magnum Photos; pages 58-59: Collection Archives Audiovisuelles de Monaco; page 60: © Howell Conant/Bob Adelman books; page 61, clockwise from top left: © Bettmann/Corbis, photo Edward Quinn, © edwardquinn.com, Collection Archives Audiovisuelles de Monaco, © Fausto Picedi/Archives du Palais de Monaco; page 62: © Howell Conant/Bob Adelman books; page 63: © Fausto Picedi–Archives du Palais de Monaco; page 65: © Howell Conant/Bob Adelman books; pages 66-67: © Elle Berdy; pages 68-69: (1) © Assouline, (2, 11, 14) Robert Oggero © Archives Monte-Carlo S.B.M, (3) DALMAS/SIPA, (4) © Georges Lukomski/Archives du Palais de Monaco, (5) © Manuel Litran/Corbis, (6) DALMAS/SIPA, (7) © Office des Emissions de Timbres-Poste, (8, 12) Photo Edward Quinn, © edwardquinn.com, (9, 15) © Bettmann/Corbis, (10, 16) Collection Archives du Palais de Monaco, (13) © Reg Wilson–Archives du Palais de Monaco; pages 70-71: © Giribaldi/Gamma-Rapho via Getty Images; pages 72-73: © Howell Conant/Bob Adelman books; pages 74-75: © Keiichi Tahara; pages 76-77: © Archives Monte-Carlo S.B.M; page 78: courtesy The Advertising Archives; page 79: © Archives Monte-Carlo S.B.M; page 80: Robert Oggero © Archives Monte-Carlo S.B.M; page 82, from top: © Michael Steele/Getty Images, Robert Oggero © Archives Monte-Carlo S.B.M; page 83: © Julian Finney/Getty Images; page 85, clockwise from top left: © Assouline, © Archives Monte-Carlo S.B.M, © Assouline (3), © Archives Monte-Carlo S.B.M; pages 86-87: © Assouline; pages 88-89: Detaille © Archives Monte-Carlo S.B.M; page 90: Sasha © Archives Monte-Carlo S.B.M; page 91: © Archives Monte-Carlo S.B.M; page 93: © Keiichi Tahara; page 94: photo by Angela Sterling, *LAC* choreography by Jean-Christophe Maillot, Ballets de Monte-Carlo; page 95, clockwise from top left: © Vinaj Jean-Charles/Visual Press Agency, Everett Collection, © Keiichi Tahara, © Archives Monte-Carlo S.B.M, photo © Keiichi Tahara/artwork © Ruben Alterio; pages 96, 98-99: © Keiichi Tahara; page 100-101: © Gamma-Rapho via Getty Images; page 102, clockwise from top left: AdB via Getty Images, © Pamela Fiori, © Keiichi Tahara, © Elle Berdy, © Keiichi Tahara; page 103: © Collection Oceanographic Museum of Monaco; pages 104-105: © Maurice Jarnoux/*Paris Match* via Getty Images; pages 106-107: © Thomas McAvoy/Time & Life Pictures/Getty Images; page 108: © Lordprice Collection/Alamy; page 109: © Phipps/Sutton Images/Corbis; pages 110-111: Robert Oggero © Archives Monte-Carlo S.B.M; page 112: © Archives Monte-Carlo S.B.M; page 113, clockwise from top left: © Hoch Zwei/Corbis, photo Edward Quinn © edwardquinn.com, Robert Oggero © Archives Monte-Carlo S.B.M, © Hoch Zwei/Corbis, © Archives Monte-Carlo S.B.M, © Assouline; pages 114-115: Ploton © Archives Monte-Carlo S.B.M; page 116, from top: © Patrick Hertzog/AFP/Getty Images, © Phipps/Sutton Images/Corbis; page 117: © Pascal Le Segretain/Sygma/Corbis; pages 118-119: © Monaco Media Bureau, Charly Gallo; pages 120-121: © Monaco Yacht Show; page 122: © Walter Carone/*Paris Match* via Getty Images; pages 124-125: © Harry Gruyaert/Magnum Photos; page 126: © Stephen Nitkin; page 127, clockwise from top left: © Bauer-Griffin.com, photo by Remi Ferrante, model: Aude Pépin, art direction: Patrice Meignan, courtesy *Intersection* magazine, © Archives Monte-Carlo S.B.M, © Splash News/Corbis, © Pamela Fiori; page 128: Jacques Enrietti © Archives Monte-Carlo S.B.M; pages 130-131: © Foster+Partners; page 132: AP Photo/Bruno Bebert, Pool; pages 134-135, clockwise from top left: © Pascal Guyot/AFP/Getty Images; Rex USA/Villard/PDN, © Pool/Getty Images, Rex USA/Villard/PDN, © Daniele Venturelli/WireImage, © Manuel Queimadelos Alonso/Getty Images, © Pascal Le Segretain/Getty Images, © Didier Baverel/WireImage; pages 136-137: © Monaco Media Bureau; page 138: © Tony Barson/WireImage; page 139: © Elle Berdy; pages 140-141: Rex USA/People Picture; page 142: SBM via Getty Images; page 143: © Alain Benainous/Gamma-Rapho via Getty Images; page 144: Robert Oggero © Archives Monte-Carlo SBM; page 145: Rex USA/Villard/PDN; pages 146-147: Rex USA/Villard/PDN; pages 148-149: © Keiichi Tahara; page 151: © Keiichi Tahara; page 152: © E. Cuviller, courtesy Hôtel Métropole Monte-Carlo; page 153: © Fred de Noyelle/Godong/Corbis; pages 154-155: © Pamela Fiori; page 156: © Assouline; page 159: Rex USA/ITV.

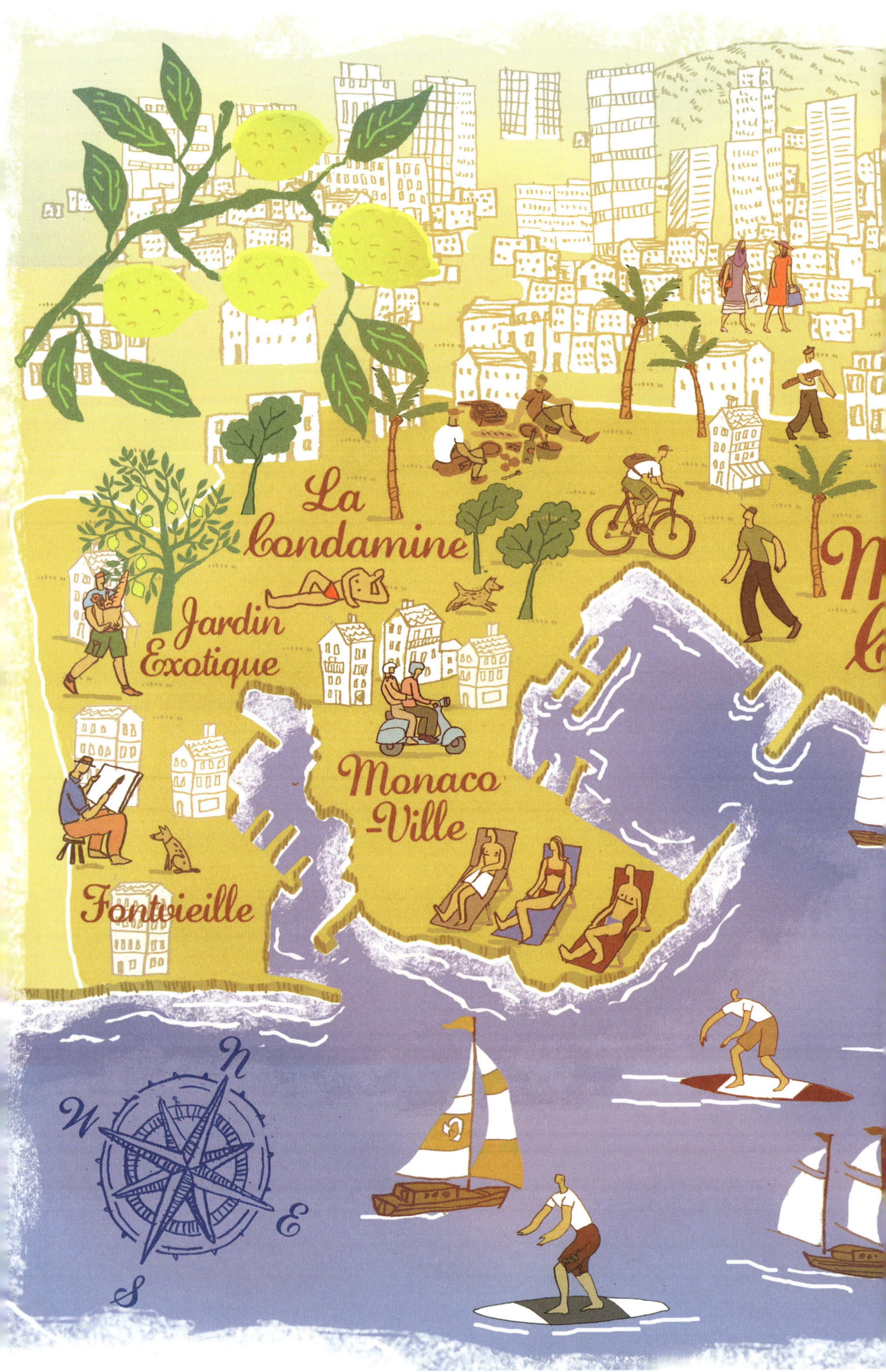

La
Condamine
Jardin
Exotique
Monaco
-Ville
Fontvieille
N
W
E
S